D1104036

Coaching and Mentoring at Work

Second Edition

"As a coach and as an HR Director, this book has become a main source of reference since I first read it. It's an accessible and absorbing read. It has helped when preparing for difficult coaching sessions, and later, when reflecting on my practice. It provides a huge amount of information on the principles of coaching and mentoring and some really practical advice on how to apply these principles to improve performance at work. The new edition adds further superb insights and a more reflective dimension – together with concise answers to some frequently asked questions. My favourite coaching and mentoring book!"
Sue Covill, Coach and former director of Human Resources

"With teams of teachers and school leaders The Skilled Helper Model has proved itself to be a robust and flexible tool for frameworking coaching conversations. I use it frequently both implicitly and explicitly with learners. The questions in the 2nd edition of Coaching and Mentoring at Work help explain the stages of the model to learners and provide invaluable prompts for leaders new to coaching."
Hannah Jones, BlueKiteCoach

"Mary Connor and Julia Pokora clearly live by one of the central tenets of their new book - "effective practice is reflective practice". They have listened to feedback on the 1st edition and made some pivotal changes. The book has a new structure of four sections that give a cohesive, interlinking framework that works. They have reconfigured the core of the earlier book and augmented it with some new material. I really like the way they have incorporated their own voices into the narrative - there was a real sense of how their current practive has emerged from a range of influences and approaches and is still developing.

There is an excellent new chapter on reflective practive and supervision that I anticipate I will read and re-read many times. They have also brought clarity to me about the confusing world of coaching accreditation in another new chapter. Finally, the FAQ's in the final section are a distillation of pure wisdom. The new edition has exceeded all my expectations."
Alan Swann, Consultant Old Age Psychiatrist/Clinical Director for Revalidation & CPD, Newcastle Older Peoples' Mental Health Services

Coaching and Mentoring at Work

Developing Effective Practice

Second Edition

Mary Connor and Julia Pokora

 Open University Press

Open University Press
McGraw-Hill Education
McGraw-Hill House
Shoppenhangers Road
Maidenhead
Berkshire
England
SL6 2QL

email: enquiries@openup.co.uk
world wide web: www.openup.co.uk

and Two Penn Plaza, New York, NY 10121-2289, USA

First published 2007
Reprinted 2010, 2011
First published in this second edition 2012

Copyright © Mary Connor and Julia Pokora 2012

All rights reserved. Except for the quotation of short passages for the purpose of
criticism and review, no part of this publication may be reproduced, stored in a
retrieval system, or transmitted, in any form or by any means, electronic,
mechanical, photocopying, recording or otherwise, without the prior written
permission of the publisher or a licence from the Copyright Licensing Agency
Limited. Details of such licences (for reprographic reproduction) may be obtained
from the Copyright Licensing Agency Ltd of Saffron House, 6–10 Kirby Street,
London, EC1N 8TS.

A catalogue record of this book is available from the British Library

ISBN-13: 978-0-33-524385-3 (pb)
ISBN-10: 0335243851
eISBN: 978-0-33-524386-0

Library of Congress Cataloging-in-Publication Data
CIP data applied for

Typesetting and e-book compilations
by RefineCatch Limited, Bungay, Suffolk
Printed and bound in the UK by Bell & Bain Ltd, Glasgow

Fictitious names of companies, products, people, characters and/or data that may be used
herein (in case studies or in examples) are not intended to represent any real individual,
company, product or event.

The **McGraw·Hill** Companies

Contents

Authors and contributors

Dr Mary Connor

Mary is an independent consultant. She has been providing coaching, mentoring, training, supervision and research to both public and private sector organizations for more than 20 years. Previously, she was head of Individual and Organization Development Studies at York St John and honorary fellow at the Centre for Leadership Development at the University of York. She has considerable experience of working with Professor Gerard Egan, of Chicago, USA, author of The Skilled Helper model. She has a particular interest in ethical practice and professional development, and serves on an NHS research ethics committee.

Julia Pokora

Following an early career with BP and Exxon, Julia established an independent organization and management development consultancy, and at that time was an associate with Ashridge Teamworking Services. She has many years' experience of consultancy and has worked with private and public sector organizations. Recently, she has focused on leadership development for teams and individuals, and on developing mentoring and coaching capability in the health service. She holds an MSc in occupational psychology and a Graduate Diploma in counselling.

Wendy Briner is a leadership coach and researcher at Ashridge Management College. She was director of leadership coaching for the Ashridge Leadership Process, introducing coaching as an integrated part of leadership development. Her main activities are designing, participating in and researching leadership coaching processes for the BBC, further education colleges, the World Health Organization, the UAE civil service, the Qatar health service and other private and public sector organizations.

David Harrison is currently headteacher of a primary school, with 23 years' experience in the education sector. He has established a coaching and mentoring culture among the staff in his school and continues to further develop this, within his role as a consultant headteacher to other schools in the local authority where he works.

Malcolm Hurrell is founder and director of New Mindsets Ltd. He works with leaders across both public and private sectors as an individual and team coach alongside work in education, developing coaching and mentoring skills with senior teams in schools. He previously worked as vice president of HR UK at AstraZeneca where he was an active practitioner of coaching and mentoring in business. He is a passionate advocate of coaching, seeing this type of tailored and focused learning as the most impactful development intervention available to senior leaders in organizations.

Shaun Lincoln specializes in training coaches and mentors, and introducing and building coaching and mentoring capability in organizations as diverse as ACAS, the Metropolitan Police, the NHS and further education colleges. He has been an executive coach for over 10 years, specializing in using solution-focused and 'fierce conversations' approaches in one-to-one and team coaching together with MBTI and Insights. He is a founding member of SFCT.

Dr Nancy Redfern is a consultant anaesthetist in the Newcastle upon Tyne Foundation Trust and was associate dean and then dean director at the Northern Postgraduate Medical and Dental Deanery. Between 1995 and 2009 she led the Northern Mentoring Programme for doctors, dentists, nurses and other healthcare professionals. She supports other deaneries, royal colleges and trusts in the UK in establishing mentoring programmes and schemes. As a member of the National Clinical Assessment Service she has wide experience of using mentoring to support doctors in difficulty.

Preface to the second edition

When the first edition of this book was published in 2007, we could not have anticipated the dramatic growth in coaching and mentoring activity and the deepening understanding of what they can offer to the individual and to the organization. There is increasing evidence that coaching and mentoring help people to learn and change, and help organizations to develop and to increase effectiveness. This is the background to our second edition, which revises, updates and supplements the previous edition. We have aimed to enhance the material which readers found particularly useful. We have expanded some sections and added others. We have added two new chapters, discussing reflective practice, supervision, accreditation and frequently asked questions.

We hope that the book will be a source of encouragement and stimulation, whether you are a client, a coach, a mentor, a sponsor or someone who may one day be one of these.

Acknowledgements and permissions

We could not have written this second edition without the support of our immediate families, Bruce, Annie, Luke and Martina. Annie has been a skilful mentor and meticulous proof-reader. Martina has been a gentle strength.

We thank those who have directly helped in the development of this book: Nuala Brice, Geraldine Bynoe, Terry Connor, Sue Covill, Hilary Farrar, Pamela Hartshorne, Marie Johnson, Helen Jones, Marian Orchard and Alan Phillips. We especially thank Professor Gerard Egan for inspiring our thinking and practice over more than two decades. Clients and participants on training programmes have greatly appreciated the value of his Skilled Helper model.

We appreciate the enthusiasm and commitment of all the sponsors and facilitators with whom we work. We thank our clients, and all those who have coached and mentored us, whether knowingly or otherwise. Learning with you, and from you, has informed and encouraged us.

We are grateful to Cengage Learning for permission to reproduce Figures 3.1 and 3.2 from *The Skilled Helper*, ninth edition, by Gerard Egan © 2010. Reproduced by permission: www.cengage.com/permissions.

We are grateful also to the Chartered Institute of Personnel and Development (CIPD) and to Kate Hilpern, for permission to quote from *Coaching at Work*, Volume 1, Issue 2, January/February 2006, pp. 42–5. The extract quoted is from an article 'Bringing Law to Order' written by Kate Hilpern.

Introduction

For more than 20 years we have been involved in coaching, mentoring and supervision at work, both informally and in more structured settings. We have designed and delivered coaching and mentoring training throughout the UK. We have written this book to address, practically, all the aspects of coaching and mentoring at work that seemed important to us. Feedback from colleagues and participants was that they wanted a text which encapsulated the learning from training programmes and sustained them when they were on their own, back at work, trying to be effective coaches and mentors. So we have written this book partly for them.

However, we also wanted to write a book which could be read by clients. Much is said about the partnership nature of coaching and mentoring, yet most of the literature and most training programmes focus on only half of that partnership. The book is written, therefore, for the other half also – the clients – to help them get the best out of coaching and mentoring.

In addition, we wanted to have a voice. We noticed the ongoing debate about coaching versus mentoring, and in our everyday experience we found that these activities had much in common. Conversations with colleagues in both the public and private sectors revealed that while terminology differs, there is considerable overlap in what many coaches and mentors actually do. So, this book seeks to identify the common ground, and to explain the key principles that underpin both effective coaching and effective mentoring.

Another reason for writing this book was to answer frequently asked questions. We wanted to write a book that was accessible to busy people. A book that was full of practical examples and exercises, with ideas that could be used in everyday life and work. The chapters address the topics that are often raised by clients, coaches or mentors, and the penultimate chapter specifically addresses frequently asked questions.

Anyone who has tried to coach or mentor knows just how demanding the work can be. It seems straightforward enough to suggest that someone can be helped to help themselves, rather than being told or advised what to do. However, it can be hard work and it is certainly not commonplace. Spend a few minutes listening to the conversations around you in the workplace and you will see what we mean. Nevertheless, when we have experienced skilful coaching and mentoring from friends, colleagues and professionals, it has made a world of difference. So we hope that this book will support the reader in developing their skills and making a difference.

We are concerned about maintaining high standards in an emerging profession. The serendipity that has been prevalent in the provision of coaching and mentoring services is being rightly challenged by the current focus on competent, ethical and professional practice. In this book we aim to make the connection between everyday practice and ongoing professional development.

Both of us have benefited from wise mentors and coaches, some formal and some informal, some qualified and some not. We hope in this book to share something of their wisdom, which we have found to be more easily 'caught' than 'taught'. It is not easy to capture the essence of wisdom, but we experience a wholeness and a sense of deep integrity in those coaches and mentors who have, in brief moments as well as over many sessions, transformed aspects of our lives.

The structure of the book

Part 1 focuses on effective coaching and mentoring at work. In Chapter 1 we define coaching and mentoring at work, and the key principles which underpin effective practice. In this edition, we have added a description of the influences on our own practice, as well as a more detailed consideration of some approaches that are used by coaches and mentors. In Chapters 2 and 3 we focus on the coaching and mentoring relationship, looking at how the reader can become an effective coach, mentor or client.

Part 2 addresses coach and mentor development. Additions in this edition highlight the growing importance of developing reflective practice and supervision, alongside training, accreditation and professional networking. In Chapter 4 we consider coach and mentor development, reflective practice and supervision. Chapter 5 is an interactive case study exploring aspects of reflective practice and issues to take to supervision. Coaching and mentoring are becoming more professional, helped by the work of the international associations and their accreditation and certification procedures, and Chapter 6 describes the role of training and accreditation and outlines some competency frameworks.

Part 3 explores and illustrates the practicalities of using a model and discusses the use of 12 tried and tested tools and techniques. In this edition we have reworked and updated the two chapters on The Skilled Helper model. In Chapter 7 we explore the model in detail. We get consistent feedback that, when used wisely, it provides a valuable framework for the coaching and mentoring process. Coaches and mentors like it because both the framework and skills are transferable to any aspect of work and life. Clients like it because they can use it on themselves. We like it because it embraces so many different approaches to coaching and mentoring. In Chapter 8 we show how the model can be used in practice with an interactive case example that invites you to be the coach. The case example illustrates the development of a learning relationship and how you might use the stages of the framework and key skills. Chapter 9 presents some useful tools and techniques which can support coaching and mentoring, with a discussion of their advantages and disadvantages.

Part 4 considers important questions, issues, and recommendations about developing coaching and mentoring in practice. Chapter 10 explores ethical issues. Chapter 11 offers responses to 10 questions which we are frequently asked when training coaches and mentors. In Chapter 12, five contributors describe their experiences of culture change through coaching and mentoring. We reflect on developments since the first edition, and draw together some key questions for assessing the coaching and mentoring culture in your organization.

A note about examples used in the book

We have tried to make this book as practical and relevant as possible, so you will find that it is full of examples, many of which are interactive. Confidentiality in coaching and mentoring is key. For this reason, throughout the book we have constructed the examples rather than use client case material.

PART 1
Effective Coaching and Mentoring

1 What is effective coaching and mentoring at work?

- Introduction
- Nine key principles for effective practice
- Coaching and mentoring in context
- Influences on our practice
- Some useful approaches
- The wise coach or mentor
- Summary

Introduction

Our aim in writing this book is to capture the essence of coaching and mentoring, and to energize and equip the reader, whether as coach, mentor or client, and whether coaching or mentoring formally or informally.

There are increasing numbers of full-time professional coaches and mentors for people at work. In addition, many managers and professionals offer coaching and mentoring within their organization or profession. Even more of them use the skills in leading and managing individuals and teams. This book is addressed to all these groups, and to those who are not yet actively involved in coaching and mentoring. It is for those who want to find out more about effective coaching and mentoring, and who:

- are already a coach or mentor;
- want to become a coach or mentor;
- are looking for a coach or mentor;
- use coaching or mentoring skills at work;
- are participants on coaching or mentoring programmes;
- train or supervise coaches and mentors;
- want to establish or review the provision of coaching and mentoring in their organization or profession;
- see coaching or mentoring as part of leadership, management or professional development.

Terminology can be problematic and so in this book we generally use the term 'client' to refer to the person with whom the coach or mentor is working. We acknowledge that in real life they may be called, for example, 'mentee' or 'colleague'.

There has been considerable debate in the literature about the differences and similarities between coaching and mentoring. It is evident that what is described in one organization as mentoring might be known in another as coaching. Recently, with acknowledgement that use of the terms varies widely, attention has turned to the common ground, and it is to this common ground that our book is addressed.

What is this kind of helping, this kind of learning, which is not teaching or telling or advising or instructing? Whatever it is, it is certainly in demand, and the number of coaching and mentoring articles, journals, special interest groups and training courses has increased rapidly in recent years.

We define coaching and mentoring as *learning relationships* which help people to take charge of their own development, to release their potential and to achieve results which they value (see Figure 1.1). We believe that the learning relationship is central to both coaching and mentoring, which are more than just a set of activities or skills. Through the relationship, the client develops and changes, as, indeed, does the coach or mentor.

Clients are helped to take charge of their own development. The coaching or mentoring relationship facilitates insight, learning and change. Through this relationship, potential is identified, possibilities become reality and tangible results are delivered. Coaching and mentoring help a person to see the present as a springboard to the future, and to be strategic about their development.

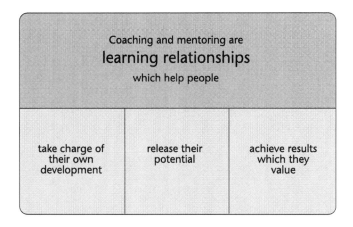

Figure 1.1   Definition of coaching and mentoring

Whether the person seeks help with a specific current work issue, or a longer-term career question, the coach or mentor will facilitate exploration, help in the formulation of goals and provide support while action is implemented.

Nine key principles for effective practice

Effective coaching and mentoring are underpinned by nine key principles (summarized in Figure 1.2). These principles, derived from our experience, have informed and guided our coaching and mentoring. We introduce them here. In subsequent chapters, they are explored in greater depth and linked to case examples and interactive exercises.

1   The LEARNING relationship is at the heart of change
2   The CLIENT sets the agenda and is resourceful
3   The COACH OR MENTOR facilitates learning and development
4   The CONTEXT is work
5   The OUTCOME is change and action
6   The APPROACH OR MODEL provides movement and direction
7   The SKILLS develop insight, release potential and deliver results
8   The QUALITIES of the coach or mentor affirm, enable and sustain the client
9   ETHICAL practice safeguards and enhances coaching and mentoring

Figure 1.2   Nine key principles for effective practice

1 The learning relationship is at the heart of change

The central principle is that learning, change and transformation occur through the relationship with a coach or mentor. Coaching and mentoring are not just an interaction, an event, an opportunity. Two people meet. They share knowledge, values, attitudes, skills and experience. They engage with one another, they relate to one another and if the coaching and mentoring is effective, they *connect* with one another. Dialogue is important in establishing and maintaining the connection. In a learning dialogue there is, on both sides, a willingness to share perspectives, to listen, to understand, to be open to new ideas and to take joint responsibility for the conversation and the outcomes. Dialogue sustains the connection and it follows, therefore, that the learning relationship is a partnership, and not an activity imposed by one person on another.

2 The client sets the agenda and is resourceful

Centre stage in the learning relationship is the client and their agenda. Being centre stage and being the focus of attention can be both challenging and empowering for the client. Some clients are reluctant, some are eager. Where a client is referred, they may have little interest or belief in creating their own agenda. Some clients have clear goals, some only vague ideas. In all cases, the start point of the effective coach or mentor is to work with the client to help them figure out what they want. This process, the first step in facilitating the client's learning and development, can be relatively straightforward, or may be one of the most demanding parts of the coaching and mentoring relationship. However, unless the client chooses to be a partner in the learning relationship, and has a sense of purpose, the relationship cannot be successful.

Once the agenda is clear, the task of the coach or mentor is to help the client to identify and use the resources, both internal and external, that will enable them to change and develop. Affirming the client's resourcefulness, and communicating this affirmation to the client, is an important role. When the client seems to lack energy or focus, or ideas, or direction, or creative alternatives, the coach or mentor can communicate hope and possibility, and work with the client to make these real. A coach or mentor can enable a client by believing in them at times when the client's self-belief falters.

3 The coach or mentor facilitates learning and development

The coach or mentor is a facilitator, not an instructor. They support and challenge the client to learn and to develop. The client learns by acquiring new awareness, insight, skills, ideas and knowledge. Development involves integrating this learning into their everyday working and way of being. It is important that the facilitator asks questions which provoke new perspectives and change in the client.

The effective facilitator reviews the learning relationship and the learning process, and does not take these for granted. The client is asked what might help their learning and development. The effective facilitator finds learning methods that suit the client. They help the client to clarify how they learn best, and how to make coaching or mentoring work for them.

Finally, the effective facilitator understands the importance of what happens between sessions. They know that coaching and mentoring sessions should be a catalyst for learning and action, not a substitute.

4 The context is work

This book is about coaching and mentoring at work. The focus is on the relationship with an individual client, although the principles apply also to team coaching. The client may want or need to improve their work performance in the short term, or they may be concerned with broader issues of personal, professional and career development. Short- and long-term issues are often interrelated. The effective coach or mentor values the client as a whole person within their work context. The focus of coaching and mentoring is the client's present and future experiences, problems, opportunities and development. The best results are produced when there is a balance between developing strengths and resources and addressing areas for development.

The effective coach or mentor knows enough about the work context to be able to facilitate exploration of issues and is aware that opportunities and resources in the workplace differ from person to person.

Coaching and mentoring are not career patronage, neither are they counselling or therapy. The effective coach or mentor agrees with the client the boundaries of their coaching or mentoring work, and is aware of other resources and networks beyond these boundaries.

5 The outcome is change and action

Coaching and mentoring enable reflection leading to change which produces valued outcomes. The client achieves something that they care about, that makes a positive difference in their working life or career. The real significance of change should be judged in relation to the client agenda and their goal. A minor change in attitude for one client may be just as transforming as a major job promotion for another. Insight and understanding are important in coaching and mentoring in so far as they lead to change. Of course, change is hard work. Change provokes resistance, a normal reaction to facing up to difficult issues. Resistance can be viewed as a sign that the coaching or mentoring dialogue is on track and that it is touching on important issues for the client. Effective coaches and mentors work with client resistance, rather than try to overcome it. They use resistance to help the client to clarify their values and their goals, and to explore what will help or hinder them in making changes.

6 The approach or model provides movement and direction

If coaching and mentoring are about change, then the approach or model used provides a map for the journey, for both client and coach or mentor. It does not fully describe the landscape of the journey, but rather it provides reference points and a sense of direction. It can help if either party gets stuck or loses direction. Any approach, model or framework should be used with a light touch, or even set aside, if that is what would be most helpful for the client. It should not be used to constrain or limit exploration of the landscape.

7 The skills develop insight, release potential and deliver results

The effective coach or mentor uses skills appropriately to enable the client to develop insight and release potential. The effective coach or mentor is competent, using the skills in an integrated way within the learning relationship, not merely applying a set of competences. The skills communicate the coach or mentor's belief in, and valuing of, the client. Wise and judicious use of the skills ensures a balance of support and challenge, of reflection and action. The effective coach or mentor has a repertoire of tools and techniques which they offer appropriately to the client to support their learning and development.

8 The qualities of the coach or mentor affirm, enable and sustain the client

The distinctive style, personality, values and experiences of the coach or mentor are shared as 'self'. Moreover, when the chemistry between coach or mentor and client really works, there is a sense of deep connection. The paradox of this connection is that it is not tangible and yet it is powerfully present and effective in bringing about client self-belief, hope, courage and action.

Effective coaches and mentors are not only smart, but also wise. They have the wisdom to make sound judgements about what they see, hear and experience in the learning relationship. They communicate caring, valuing, respect and empathy. They model a way of being which is both human and professional. This is not deliberately taught but is often 'caught'. Learning is not just 'from' the coach or mentor, but also 'with' and 'through' them. Learning 'through' the coach or mentor is often overlooked, yet it may be the most powerful learning of all.

9 Ethical practice safeguards and enhances coaching and mentoring

The client is safeguarded if ethical principles inform and guide practice. Such principles might include: respect for client autonomy; faithfulness to promises made; acting in ways which are beneficial to the client; not doing harm; and acting fairly. When these principles are in operation there is an openness and transparency in the coaching and mentoring relationship. This not only safeguards the interests of both parties, but also enhances the quality of their work together. Effective coaching and mentoring start with clear expectations and a working agreement, continue with ongoing review, and finish with well-prepared endings. Ethical coaching and mentoring are informed by legal requirements and professional codes of practice. Working within agreed limits and boundaries helps the client to feel secure, for example in relation to issues of confidentiality or conflicts of interest.

Coaching and mentoring in context

Since writing the first edition of this book, plenty of evidence has emerged that both coaching and mentoring are becoming embedded in organizations. Cultures are changing. Senior leaders are relying less on external coaches to help transform teams and departments. There is now increasingly the expectation that all managers and leaders should use coaching skills to encourage learning and development throughout the organization, as well as to increase productivity. Coaching is used alongside appraisal, work planning and performance review. Experience is showing that the positive approach of helping people to 'astound themselves' is far more beneficial than the type of coaching which focused on remedying performance deficits. Rogers (2008: 7) puts it this way: 'The coach works with clients to achieve speedy, increased and sustainable effectiveness in their lives and careers through focused learning. The coach's sole aim is to work with the client to achieve all of the client's potential – as defined by the client'. The rise in executive coaching has given a strong message that the most successful leaders are also clients who benefit from working regularly with a coach. Meanwhile, mentoring has also been developing, away from the concept of patronage and sponsorship in which the use of power and influence worked for some but not for all, to a more inclusive concept of exchange of experience, resources, knowledge and information. Megginson *et al.* (2006) highlight two contrasting models of mentoring: sponsorship versus developmental. The trend now is away from sponsorship in which the mentor actively champions the client with the primary motive of career or professional success. It is towards more developmental mentoring where the mentor may be experienced but not necessarily more senior and their aim is to facilitate learning rather than being the 'expert' who provides the answers.

Mentoring may be used to support the development of newly recruited staff, or as a means of identifying and sustaining talent at different levels of an organization. The mentor may, or may not, be someone more experienced or senior in the organization or profession. Often their services are offered and taken up voluntarily, through mentoring networks and schemes. Mentoring can be either short term or long term and may involve aspects of personal, professional and career development. It is frequently used at times of induction or transition in organizations, particularly when the client is promoted or demoted. In some mentoring schemes, clients are offered a limited number of sessions over a set period of time. In other organizations the mentor is available in a more developmental role over a longer period of time. This mentoring may be less structured and more informal, but nevertheless greatly valued. Parsloe and Wray (2000: 82) summarize mentoring as 'a process which supports learning and development, and thus performance improvements, either for an individual, team or business. Mentoring is usually understood as a special kind of relationship where objectivity, credibility, honesty, trustworthiness and confidentiality are critical'.

We have found overlap in what is described as coaching, and what is presented as mentoring. Some of these similarities have been identified by Zeus and Skiffington and are summarized in Figure 1.3. Both coaching and mentoring base their assumptions on basic values and beliefs: that humans have the ability to change; that they make the best choices available to them; that helping is not a quick fix – 'it is a journey where the process of learning is as important as the knowledge and skills gained' (Zeus and Skiffington 2000: xv). Zeus and Skiffington talk about coaching and mentoring as essentially a conversation where learning takes place through asking the right questions rather than providing answers. This leads to personal and professional transformation and reinventing of oneself.

- Both require well-developed interpersonal skills
- Both require the ability to generate trust, support commitment, generate new actions through listening and speaking skills
- Both shorten the learning curve
- Both aim for the individual to improve his or her performance and be more productive
- Both encourage the individual to stretch, but can provide support if the person falters or gets out of his or her depth
- Both provide support without removing responsibility
- Both require a degree of organizational know-how
- Both focus on learning and development to enhance skills and competencies
- Both stimulate personal growth to develop new expertise
- Both can function as a career guide to review career goals and identify values, vision, and career strengths
- Both are role models

Figure 1.3   Similarities between coaching and mentoring (Zeus and Skiffington 2000: 18)

The Chartered Institute of Personnel and Development (CIPD 2010) attempts to differentiate coaching and mentoring but acknowledges that the same skills and models are used in both. The CIPD notes that coaching is often shorter term, focused on skills and knowledge leading to improved performance, and ultimately linked to achievement of organizational objectives. On the other hand, mentoring relationships can be longer term and more broadly developmental, and traditionally mentoring has referred to a more experienced person helping a more junior or inexperienced colleague. Table 1.1 provides a summary of some of the differences highlighted by the CIPD (Jarvis 2004: 19).

We understand the distinction made between coaching as shorter term and performance focused, versus mentoring as longer term and focused on career and professional development. However, we are aware that, in real life, specific performance development issues and broader professional development are often inextricably linked. In this discussion of the context of coaching and mentoring at work, we have included differing perspectives. Our own view, having worked in this field for some considerable time, is that:

- in practice, coaching and mentoring often overlap;
- nomenclature is often context driven rather than activity driven – for example, the activity which is called 'coaching' in the business sector may be referred to as 'mentoring' in the health, education and public sectors;
- both coaching and mentoring may encompass the transmission of knowledge or skills and this should be accomplished in a facilitative, rather than a directive, way;
- our definition of coaching and mentoring, and our nine principles for effective practice, apply equally to both activities.

Coaching	Mentoring
Relationship generally has a set duration	Ongoing relationship that can last for a long period of time
Generally more structured in nature; meetings are scheduled on a regular basis	More informal; meetings can take place as and when the client needs some advice, guidance and support
Short term (sometimes time-bounded) and focused on specific development areas/issues	More long term and takes a broader view of the person
Coaching is generally not performed on the basis that the coach needs to have direct experience of their client's formal occupational role, unless the coaching is specific and skills-focused	Mentor is usually more experienced and qualified than the client, often a senior person in the organization who can pass on knowledge, experience and open doors to otherwise out-of-reach opportunities
Focus is generally on development/issues at work	Focus is on career and personal development
The agenda is focused on achieving specific, immediate goals	Agenda is set by the client, with the mentor providing support and guidance to prepare them for future roles
Coaching revolves more around specific development areas/issues	Mentoring revolves more around developing the client professionally

Table 1.1   Differences between coaching and mentoring

Influences on our practice

We have found that the most important thing we bring to our work with clients is ourselves. In this section, we discuss approaches which have particularly influenced us and which we have incorporated into the way we work. These approaches have been experienced by us as clients and as helpers in both formal and informal coaching and mentoring contexts.

A significant influence on our work is that of humanistic approaches and particularly the work of Carl Rogers (1961, 1983). Rogers emphasized the importance of psychological 'contact' between helper and client, and particularly the presence and communication of the core conditions of respect, empathy and genuineness. Humanistic or person-centred approaches describe the innate positive tendency of people, given the right conditions, to grow and to develop, to fulfil their potential and to self-actualize. Maslow's research (1970) highlighted the importance of the core conditions. He found that unless basic needs for acceptance, respect and trust were met, then higher-order needs for achievement and self-actualization were unlikely to be realized. Many later research studies (e.g. Lambert 1992) have confirmed the importance of the core conditions and found that a positive relationship between helper and client is one of the predictors of positive outcomes.

Interestingly, very few coaching and mentoring approaches nowadays agree with Rogers that the core conditions are both necessary and *sufficient* for change to occur, although a great many of them cite the core conditions as important cornerstones upon which to build their particular approach. This has resulted in the downplaying of the importance of relationship, and we are pleased that in recent times there have been signs that this downplaying is being questioned.

What we value from the person-centred approach is the emphasis on relationship and connection between two people, and on the intrinsic human capacity for growth. We experience again and again in our work the transforming power of being fully present with, and listening to, a client, and in so doing enabling them to access their own resourcefulness.

The non-directive element of the humanistic approach can be thought to imply, erroneously in our view, 'not really going anywhere', and in the work context, with an emphasis on performance and results, more upbeat-sounding 'going somewhere' approaches may have greater face validity and acceptability. In this context, we wonder whether the term 'coaching' has become more acceptable in the business world because it is viewed as more performance-oriented than the term 'mentoring'.

The humanistic view of the individual as growth-oriented and resourceful is also found in the field of positive psychology, with the emphasis on using client strengths and resources to enhance well-being (Seligman 2002). As coaches and mentors we value this reminder that our work is developmental not remedial. We find this particularly useful with clients who are in difficulty at work. These could include clients who are 'sent', having been identified as underperforming, or clients who self-refer, perhaps seeing themselves as undervalued in their organization. Positive psychology encourages clients to identify and apply their strengths to achieve their goals. It should not be misunderstood as offering bland reassurance to clients that all will be well or as glossing over difficult or important issues. Rather, it uses intentional interventions to help clients build their resourcefulness and lead more fulfilled lives. We find such interventions are particularly useful in helping clients to access resources and creativity at times when, if they are stuck with a problem, they may not feel very creative or resourceful. A simple prompt – for example, 'How can you use your strengths in this situation?' – may be enough to catalyse client thinking and action.

Similarly, appreciative enquiry (Cooperrider *et al.* 2003) emphasizes helping the client to appreciate what *is*, and to build on successes and strengths. It employs specific questions about existing strengths and current positives, and we find that this can work well. Brief or solution-focused therapy (Berg and Szabo 2005) employs some similar approaches, with an emphasis on exploring the client's 'preferred future' and identifying any pieces of that future that are already happening. Associated with these approaches is the so-called 'miracle question', which might be asked thus: 'If you were to wake up tomorrow morning and a miracle had occurred and the problem was sorted, what would things look like, what would be different?' For us, a strength of these approaches is that they help the client to focus on the future and on positive goals, rather than negative ones. So, for example, a client who states that their goal is 'I will stop feeling anxious in meetings' can be asked to restate it in a positive way: 'I will feel confident and assertive in meetings'. Positively stated goals are more likely to be achieved. Similarly, some clients get stuck going round and round analysing and dwelling on their problems. They are unwilling or unable to contemplate the future because the difficulties in the present absorb their energy and attention. Techniques such as brainstorming a preferred future, or even a gentle prompt ('So what would this look like if it were just a bit better?') can enable clients to move forward.

Motivation theory asserts that appropriately stretching goals are most powerful in changing behaviour. A 'stretch' goal is neither too hard nor too easy to achieve, and is a powerful motivator when it is self-determined and not imposed. As coaches and mentors we have experienced the powerful impact for clients of identifying personally meaningful, realistic goals. Research by Gail Matthews (undated) indicates that when goals are written down, and shared with a trusted person, they are more likely to be achieved, and we notice that this simple intervention can increase the probability of client success.

While we value motivational and goal-setting approaches, we realize that goal-setting is neither simple nor straightforward for many clients. There is an interesting debate among coaches and mentors: some think that helping should start with asking the client what their goal is, as in the GROW model (Whitmore 2002), while others think that the client benefits from telling their story and imagining their preferred future in order to arrive at a meaningful goal, as in The Skilled Helper model (Egan 2010). Our experience has been that some clients are not ready or able to set substantial goals, even after more than one session. However, after each session we expect that a client will act in some way, whether that is a significant change, simply reflecting on the session, or taking a small step.

We have been influenced by cognitive behavioural coaching (CBC) which asserts that the way a person thinks about events influences the way they feel, and how they behave (Neenan and Dryden 2002). We find these ideas particularly useful in enabling clients to self-challenge. A client can ask themselves whether their thoughts and beliefs are justified and whether they are helping or hindering in the situation. Self-limiting beliefs can be questioned and replaced with ones which help rather than impede performance. The client who asserts 'I'm hopeless at job interviews' restates this as 'Some interviews have gone well for me and others not', and similarly 'I always fall to pieces under pressure' becomes 'When I am well prepared I can withstand interview pressure'.

Taking the time to help clients explore their stories and underlying themes and patterns in their lives is a powerful intervention. An awareness of psychodynamic approaches has helped us here (Johnson 1985). When unconscious beliefs and assumptions (perhaps formed very early on in life) are limiting the client's capacity to manage problems and make the most of opportunities, it can be a welcome relief to examine and challenge these beliefs in a safe and supportive context. However, we would caution against too much interpretation, or seeking underlying patterns or meanings which may not exist. We once heard a sound piece of advice for the coach or mentor: 'Always work at the least interventionist level necessary to help the client to achieve change.'

Helping clients to become aware of their personal stories and how these shape their identity and behaviour is emphasized in narrative-based approaches to coaching and mentoring. Launer (2002) describes six concepts taken from family therapy, and from these we draw some useful reminders for our work: being fully attentive in the conversation and listening to what the client actually says rather than what we think they mean; staying both curious and neutral as the story unfolds; asking reflective questions which encourage the client to examine and expand their perspective; talking with the client about how we work together, not just focusing on the content of the client story; and working *with* the client rather than applying a particular approach *to* them, irrespective of whether it is right for them.

It may be tempting to see our coaching and mentoring conversation as talking 'about' change, while the real change happens 'out there' back in the client's world. Hawkins and Smith's model of transformational coaching (2006) challenges this view, and describes the 'shift in the room' when a fundamental shift in client thinking, feeling and behaving occurs in the coaching or mentoring session. The emphasis is on the here and now, and the relationship in the room, in order to change things 'out there'. These ideas have helped us to be brave in challenging ourselves and our clients when things get stuck. Hawkins acknowledges that to work in this way may seem risky, but the impact is potentially very powerful. Similarly, Gestalt approaches describe the importance of heightened awareness of the here and now. The Gestalt paradoxical theory of change asserts that change occurs when one is fully in contact with what is, rather than trying to be different or disown parts of ourselves (Bluckert 2010: 83). We have found techniques which originated in Gestalt, such as 'role reversal' and 'empty chair', to be particularly helpful for clients in bringing immediacy to the session, so that rather than 'talking about' an issue, they *experience* it.

Another important influence on us has been the work of Isabel Briggs Myers, and her mother, Katharine Briggs, in developing the Myers-Briggs Type Indicator® questionnaire.[1] Their aim was to make Jungian Type theory accessible and useful to individuals and groups (Myers with Myers 1980). We find the MBTI questionnaire a useful way of working with differences and similarities between ourselves and our clients. Clients find it helpful in thinking about their relationships and how they lead, manage and influence others (Bayne 2004). For example, the client who likes to keep their options open and gather more information may be irritated by their colleague who prefers to reach conclusions and make decisions. An awareness of 'type' can help the client to work with difference rather than seeing it as an obstacle, and appreciate that both approaches have value. However, we are aware that questionnaires don't suit all clients and this one does not, nor does it claim to, explain all differences between people or capture each person's unique individuality.

Many successful leaders and managers are also coaches and mentors. We are intrigued by research (Boyatzis *et al.* 2006) that highlights the benefits for a leader of being a coach. Coaching others and experiencing compassion serves to balance at a physiological level the effects of the stresses of the leadership role. We find that leadership research often resonates powerfully with clients. For example, Goleman (1998) describes the link between successful leadership and emotional intelligence (EI). He defines EI as 'the capacity for recognizing our own feelings and those of others, for motivating ourselves and for managing emotions well in ourselves and in our relationships'. He describes five EI competencies: the personal competencies of self-awareness, self-regulation and motivation, and the social competencies of empathy and social skills. These competencies can be developed and we find many clients are able to use these ideas in their personal and professional development.

This section would not be complete without futher reference to The Skilled Helper model (Egan 2010). While some coaches and mentors may experience the framework as constraining or too simple, we find it both liberating and embracing complexity. Used wisely, it has enabled us to apply the ideas and approaches we have described above. Our experience of using the model is rather like two people going for a walk in the countryside with a good map. Both can look at the map. It doesn't dictate their journey. It doesn't prevent

---

1 MBTI and Myers-Briggs Type Indicator are registered trade marks of the Myers-Briggs Type Indicator Trust.

them from slowing down or speeding up or taking shortcuts or meandering away from the path. Rather, it helps them to know where they are, albeit that they may choose sometimes to get pleasantly lost. It helps them to judge wisely the best route for them for that day, given the weather, their stamina and how much time is available. And they can return another day, map in hand, with a clearer sense of the terrain, to choose which direction they will then take.

Some useful approaches

Coaching and mentoring are learning relationships which help people to take charge of their own development, release their potential and achieve results which they value. In this section we explore several approaches which contribute to coach or mentor effectiveness in relation to:

- releasing potential for change;
- working with the relationship;
- focusing on performance;
- team coaching.

Releasing potential for change

In the previous section, we referred to humanistic and positivist approaches. These describe the core conditions for effective helping as belief in the client and communication of genuine interest, respect and empathy. The co-active coaching model is based on these conditions. There are four 'cornerstones' that are the foundation of co-active coaching (Whitworth *et al.* 1998: 3):

1   The client is naturally creative, resourceful and whole.
2   Co-active coaching addresses the client's whole life.
3   The agenda comes from the client.
4   The relationship is a 'designed alliance'.

The aim of the 'designed alliance' is that both client and coach have joint responsibility that the coaching will meet the client's needs. Clients learn to be in charge of the changes they will make in their lives. Coaches and clients use listening, intuition, curiosity, action learning and self-management. Two forces are used to create change: action and learning.

> Because the notion of *action* that moves the client forward is so central to the purpose of coaching, we make 'forward' a verb and say that one of the purposes of coaching is to 'forward the action' of the client. The

other force at work in the human change process is *learning*. Learning is not simply a by-product of action, it is an equal and complementary force. The learning generates new resourcefulness, expanded possibilities, stronger muscles for change.

(Whitworth et al. 1998: 5)

When using this model the coach or mentor can focus all their attention on listening to the client and moving in whatever direction the client wants. Experience and skill are needed to 'freewheel' in this way.

Releasing potential for change is an important aspect of positivist approaches, which include appreciative enquiry and solution-focused coaching. In appreciative enquiry, the aim of the mentor or coach is to help the client through a four-stage cycle (Pask and Joy 2007: 212):

1   *Discovery*: through dialogue involving systematic enquiry the client is helped to identify within a particular focus the elements that they find challenging, interesting and energizing and to which they can commit.
2   *Dream:* the client is encouraged to project positive elements of the existing situation into a positive vision or dream of how the future ideally might look.
3   *Design*: the client thinks through and designs a strategy to achieve the articulated vision or dream.
4   *Destiny:* the client focuses on implementing the vision, and, importantly, sustaining and developing the energy, hope and enthusiasm and positive relationships underpinning the design.

In this approach the mentor or coach focuses on change from the outset. Below is an example of some appreciative enquiry questions for a client who is having problems with their team. Rather than asking what is wrong with the team, the mentor or coach invites the client to think about the strengths of individual members and a time when they worked to achieve something that the client valued. This might include questions such as:

- 'Describe a high point experience in your senior leadership team – a time when you were most engaged or excited!'
- 'Without being modest, what is it that you most value about yourself and your contribution to the team?'
- 'What do you most value about the team and its contribution to the organization?'
- 'What do you think are the core factors that give life to the team?'
- 'If you had three wishes to heighten the vitality and health of the team, what would they be?' (Pask and Joy 2007: 215 from Cooperrider *et al.* 1999: 11–12).

Such questions (Cooperrider *et al.* 1999: 11–12; Pask and Joy 2007: 215) are valuable in trying to develop new perspectives and uncover blind spots which prevent the client from moving forward. They energize and give hope. There are some similarities between the discovery, dream, design and destiny cycle and the stages of The Skilled Helper model. The latter model is described as 'A problem-management and opportunity development approach to helping'. In the model there are three stages:

1   Current picture: *What's going on?*
2   Preferred picture: *What do I need or want?*
3   The way forward: *How do I get what I need or want?*

The client is invited to tell their story, identify an aspect they would value working on, brainstorm their preferred scenario, choose and commit to a goal and then develop strategies and a manageable plan that will lead to valued outcomes. These stages help to release client potential by creating the opportunity for them to identify what they really value and then encouraging them to 'dream' about their preferred future.

Another approach which releases the potential for change is solution-focused. This has some similarities with appreciative enquiry and focuses on practicality and simplicity. It is positive and pragmatic (Jackson 2002). The methodology is based on:

- finding what works and doing more of it;
- finding what doesn't work and doing something different;
- finding and using resources;
- finding and building on successes.

Some of the techniques which are used to help people include focusing on what clients say they will do, not on what they won't do, and using questions of scale, such as 'On a scale of 1 to 10 where are you now? What would it take to move you from where you are now to where you would like to be on this scale? How much is good enough?' Questions about how well a person is coping with a difficult issue at work would not concentrate on the problem but would focus on client resources to solve it: 'I can see that . . . is very difficult at the moment . . . and I am noticing that you have still managed to . . . I am wondering how you have managed to do that?' In this example, helping the client to be aware of their strengths may make them feel more positive about moving forward. There are the classic questions: 'Tell me, what is already going well for you? and 'When . . . worked well, what was it that was different?'.

An exercise in positive psychology, to help clients move towards a goal that seems unattainable, is explained this way: 'Visualise yourself on one side of a gap, with the goal on the other side. Now let's construct bridges over that gap. Let's consider your top five strengths, and see how each one can be used to connect you to what you truly want to be' (Kauffman *et al.* 2010: 161). The coach begins with the client's top strength, for example persistence. They then invite the client to develop an action plan, *a road map for crossing the bridge*, using that strength of perseverance. Then the client is asked to create another bridge with their next highest strength and the process is repeated with the other four strengths. Two other techniques are useful: the first is to help the client to get into the habit of affirming what is going well, the second is to encourage the client to remember that tiny steps make a big difference.

Working with the relationship

Relationship is the way in which two or more people are *connected*. There is currently an interest in relational coaching, partly, we suggest, growing out of the experience of those who have found that models of performance coaching leave certain questions unanswered. 'Relational' tells us about the way in which the two people, coach or mentor and client, *relate to* one another. Whereas some approaches focus on what is happening in the client, relational coaching is equally interested in what is happening in the coach, and indeed in the way coach and client are both *relating to* one another. Coaches and mentors who have had a background in psychological (Berne 1976), psycho-therapeutic (Perls 1951; Jacobs 1989), sociological (Mead 1967) or construc-tivist (Gergen 2003) perspectives have realized the importance of understanding how meaning is communicated between coach and client. In this section we share some perspectives on the dynamics and transactions which may occur in the here-and-now of a coaching or mentoring session.

In relational coaching there is an ever-present awareness that past experi-ences of attachments and relationships with significant others are likely to influence the current ways of relating, between coach or mentor and client:

> When a coaching client meets his or her coach, he/she brings into the encounter, both consciously and unconsciously their experience of primary relationships, their expectations of someone who is supposed to be there for them . . . This relational approach requires the coach to be capable of self-awareness and reflexivity, to allow him or herself to be subject to the process of relating, rather than to be in control of it, and hence to being changed by the interaction. It is also risky in the sense that precise outcomes cannot be forecast. Working fully in the relation-ship increases the possibility of emergent novelty at the necessary expense of predictability.
>
> (Critchley 2009: 26, 29)

Relational coaches notice and respond to the dynamics between coach and client as they are actually happening in the session.

Berne (1987) helps us to understand, and work with, the way that the past impinges on the present. He examined communications or 'transactions' between people and his analysis suggested that most communication arises from three ego states: parent, adult and child. These ideas form the basis of transactional analysis (TA). TA ideas and techniques are widely used in coaching and mentoring, and coaches and mentors who use TA may notice certain 'scripts' which come from these ego states, such as 'I must always be perfect', 'I cannot succeed' and 'One day I will be found out'. People learn scripts early on in life, and these can become unhelpful 'games' in later life; however, the effective coach or mentor can enable the client to identify and challenge these.

The Karpmann Drama Triangle (1968) illustrates this by showing how the roles of persecutor, victim and rescuer get shifted around in such a game. So, it can happen that the well-meaning coach or mentor is perceived by the client as the persecutor, while the client sees themselves as the victim. For examples of scripts and games in coaching and supervision see Hay (2007). Coaches and mentors find TA valuable as a way of noticing the transactions taking place within the session. It is also useful when exploring difficulties which the client is having in relationships at work or elsewhere. The wise coach or mentor reflects to the client what is heard and experienced, but in a spirit of enquiry and invitation to explore, rather than offering expert interpretation. *The aim is for interpretation to come from the client, not from the coach or mentor.* Working with scripts, games and transactions can lead, in the session, to rehearsal of different ways of communicating with others back at the workplace (for further detail on TA and the Drama Triangle, see Chapter 9).

When the coach or mentor is fully aware of what is going on in the here and now, they work in an appropriately immediate way. This can make a real difference to the client. They can learn that it is safe to be authentic with the coach or mentor, and so they are more likely to be authentic in their other relationships. The importance of this authenticity is evident in the Gestalt relational approach. Bluckert (2010) suggests that this approach would not be appreciated by all clients, but that it is useful with those who are flexible, reflective and interested in both their internal and external worlds. He outlines some core assumptions: that clients are always doing the best they can; that change occurs when the client is fully in contact with 'what is'; that heightened awareness helps people into new ways of seeing, choosing and acting; that each context and situation has its own dynamic which needs to be understood; that so-called 'unfinished business' holds clients back from realizing their potential; and that exploring the 'here and now' provides 'the best opportunities for learning and growth by such questions as *What are you aware of now?*' (Bluckert 2010: 83). So clients are helped to develop an honest awareness of what is happening in themselves in the moment-to-moment encounter with the coach or mentor. They are encouraged to 'make contact' or 'meet' all parts of themselves, their work and workplace, their colleagues and friends.

Gestalt theory asserts that change occurs, paradoxically, not by moving to the future, but by remaining fully in contact with the present. However, making contact with 'what is' means getting in touch with parts of the self which have been disowned or denied, maybe because important basic needs have not been met or satisfied in earlier experiences. The difficulty of doing this cannot be overestimated and in Gestalt theory there are four major obstacles to making contact with the self. Two of these are introjection and retroflection. Introjects are the 'shoulds' and 'oughts' which may have been acquired from parental and other adult expectations. These interrupt contact with what the client 'wants'. Retroflection occurs when clients turn inwards with their real thoughts and feelings, perhaps in the workplace, where they do not feel safe to express themselves and where, for example, they may have allowed themselves to become invisible or overlooked. A client may have lost contact with what they really think and feel. If the coach or mentor can stay fully present with them so that they feel safe enough to 'make contact' with what they really want and need, this can be powerfully liberating for the client. Contact leads to the sort of 'connectedness' that develops from this shared vision of honesty and transparency and from the willingness to empathically challenge when 'contact' is being interrupted. It is this quality of connectedness which enables the relationship to be transforming for the client.

Focusing on performance

Approaches which focus on achieving specific performance outcomes are often informed by cognitive behavioural psychology. They use knowledge of the ways in which thinking, feeling and acting are interrelated and affect client outcome. They focus upon present experience and future possibilities. They use techniques of behavioural reinforcement to accentuate positives and reduce negatives. They have a common aim to help clients formulate and achieve specific, measurable, realistic goals within clear timeframes. Neenan and Palmer (2001: 17) describe the coaching relationship as 'a collaborative relationship that helps individuals to focus on problem-solving in a structured and systematic way'.

GROW is a popular coaching model developed by Whitmore (2002) for performance coaching. It has been used extensively in executive coaching and coaching at work. With the emphasis on performance and outcome, the GROW sequence starts by asking the client to identify a *Goal* or outcome which they want to achieve. Once this is identified, the coach helps the client to track back to their current *Reality*. Once the client has explored where they are now and where they want to be, they are then helped to explore all the *Options* for getting there. Finally, having decided upon options the client explores the *Will* to act.

Several writers on performance coaching and executive coaching base their ideas on the 'inner game'. Much of the thinking in performance coaching originated from sports coaching, including the difference between the 'outer game' of performance and the 'inner game' of attitude and psychology. Gallwey (2000) states that the outer game of improved performance will only be possible if there are changes in the inner game of thinking and feeling. The power of positive thinking is at the heart of the inner game approach. The important concept is that *potential minus interference equals performance*. Downey (2003: 11) is an advocate of this approach and explains that time and time again he has noticed that what prevents successful performance is the emotional interference that comes between potential and achievement. He cites the following examples of interference that get in the way and stop us focusing on the goal: fear, doubt, lack of confidence, the 'be perfect' driver, anger, boredom and frustration.

The coach helps the client to identify interference and then to work with it to minimize its impact. This leads to 'relaxed concentration', which in turn leads to performance that flows. The relationship between this approach and sports coaching is obvious. We all recognize 'flow' in excellent performance, whether it be playing tennis, playing the piano or public speaking. Downey gives useful examples of listening for emotions when the client tells their story. Like Whitmore and Gallwey, he starts by asking about aspiration. When the client starts talking about their dream, the coach or mentor listens not only to the external reasons why the client thinks this cannot be achieved, but also the internal reasons, 'the interference', which perhaps have never been articulated before. Although Whitmore, Gallwey and Downey keep their focus very much upon outcome in coaching, they also use skilled listening and questioning to be facilitative with the client, rather than direc- tive. In fact, Downey calls his approach 'non-directive coaching': 'Coaching is the art of facilitating the performance, learning and development of another' (2003: 21).

Coaches who use the neuro-linguistic programming (NLP) approach draw attention to similiarities between the 'main pillars' of NLP and the stages of the GROW model. Grimley (2010: 190) states that the NLP coach focuses on three main questions:

- Does the client know specifically what they want?
- Can they keep their senses open so they know what they are presently getting?

- Do they have the flexibility to keep changing until they get what they want?

Grimley suggests that the goal of NLP coaching is maximizing client resourcefulness and increasing choice. This is to be done with an awareness of context. The coach helps the client to see that if they get stuck it is because of the way they are construing the world. Self-awareness is key, with goal achievement as an important outcome.

There are several features in common between Whitmore's GROW model and The Skilled Helper model (Egan 2010). Both approaches highlight the important relationship between wanting and acting. Both focus on articulating specific goals for change. Both test commitment to the goal. However, the differences are in the sequencing of events. In Egan's approach, commitment is tested before options and action plans are drawn up. In both models it is important for the coach or mentor to be flexible and not to follow the model rigidly. The Skilled Helper model is explored in Chapters 7 and 8. It provides a framework for the coaching and mentoring process which can be used with some of the ideas and approaches which have been presented in this section.

Team coaching

While this book is primarily about the learning relationship between the individual client and the coach or mentor, in team coaching the client *is* the team. Team coaching is growing in popularity as a way of developing high-performing teams, which are often found to: have a high level of agreement about their common purpose; work closely together; be 'mutually accountable'; and value and respect individual differences (Katzenbach and Smith 1993). Team coaching helps to align individual, team and business goals.

Definitions of team coaching vary; however, many authors agree that task performance and team development are both important components of successful coaching. Therefore, a team coach might be expected to have an understanding of group dynamics (Bion 1961), group development (Tuckman 1965) and team roles (Belbin 2003), as well as an awareness of organizational culture and its impact on team learning (Pokora and Briner 1999).

Team coaching may be used to: encourage more effective teamworking in an existing group; accelerate the development of a newly-formed group into a working team; enhance the coaching skills of team leaders; and develop cross-boundary teams which address organization-wide issues. Barden (2006: 6) outlines how team coaching may be useful with a team which already works together:

a team may be coached when it is no longer aligned with its purpose. That can occur when the organisation has changed its focus and a key team is having difficulty in following suit. The team leader has – perhaps through individual coaching – become aware of the need for a new purpose and the team needs to revisit its key elements.

In practice, the team coach will often work with one or more management sponsors, as well as with the team, and may coach individual team members to enhance their participation in the team. Executive coaches may start work with an individual executive client and then be asked to coach the client's team. In this scenario, boundary issues and conflicts of interest need to be clarified.

The skill of the team coach includes firstly, aligning team outcomes and achievements with business expectations and targets, and secondly, maximizing the distinctive contributions of individuals to ensure high performance of the team as a whole. Although team coaching can be cost-effective and rewarding, it is not an easy option. It requires sensitivity, skill and adaptability on the part of the team coach who manages a variety of individual and organizational expectations.

The wise coach or mentor

So far we have defined coaching and mentoring at work, explained the nine principles underpinning effectiveness and shared some approaches and models which have influenced us and which are commonly used. Now we turn to consider what it is that makes a coach or mentor not just competent, but also effective, and wise.

Clutterbuck and Megginson have observed numerous coaches and mentors at work and conclude that mature practitioners are those who, although informed by particular models and approaches, do not stick to them rigidly. Instead, they constantly ask themselves three key questions when working with a client: 'Are we both relaxed enough to allow the issue and the solution to emerge in whatever way they will? Do I need to apply any processes or techniques at all? If I do, what does the client context tell me about how to select from the wide choice available to me?' (Clutterbuck and Megginson 2010: 7). They call this way of working 'systemic eclectic'. These mature coaches or mentors are demonstrating the confidence to be able to 'let go' and 'freewheel' with the client. This requires the wisdom to make difficult choices from moment to moment in the session. When we have experienced as clients the help of a 'wise' coach or mentor, what has made the difference? For one of us, it was like this:

My mentor was just a natural. So natural that I didn't even notice his skills, but they were certainly there. He wore his experience lightly, keeping himself in the background. But he was himself, he showed me that he cared, he gave me enough time to talk and think. He could be very challenging too, but he seemed to consider carefully when to be like this, watching me closely for my reactions. I was continually surprised at how well he seemed to know me. He would know just when to push and just when to hold back. I felt like I was moving along with my issues and targets and he seemed to intuitively understand when to say something and when to just stay quiet.

I wanted to learn from him. I chose him because he knew how my organization worked and he knew the politics there. He shared his own experiences with me so that I felt I was with a real person and not just some 'professional front'. He gave me time. That was a big thing. I needed to make some changes at work, but wasn't ready at first. He never tried to move me too quickly into making those changes. There were moments when something would click. I may have suddenly opened my eyes to something and we would share that eureka moment together, he would be as pleased as I was! There were other difficult moments when we seemed temporarily to be not connecting and he would take his time, give me time, and then ask if I would like to look at what was happening, together. This we would do and each time, although difficult, it brought our relationship to a new level of trust. The times when I sensed he had really understood, he didn't need to say anything, there was just a certain twinkle in his eye, a smile, a quizzical expression and in that moment I knew he was 'with' me.

So, what is this wisdom? Competencies are tangible, wisdom less so. Wisdom seems to be about discerning what is needed at any one time and using sound judgement. To make such wise choices, the coach or mentor needs to be able to tune into the client on several levels at once. Such sensitivity, combined with caring, gives a special quality to the relationship. People talk about 'connecting', being 'in tune with one another', moving together 'in harmony'. These expressions attempt to capture the essence of being with a coach or mentor who is wise as well as competent, who trusts their instincts and intuition as much as their knowledge and skills, who knows when to hold back and do nothing, and when to move forward and actively engage, who uses all their senses to communicate a real belief in the worth and capacity of the client to achieve what they want and value.

Summary

In this chapter we have:

- Proposed a definition of coaching and mentoring as learning relationships which help people to take charge of their own development, to release their potential and to achieve results which they value.
- Outlined nine key principles which underpin effective coaching and mentoring.
- Explored the context of coaching and of mentoring.
- Shared some influences on our practice.
- Discussed some useful approaches to coaching and mentoring.
- Concluded with thoughts about effective and wise practice.

2 How can I be an effective coach or mentor?

Introduction

The purpose of this chapter is to help you to be an effective coach and mentor, and to use coaching and mentoring skills effectively at work. You may already be a coach or mentor, or wondering whether you want to become one. You may be interested in how coaching or mentoring skills could help you to be more effective as a leader or manager. You may be considering whether coaching or mentoring could benefit your organization or profession. This chapter helps to answer these questions. It addresses, from the coach or mentor perspective, questions about how coaching and mentoring work in practice.

In this chapter we describe the qualities and characteristics of effective coaching and mentoring and how it differs from other helping relationships. We show how key coaching and mentoring skills can be used to help the client. We explore how the learning relationship is established, sustained and concluded. We discuss how frameworks and tools can help coaches, mentors and their clients to make the most of coaching and mentoring.

We include practical exercises, checklists and activities, as well as case examples designed to illustrate key points.

 Where you see this sign, there is an activity for you to complete. The questions are written assuming that you are already involved in coaching or mentoring. However, even if you are not yet actively involved, you can reflect on what your answers might be.

Why be a coach or mentor?

In the previous chapter we defined effective coaching and mentoring, and explored the common ground and key principles. In both coaching and mentoring, one person is helping another with either short-term work issues or longer-term development, or perhaps a mixture of both. Their relationship, a learning partnership, is crucial in releasing potential and producing results. One person becomes a trusted and faithful guide for another on a journey of personal, professional and career development which may last for many weeks or months or perhaps for only one meeting. Whether the journey is long or short, the objective is the same: to help someone to achieve change which they value.

While reading this description you may have recognized work you are already doing, or work in which you would like to be involved. Take a moment to think about your motivation by completing the following activity.

 Complete the following sentences.

- I'm interested in coaching/mentoring because . . .
- What I have to offer as a coach or mentor is . . .
- My experience of coaching or mentoring (whether formal or informal) is . . .
- I value coaching/mentoring because . . .
- What I want to achieve as a coach or mentor is . . .
- The benefits for those I coach or mentor are . . .
- The benefits to my profession/organization are . . .
- The benefits for me are . . .

What do your answers tell you about your motivation? What do you want to achieve though coaching or mentoring? Any surprises? Any questions raised?

The benefits of coaching and mentoring for both individuals (coaches, mentors and clients) and organizations are well documented (Garvey and Garret-Harris 2005; Steven *et al.* 2008). A survey of mentoring research papers from the USA and Europe reported that benefits were not only for the client (40 per cent) and the business (33 per cent), but also for the mentor (27 per cent) (Megginson *et al.* 2006: 30). A mentoring guidance pack (NHS Finance Staff Development 2004: S1.2) lists potential mentee benefits, describing how mentoring can develop the ability of the mentee to:

- understand how they think, how they see the world and how this impacts on how they behave;
- think creatively and from multiple perspectives;
- manage their own learning and understand how they learn best;
- be self-managing and self-reliant, using techniques such as self-directed reflection and self-analysis to identify issues and understand themselves;
- understand how to manage change and manage their own transitions;
- analyse issues/problems and apply effective decision-making approaches to problem-solving;
- be confident in dealing with others, in networking, interpersonal scenarios, managing people and situations, influencing, etc.

Organizational benefits can include attracting and retaining staff, reduced stress levels, improved performance of staff, the development of a more supportive culture, improved equal opportunities and reduced training costs. Mentor benefits include increased personal satisfaction gained from developing others, increased knowledge and skills, recognition by others and greater self-insight.

Here are some examples of coaches and mentors talking about the benefits, and the costs:

> **Jo, a senior nurse and experienced mentor, and someone who is keen to continue her own development:** I've helped several people to get clearer about their career direction, and to become more focused in their thinking. Now, I see them being successful and fulfilled. I hope I've put something back into the profession and encouraged people. I know how important that is, and it wasn't around for me when I started out. I've also learned a lot about myself, for example, just because I'm more senior doesn't mean that I know what's best for someone. Mentoring has made me more aware of how I deal with colleagues and patients. It does take time and it competes with other demands, but for me it is worth it.

Ryan, an HR director, who has developed a coaching skills programme for senior staff, and wants to develop a coaching culture: Obviously, there are significant direct and indirect costs incurred in running a training programme. A benefit is that we have seen, over the years, a transfer of participants' coaching skills into everyday work situations and 'the way we do things around here'. We haven't yet tried to quantify the benefit, but qualitative evaluation shows that staff are using the skills and the mindset in both formal coaching and also in day-to-day work. For example, a colleague remarked to me that 'you can tell if someone has been on the coaching course – it shows in the way they approach problem-solving in meetings'.

Nita, a manager: Coaching is an integral part of my job, not a separate function. I'm responsible for developing my staff, and we have a very positive coaching culture here. I see myself as a resource for staff, and the benefits are tangible in terms of improvements in performance and the development of individuals. What are the costs to me? Well, reminding myself that sometimes I need to bite my tongue and not rush in and fix things!

You can see from these examples that costs and benefits may be both tangible, for example, time or money, and intangible, for example, personal satisfaction.

 What are the benefits for you of coaching or mentoring? What are the costs?

Helping without telling

Coaching and mentoring are different from *patronage* and from *therapy*. In patronage, a senior person nurtures the career advancement of a more junior colleague. The patron may act as a sponsor for the individual and may use their own professional networks to aid the person's career or development. In therapy, a qualified professional helps to resolve difficulties which may be long-standing, personal and not necessarily work-related.

In coaching and mentoring the focus is on the individual at work, and while this may encompass personal issues, coaches and mentors do not work in depth in the way that therapists might work. Table 2.1 describes some of the ways in which coaching and mentoring differ from patronage and from therapy.

Patronage	Coaching and mentoring	Therapy
Career advancement	Problems and opportunities	Personal problems and difficulties
Career-related	Work- or career-related	Issues may be deeply personal/unrelated to work
Patron unlikely to be trained	Coach/mentor uses skills and framework	Therapist is qualified practitioner
Boundaries less important – may be intentional overlap	Coach/mentor agrees boundaries	Therapist operates strict boundaries
May be same profession/ field	Coach/mentor may be internal or external	Therapist is outside organization
Patron opens doors	Emphasis is on learning and development	Therapist helps to resolve problems
Patron is senior	Coach/mentor may be senior/colleague/junior or independent	Therapist is impartial and independent
Patron may not expect feedback on relationship	Feedback is part of learning relationship	Amount/use of feedback dependent on therapeutic approach

Table 2.1   Patronage, coaching and mentoring, and therapy

Emil, a mentor: I've been a mentor for several years for fellow professionals, helping them think through career and work issues. Of course, I have a good network and sometimes that's helpful, but my role isn't to smooth their career paths. In fact, over the years one or two have left the organization, and that's been right for them, they've moved on to new pastures. Occasionally someone brings something that I'm not skilled to deal with, for example a relationship issue or a health problem, and then we talk about how they might get help elsewhere.

Angela, a coach, has a career background in counselling. She reads a list of coaching competences. One item on the list refers to paying attention to the client's agenda, rather than what the coach thinks the agenda should be. Angela is an excellent listener and she is respectful and pays close attention to what her clients say. However, she has been wondering whether she sometimes steers her coaching clients, in her words, 'to get to the bottom of things' rather than 'to get on with things'. She says, 'Maybe I'm more interested in insight than action!' She decides that in future she will pay particular attention to this, and ask clients what they want to focus on in each session, and what outcomes they want.

 How do you see your role as a coach or mentor? Is it different from that of patron or therapist? Are there any topics that you think are outside the scope of coaching or mentoring?

Box 2.1 is a list of possible roles for a coach or mentor.

Box 2.1 Some roles of the coach or mentor

- **Supporter:** a confidential respectful listener who does not judge or evaluate
- **Challenger:** helps the client to challenge themselves, and offers empathic challenge
- **Sounding board:** helps the client to explore 'half baked' ideas and thoughts
- **Networker:** helps the client to identify key connections and develop relationships
- **Coach:** helps the client to develop skills and confidence
- **Role model:** has qualities or attributes to which the client aspires
- **Critical friend:** offers constructive feedback
- **Strategist:** helps the client to look at the broad picture and think long term
- **Catalyst:** helps the client to develop new perspectives and harness their creativity

---

While the list shows how varied the coaching and mentoring role can be, you might notice that one role, that of *expert*, is missing. Coaching and mentoring are different from the help which many of us offer in everyday working life, when we give advice to people who benefit from our expertise. Expertise is at the heart of many jobs and professional roles. The expert helper, by and large, knows more about the topic under discussion than the person being helped.

As a coach or mentor, although we may have experience and expertise, our primary role is to help the client to find *for themselves* resourceful ways forward in dealing with issues facing them. The coach or mentor helps the client to explore their experience and resources. In this way, the client gains insight and generates *their own* solutions. These are more likely to be successful than solutions proposed by a coach or mentor. Table 2.2 illustrates the differences between expert and coach or mentor.

Expert	Coach or mentor
Emphasis on knowledge	Emphasis on process
Expert insight is key	Helping skills are key
Provides direction	Provides a 'map'
Puzzle-solver	Facilitator/enabler
Gathers/analyses information	Enables information-gathering
Facts and logic	Facts, logic and feelings
Diagnoses the problem	Explores the problem
Problem can be solved	Problem can be managed
Definition of problem is objective	Definition of problem is subjective
Expert knowledge important	Client insight important

Table 2.2 Some differences between coach or mentor and expert

So, if coaches and mentors seek to enable and empower, rather than to offer answers or advice, how does that work in practice? Here are some examples of client dilemmas. These might arise in an everyday work conversation, for example between a manager and an employee, or in a more formal coaching or mentoring session.

- How can I be more assertive at work?
- How can I develop my career?
- Is this job offer right for me?
- How can I manage a difficult colleague?
- What's the best way to deal with this demanding customer?
- How can I better manage my work–life balance?

The 'right' answer or way forward with each question depends to a large degree on the person asking it. Each question does not have one 'correct' answer. So, for example, looking at the first dilemma: the best way for person A to be more assertive at work may be very different from the way that works best for person B. These questions or dilemmas are examples of what Revans (1983), writing about action learning, calls 'problems'. He uses the word 'problem' to describe an issue which can be dealt with in different ways by different people. He sees 'problems' as different from 'puzzles'. Puzzles have one right answer, just like a crossword puzzle. Expert advice is important, and even vital, in finding the right answer to a puzzle – for example, a complex medical diagnosis. Problems, however, require a different approach, and coaching and mentoring is often more appropriate than expert advice. Of course, expert knowledge can play a part in coaching or mentoring. However, the role of the coach or mentor is primarily that of facilitator or enabler, rather than expert, as the following examples illustrate.

> **Jack is an interpersonal skills coach** for senior executives. He helps clients to improve their influencing and conflict resolution skills. He is familiar with research on these topics, and shares this 'expert' information with them when appropriate. However, Jack focuses initially on each client's experience of what is helping and hindering their effectiveness. He helps each client to identify what changes are important to them and their organization, and to look for appropriate situations where they can try out and refine new skills. He shares expert research with a 'light touch', rather than imposing it.

> **Ruth, a doctor,** uses a coaching approach to develop the junior doctors who work in her unit. She is highly experienced, and has realized over the years that 'If I just tell them the answer, or do it for them, then they don't really learn. I have to get alongside my trainees, to ask them questions which challenge and develop them, and of course I'm there as a safety net if they need it.'

The next activity will help you to reflect on how much expert helping you do at work.

 How much expert helping do you do at work?

To what extent are the following usually true, or not? In what ways are coaching or mentoring different from your usual helping role?

- I know more about the subject than the person I'm helping
- People seek out my knowledge and experience

- I know what facts or information are relevant to solving things
- I ask questions to gather relevant information
- I can usually give people the right answer or some options
- I gather facts and evidence
- I sort irrelevant from relevant information
- I generate options for people
- I propose solutions for people

Finally in this section, Shaun Lincoln (Sulaiman 2006) suggests an activity for those considering becoming mentors: 'Test yourself. Can you listen for more than ten minutes without giving advice? If you can't you might want to hesitate.' We would add here that, after hesitating, you might seek some training or development to enhance your skills!

Building a learning relationship

How clients perceive the coaching or mentoring relationship is important. When their view of the relationship is positive, then coaching or mentoring is more likely to be effective. What is the learning relationship? Clients can learn:

- *from* the coach or mentor, from their experiences, knowledge and insights;
- *with* them, during the learning conversation;
- *through* them, from the way they are, sometimes called their 'way of being'.

Some of these more intangible qualities of the relationship are not easy to capture in words. Carl Rogers, writing about helping relationships, describes how, in striving to be trustworthy, he sought to fulfil the 'outer conditions of trustworthiness' (1961: 50), for example being punctual, maintaining confidences and being consistent. Over time, he realized that it was equally important to be 'dependably real' or *congruent*, a quality often described nowadays as *genuineness*. Genuineness involves being aware of our own feelings and being able to use them to connect with the client, rather than hiding behind a façade or professional veneer. Genuineness does not mean blurting out everything we are thinking or feeling. It does mean being aware of ourselves and our reactions and being willing to engage with the client, to be fully part of the learning partnership. The more we are fully present and genuine in the relationship, the more the client is freed up to be likewise.

In the following example we see that genuineness may be challenging for the client, but may lead to learning. Notice how the coach is not judgemental. He simply states the impact of the client's words on him as listener, and asks a question.

> My coach interrupted me and said, 'I know that this is really important to you, but you're giving me so much detail that I'm having difficulty in following you. Is all this detail helping you?' I was taken aback. Was it helping me? No, and it wasn't helping him either! I'd just assumed that it was useful and I realized I do that at work too. I flood people with data before asking them what they want. Although it was a bit of a jolt, it was powerful learning for me when he didn't pretend to be interested. Maybe that's what people at work do, they just pretend to be interested.

Respect means accepting and affirming the person as they are. As coach or mentor we may not agree with or like all aspects of the client's behaviour or views, but we aim to suspend our judgement and evaluation. Demonstrating respect can be difficult when the other person makes decisions that we would not choose, as the following example illustrates. However, at times like these it can be most powerful.

> Eventually, I ended up telling my mentor that, despite everything the firm had done for me, I still thought that this wasn't the right career for me. I know people find that hard to hear. They see my success and think that I'm being ungrateful or self-indulgent, but he was different. He listened very quietly and attentively. I guess I was expecting disapproval, but there wasn't any. I know he sees things differently, but he respects my view, and that means a lot.

The third important quality identified by Rogers is *empathy*, which is different from sympathy. Though both words derive from the Greek word *pathos*, meaning 'feeling' or 'suffering', the prefix s*ym*- indicates 'sharing' or 'being in agreement', whereas the prefix *em*- indicates being 'in'. When we communicate empathy, we try to appreciate how it is to be the other person, to walk in their shoes, to experience the situation as they experience it, from within. Rogers describes how communicating empathy involves more than trying in a detached way to understand 'about' someone.

Empathy is a powerful tool in coaching and mentoring because it communicates to the client that we have understood, or at least tried to understand, their unique experience, rather than imposing our view or making assumptions.

A colleague is talking. Below are two potential responses. One is empathic, one is sympathetic. How are they different? Which is the empathic response?

Colleague: Fred is being impossible. We're jointly accountable for this project, but he's constantly passing the buck. He turns up late to meetings, hands all the tough decisions to me, and when the pressure is on, he goes off sick, whatever that means.

Response A: He sounds terrible! I don't know how you cope!

Response B: You're finding it tough – it seems as though he's not pulling his weight.

Response B is the more empathic response because it reflects the colleague's experience as seen by them. Notice that it implies neither agreement nor disagreement, but tries to communicate *understanding*. Response B is likely to be more productive in helping the colleague to address the problem, because it offers support but stays focused on the colleague.

Response A is more sympathetic because it implies *agreement* with the colleague. It is likely to lead to a conversation with the colleague about Fred, but not necessarily about what the colleague can do to change the situation. The risk with a sympathetic response is that we end up agreeing or colluding with a person, but not helping them to move forward in managing the problem.

In effective coaching and mentoring, the coach or mentor communicates empathy, respect and genuineness to the client. Sometimes this happens quite naturally. Sometimes it may be more difficult. This may be because a client is different from the coach or mentor – for example in culture, upbringing, beliefs or values. However, in effective coaching and mentoring, the client is acknowledged and valued as they are, and the challenge for the coach or mentor is to seek to understand issues in the way that the client experiences them. Communicating this willingness to understand will help to build the learning relationship, which is at the heart of change. In the next section we will look at some core skills which help us to communicate respect, empathy and genuineness.

Some core skills

Active listening

Using core skills we bring to life the coaching or mentoring framework, and create a dialogue between coach or mentor and client. In our experience of

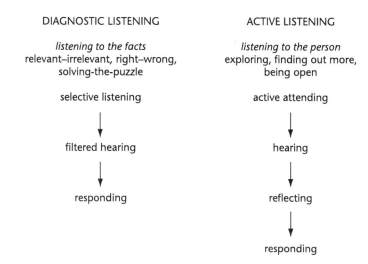

DIAGNOSTIC LISTENING

listening to the facts
relevant–irrelevant, right–wrong,
solving-the-puzzle

selective listening

filtered hearing

responding

ACTIVE LISTENING

listening to the person
exploring, finding out more,
being open

active attending

hearing

reflecting

responding

Figure 2.1   Diagnostic versus active listening (Phillips and Pokora 2004)

training coaches and mentors, the single most useful skill, which underpins all others, is that of *active listening*.

Figure 2.1 shows how active listening differs from diagnostic listening. When the coach or mentor listens diagnostically, they are trying to sift and sort information, to analyse what is relevant or irrelevant, trying to find a solution. This kind of listening can be useful when solving a puzzle, in the kind of expert helping described earlier. For example, a doctor asks a patient if a pain is stabbing or diffuse, whether it is worse before or after eating. The doctor is eliminating potential diagnoses and narrowing the search for the correct one. They are deciding what information is irrelevant and filtering it out; deciding what information needs elaboration; and gradually refining and focusing options based on their expertise and experience.

However, when the coach or mentor uses diagnostic listening, it can be less than useful, because it puts them in the driving seat and they end up leading the conversation. They ask closed questions (usually about facts) to get information to 'solve' things, and they slip into the role of expert helping. When the coach or mentor listens diagnostically, they end up generating options and solutions. In contrast, when they use active listening, they add value by helping the client to expand their understanding of the problem or opportunity so that *the client* can manage it better. When the coach or mentor listens actively, they are open to all information: feelings as well as facts. They are free to follow rather than lead the client. In effect, they are holding up a mirror and saying, 'This is what I see/hear. Is that right? Is that how it is for you?' Active listening communicates that the coach or mentor is trying to understand the client's experience, and so it builds trust and a supportive learning relationship. Active listening, with a 'credulous attitude' (Kelly 1963: 174) tries to take in all information, verbal and non-verbal, factual and emotional, and to understand from the client's perspective.

For many people, it takes considerable effort to stop diagnostic listening and to start active listening. The temptation to treat problems as if they were puzzles and to try to 'solve' them can be almost overwhelming.

When the coach or mentor listens skilfully, the experience may be like this:

> Imagine someone listening, not only to your words, but also to what's behind them – who even listens to the spaces between the words. Someone in tune with the nuances of your voice, your emotion, your energy who is intent on receiving everything you communicate. Someone who listens to the very best in you, even when you can't hear it in yourself.
>
> (Whitworth *et al.* 1998: xviii)

The following example shows how active listening can be used, and how it is different from diagnostic listening. Jane is trying to help a newly-promoted team leader who comes to her with a problem.

> **A team leader describes the problems he faces in establishing an effective team:** I feel as if I've been parachuted into a war zone. The department is divided, with factions sniping at each other, and so much unproductive conflict. We have a major deadline in four months, and it is vital that we start pulling together and stop wasting time and energy. Communication is breaking down – for example, at our weekly meeting, people become 'unavailable' at the last minute. I've inherited this situation – a hornets' nest – and I think part of the reason I was promoted was that senior management believed that I could sort it out. I suppose I should be encouraged by their faith in me, but . . .

Jane is trying to help. She is listening diagnostically and here are some of her responses:

- How many people are there in your department?
- Have you thought about involving the HR function?
- Could you try a team-building day?
- Can you renegotiate the deadline?

These questions arise from diagnostic listening, and are easy to recognize. They usually help the person asking the question more than they help the person answering it! They include:

- suggestions framed as questions;
- questions to which the client already knows the answer;
- closed questions, which invite a one-word (often 'yes' or 'no') answer.

As an alternative, here are some active listening techniques:

✓ paraphrasing the story: *'if I've understood . . .'*;
✓ prompting by echoing key words or phrases, with a question mark;
✓ creating space by counting to three (silently!) before responding;
✓ summarizing the key parts of the overall message.

 If Jane uses active listening, what responses might she make? Try to generate some responses using the skills of paraphrasing, prompting and summarizing. Some possible responses are below.

Here are some examples of how Jane might show that she is actively listening:

- *Paraphrasing:* If I've understood you, it feels like a war zone, and you've been parachuted in to sort it out, and fast.
- *Prompting:* War zone? *Should* be encouraged?
- *Summarizing:* You're finding this a pretty tough situation to handle. You're new; external expectations are high; and the team seems to be in self-destruct mode.

These examples show how Jane could communicate to the team leader that she is actively attending and trying to understand his experience without filtering, judging or evaluating it.

Encouraging self-challenge

While support is an important part of the coach or mentor role, clients want and need *challenge*. When clients are encouraged to challenge themselves, they can:

- develop insight;
- become aware of their blind spots;
- challenge self-limiting beliefs;
- notice previously overlooked strengths and resources;
- focus on the future;

- implement action;
- become more strategic and proactive.

 Think of a time when you were helped with a difficult issue, a problem. What helped you to challenge yourself? Was there anything that made it more difficult?

Active listening can serve a dual purpose. As well as supporting the client, it can help them to challenge themselves. Continuing with the previous example, let's look at how Jane's responses might help the team leader to self-challenge:

- When Jane says : *If I've understood you right, it feels like a war zone, and you've been parachuted in to sort it out, and fast* he realizes that he resents being 'parachuted in', even if he is supposed to be encouraged. At the same time, he notices that the metaphor of war is a strong one and he asks himself if things are really that bad.
- When Jane says : *You're finding this a pretty tough situation to handle. You're new; external expectations are high; and the team seems to be in self-destruct mode* he wonders if *all* the team are in 'self-destruct mode'; maybe he is overlooking some potential *allies*.

So when the coach or mentor uses active listening skills, they build trust, by demonstrating that they are trying to understand how the client sees things. They also, as the example has shown, increase the likelihood that the client will challenge *themselves*.

Sometimes active listening isn't enough and the coach or mentor may want to challenge the client more directly. Challenge is potentially strong medicine, and the coach or mentor earns the right to challenge by actively listening and challenging the client in an empathic way rather than a confronting way. As with too strong medicine, a too strong challenge will be rejected.

 Box 2.2 contains a list of challenges that might be used in coaching and mentoring. Imagine that you are Jane. Read down the list and identify some challenges which might help the team leader. How might you phrase the challenge?

Box 2.2 Areas for challenge in coaching and mentoring

- *Feelings:* what are the client's feelings in the situation? The client may focus on what they are thinking, or what's been happening
- *Others' perspectives:* how do other people see the situation? How do they see the client? The client may focus only on their own viewpoint
- *Evidence:* are there any facts to support/contradict the client's thoughts or feelings? The client may over-interpret or generalize or lack evidence
- *Blind spots:* is there anything the client might have overlooked?
- *Ownership:* in what way is the situation a problem or an opportunity for the client themselves? The client may focus on the situation in general, rather than the impact on them
- *Patterns:* has the client 'been there before'? Do they recognize a pattern in their life?
- *Goals:* is the client clear about what they want instead of what they've got? The client may find it easier to say what they *don't* want
- *Action:* is the client willing and able to do something to move towards their goals? The client may find it easier to talk rather than to act
- *The 'here and now':* is something happening in the session which mirrors how the client describes things at work? Or something that contradicts it?

 Look again at the list. Which of these challenges have you used in coaching or mentoring? Which do you find easiest? Which might be more difficult for you?

Creating a working agreement

A clear working agreement is the foundation of a productive learning relationship. It describes how the coach or mentor and client will work together, and so gets their relationship off to a good start. Importantly, it frees up both parties to focus their energy and attention on learning and development, rather than being distracted by unresolved questions or concerns. The coach or mentor models transparency by being open about what they can offer, and what they cannot, and how they want to work. This builds trust and creates the climate for learning. The working agreement is an opportunity to:

- agree with the client how you will work together;
- clarify any uncertainties;
- find out what they expect and want;

- explain what you can offer;
- answer their questions;
- deal with contractual issues.

Robert, a mentor for teachers: At the start of mentoring I ask the client quite a few 'what if' questions: What if we talk about something that can't be kept confidential? What if you don't turn up for a session? What if we think mentoring isn't proving useful? By asking these questions, I involve them in reaching an agreement, rather than imposing it.

Meg, a board-level coach: Over the years I've learned that it's helpful to be clear about the things, not many, which are non-negotiable. For example, sessions always take place away from the client's office, to free them up from job demands, and always during working hours, so that they see coaching as part of their real work. On the other hand, it is important to find out about, and be responsive to, how the client learns best, and be flexible about what will help them.

 Below is a list of items which might be included in a working agreement for coaching or mentoring. Work through the list and note your response to each item. Would you include all these items in a working agreement? Would you add any? Which do you view as negotiable? Non-negotiable?

Practical
- ❏ Pre-coaching or mentoring introductory session
- ❏ Location – where will you meet?
- ❏ Frequency – how often will you meet? Minimum/maximum number of sessions
- ❏ Length of session – what would you prefer? Agree to?
- ❏ Payment – how much? Payment procedure?
- ❏ Cancellation – policy for missed session? What if the client is late?

Working relationship
- ❏ Preferred ways of working together
- ❏ Tools and techniques you might use
- ❏ Your values and the learning relationship
- ❏ Balance of support and challenge you will offer

❏ Feedback – 360-degree, other?
❏ How client learns best
❏ Framework or model you use
❏ Your expectations – work outside of sessions

Professional
❏ Your qualifications
❏ Your experience/references
❏ Your responsibilities: legal, to the sponsor, to your profession or organization
❏ Any possible conflicts of interest?
❏ Note-taking – Who takes? Who keeps? For how long?
❏ Supervision – your arrangements

Ethical
❏ An explicit working agreement
❏ Built-in ongoing review
❏ Confidentiality: extent and limits
❏ Clear role boundaries
❏ Ending session

Many people use coaching and mentoring skills in their managerial or professional role, and a formal agreement may be unnecessary because the learning relationship is already established. However, where coaching or mentoring is an 'off-line' activity, whether the coach or mentor is internal or external, a more explicit contract is useful. This may be particularly important where third parties are involved. It may take the form of a written contract, signed by all parties, and many mentoring and coaching schemes have formal contracts describing responsibilities and boundaries. A formal contract can specify what kind of information, if any, the sponsor will receive about the content and progress of mentoring or coaching. Sometimes third parties will want more information than the coach or mentor, or client, is prepared to give.

Sustaining a productive relationship

The effective coaching or mentoring relationship is productive: it helps the client to achieve change. Regardless of whether the relationship extends over only one session or over many months or even years, it has a beginning, a middle, and an end. At each stage, beginning, middle and end, the coach or mentor works to support and enable client change. The coach or mentor pays attention both to the learning relationship and also to client outcomes. There are different issues associated with each stage and below is an introduction to some of these issues.

Managing the beginning

The coach or mentor aims to establish a productive learning relationship. Some aspects of getting started are illustrated by the case example of Harry, a coach who is meeting a potential client for the first time.

Fully attending. The coach or mentor pays attention to both the non-verbal and verbal messages from the client. They try to maintain a relaxed and attentive posture, including appropriate eye contact, facial expression, tone of voice and leaning towards the client but not invading their personal space. The coach or mentor clears their mind of other distractions, so that they can be receptive and open to the client. To communicate what they have heard, the coach or mentor reflects and paraphrases, clarifies and summarizes. All this is done tentatively, giving the client the space to correct any misunderstanding. In the example below, Harry picks up verbal and non-verbal cues from his potential client, and summarizes what he has heard.

> **Harry meets with a new client,** who is very keen to have some coaching, saying that Harry has been highly recommended by her colleagues. The client's busy schedule means that she wants coaching meetings in the early evening, as she would find it difficult to take time out of the day. Harry notices that the client is not very relaxed: she glances at her watch from time to time. Harry checks that he has understood the key points of her story and reflects to her that she seems concerned with time pressure, even during this first session together. This prompts her to talk more about how work pressures are affecting her.

Clarifying boundaries. The coach or mentor is clear about the working arrangements and what they can offer the client. They also say what they are unable to offer. As their conversation continues, Harry is clear about his boundaries, demonstrating genuineness, but also being respectful to the client by offering alternatives.

> Harry, in response to her request for evening sessions, says that he understands that she will find it difficult to make time, but that he offers sessions only between 9 and 5. The client says she is very keen to work with Harry and would be prepared to pay extra. He explains

that he is unable to do this, and suggests tentatively that perhaps finding time in the day might help her to prioritize coaching. However, he also offers her the names of other coaches who offer more flexible hours than he does. On reflection, she agrees to work with him.

Sorting out the working arrangements. This may include the framework and learning processes that might be used. Expectations and limitations are discussed, helping to establish trust and reduce uncertainties on both sides. In addition, the beginning of coaching or mentoring is the appropriate time to agree any contractual arrangements. Harry is responsive to agreeing a workable schedule with his client, and is clear about how he works as a coach.

> Harry explains the coaching process, and the framework he uses. He believes that it is important to agree goals and action plans at the end of each session, and review these at the start of the next, and he checks whether this way of working will suit his client. He suggests that they meet fortnightly, within working hours, but she is concerned that her busy schedule will result in her missing some appointments, so they agree to meet every three weeks, within working hours, initially for three months.

Focusing and prioritizing. The coach or mentor helps the client to clarify and prioritize their aims, to focus their effort and attention and to increase the chance of successful outcomes. In the first session, Harry helps the client to focus on two issues and also to commit to action before the next session.

> Harry's client manages to clear her diary and they meet for a first session in working hours. By the end of the session Harry has helped her to prioritize her aims for coaching. These are: to improve her presentation skills and her time management. They agree that these two issues are probably related. They have also discussed how coaching can help her to achieve these aims, and what she wants from her coach. She agrees some actions she will take before their next meeting.

So, by fully attending to the client's expectations, by clarifying boundaries and working arrangements and by focusing and prioritizing, a learning relationship has been successfully established. The list in Box 2.3 contains useful reminders for coaches and mentors, and summarizes the important aspects of managing the beginning.

Box 2.3 Managing the beginning: some questions for coaches and mentors

- Am I able to give the client my full attention?
- Have we both been involved, as far as possible, in the decision to work together?
- Is this the right kind of help for the client at this time?
- Are we clear about the client's priorities for coaching or mentoring?
- Have we talked about limits of confidentiality? Possible conflicts of interest?
- Have I described the framework I use? My professional background and experience?
- Have we talked about how the client learns best?
- Have we agreed time/place/note-keeping/financial arrangements?
- Have we begun to establish a working relationship? How can I tell?
- Am I concerned about anything? Any unresolved issues that might benefit from supervision or support?
- Have I created the opportunity for the client to express any concerns or questions?

The ongoing relationship

Having established the working relationship, the coach or mentor will help the client to:

- *Reflect on the work they are doing*, both during and between sessions, and learn from experience. The coach or mentor creates the reflective space that is so often missing in a busy working life.
- *Develop insight both about their situation and about themselves*. The coach or mentor enables the client to be realistic about their context, and works with them to identify what will help and hinder them in achieving goals.
- *Self-challenge, identify resources and develop their potential*. The coach or mentor helps the client to challenge self-imposed limitations, and self-limiting beliefs and attitudes. The client is supported in developing both internal and external resources which can help them achieve their goals.
- *Identify achievable change goals*. Goals vary in nature. Some may be visible – for example, achieving a performance goal; others may be harder to see – for example, sustaining a change in attitude. The value of a goal is the extent to which it helps the client to achieve the changes they want. The coach or mentor helps the client to identify and choose change goals.

- *Plan and implement actions which help to achieve goals.* The coaching or mentoring session is an important catalyst, but the proof of the pudding, so to speak, is in the changes that the client makes back at work. The coach or mentor helps the client to make realistic plans which they can implement.
- *Notice, celebrate and reinforce their successes.* The coach or mentor can support and energize the client by highlighting and acknowledging what they have achieved.

In the following example, the coach helps the client to reflect, to focus on strengths, to identify goals and to act.

John was a highly successful events organizer, until a health problem meant that he could no longer drive, which was essential in his career. He described himself as 'washed-up' and 'fit for nothing'. He needed a coach to help him to identify and exploit the talents and resources that he still had, rather than focus on his limitations. The coach helped him to generate ideas about alternative career options. Together they planned how he might explore these options, and get started on moving forward rather than looking back. Experiencing some successes increased John's confidence and enthusiasm, and the coach supported him through setbacks. Although it took time, John was able to find a fulfilling alternative career.

Box 2.4 contains some useful questions for managing the ongoing relationship.

Box 2.4 Managing the ongoing relationship: some questions for coaches and mentors

- What has the client done as a result of our initial session/s? What has helped or hindered them?
- Has the client identified change goals? Made any action plans? Tried to implement these?
- Have I drawn the client's attention to what they have achieved, and any successes?
- Am I using the appropriate balance of support and challenge?
- Have we talked about how we are working together? What is helping or hindering?
- How would I describe our working relationship? How would the client describe it?
- Am I using all my resources to help the client – for example, knowledge, skills, experience, networks?

Managing the ending

In this stage, the coach or mentor helps the client to bring the relationship and the work to a conclusion. If the session is a one-off, the effective coach or mentor will ensure there is time at the end to address the relevant items from the list in Box 2.5. As a rough guide, in a two-hour session, 10–15 minutes might be set aside for this. Where a longer relationship is coming to an end, preparation for ending may take place over several sessions and will probably form a significant part of the final session.

Box 2.5 Managing the ending: some questions for coaches and mentors

- Are we clear about why we are ending, and when?
- Have we both been involved, as far as possible, in the decision to end?
- Is the client ready for the ending? If not, what can I do to help them?
- Have we acknowledged what the client has achieved?
- Have we reviewed how we have worked together?
- Have we discussed any work still to do? Considered how the client might take this forward?
- Have we discussed how the client will move on?
- Have we agreed what will be done with any notes?
- Has the client had the chance to make a good ending for themselves?
- Would I benefit from supervision or support?

Using a framework: tools and techniques

Frameworks

A model or framework, when used sensitively, can contribute significantly to effective helping. There are many views on which framework or model is best for coaching and mentoring, but there is agreement that it is important for the coach or mentor to be clear about their approach.

Several frameworks and approaches are outlined in Chapter 1, and one, the Egan Skilled Helper model, is described in detail in Chapter 7.

 Box 2.6 lists some benefits of using a framework. Which are important to you? Are there any that you might add?

Box 2.6 Possible benefits of using a framework

- Communicates the values and assumptions of the coach or mentor
- Demonstrates a professional approach by grounding practice in theory
- Demonstrates transparency by clarifying the underlying approach
- Shares responsibility through discussion of the framework
- Creates hope by using a tried and tested approach
- Provides a reference point for deciding what work needs to be done
- Encourages change by providing a map with direction
- Focuses on key issues
- Empowers the client if the framework is transferable to other contexts
- Helps to guide purposeful coaching and mentoring conversations

---

Lucy, a mentor in a university mentoring scheme: People who come for mentoring are interested in the framework I use. I explain it to them and I think this reassures them that they are not being 'psyched out'. In fact, it's a framework which, after a time, they find they can use by themselves. I think that part of my mentoring role is to offer useful tools and techniques which people can try out in everyday work situations, and I say that right at the beginning.

Ed, an HR professional and coach: I'm a pretty good listener, but that isn't always enough. I use a framework as a map, to help me and the client to see where we are going and to check that we aren't going round in circles. It gives us both some structure which helps us to use time productively and ensure that we are moving forward.

 Use these questions to help select the right framework for you.

- What frameworks do you know about?
- Which have you used?
- Have you had training in a framework?
- What evidence exists to support the effectiveness of the framework?
- What has helped you personally in your development?
- What is congruent with your beliefs and values?
- What is relevant to your context?
- What do other coaches and mentors recommend?
- What would empower clients?

A cautionary note: a framework is only as good as the person using it. It is a useful guide, rather than a template. It should be used to help, rather than to unnecessarily constrain, the coach, mentor or client. At the beginning of Chapter 7 the disadvantages as well as advantages of frameworks are discussed in more detail.

Tools and techniques

The effective coach or mentor knows how to use tools and techniques to help clients move forward in managing problems and developing their potential. You may like to use the tools and techniques that you have found beneficial. However, coaches and mentors should be wary of overusing their favourite approaches. There is a saying that if the only tool you have is a hammer it is tempting to treat everything as if it were a nail. The most important consideration should be whether or not the tools and techniques will help the client in front of you.

A selection of tools and techniques is introduced in Chapter 9 with descriptions of how they can:

- provide a change of pace in the session;
- help the 'stuck' client to see their situation differently;
- appeal to the client's preferred learning style or way of working;
- enable the client to move out of their 'comfort zone';
- bring the 'out there' situation into the coaching session;
- access the client's hidden strengths and resources;
- offer the client a safe way of 'rehearsing' or trying out an approach;
- help the client to let go of the past and move forward.

Knowing yourself

The skilled coach or mentor understands their own strengths and style, and how these can benefit clients. Clutterbuck's '12 habits of the toxic mentor' (www.coachingnetwork.org.uk) warns quite rightly of the danger of expecting to be a complete role model in every way, but in our experience, successful coaches and mentors are often seen as role models in *some* way by their clients. They have qualities or characteristics which clients admire, aspire to or see as lacking in their own development. As discussed earlier in the chapter, the client may 'learn with' the coach or mentor, 'learn from' their experience and wisdom and 'learn through' their qualities and characteristics.

 Box 2.7 contains a list of qualities. Which are most characteristic of you? In what ways might you be a role model for others?

Box 2.7 Some qualities of a coach or mentor

- *Supportive:* a non-judgemental listener
- *Challenging:* not afraid to disagree or question
- *Networker:* identifies and knows how to develop connections
- *Respected:* by others in the organization/profession
- *Assertive:* able to state wants and needs
- *Open:* receptive to new ideas and ways of thinking, to 'half-baked' ideas
- *Transparent:* communicates their values and 'walks the talk'
- *Creative:* able to think laterally and 'outside of the box'
- *Visible:* well known in the organization/profession
- *Interpersonally skilled:* at influencing others
- *Strategic:* able to take the long-term view
- *Kind:* sensitive to others and shows care for them
- *Fair:* treats people equally, not prejudiced or partial
- *Resilient:* in the face of difficulties
- *Considered:* rather than reactive, in making judgements

In addition to differing qualities, we each have different helping styles. Table 2.3 shows some contrasting styles. All of these are potentially useful in coaching or mentoring.

 From the list in Table 2.3 select the five words that best describe you, and the five that are least like you. What does that tell you about your style? What are its strengths? Any downsides? You might ask someone who knows you well to complete the exercise and compare the two descriptions.

Another way of gaining insight into your style and helping qualities is with the use of professionally-administered psychometric instruments, such

Task-focused	Broad-ranging
Easy going	Organized
Leading	Following
Listening	Talking
Agreeing	Arguing
Supporting	Challenging
Detached	Involved
Energized	Relaxed
Realistic	Imaginative
Planned	Spontaneous
Questioning	Accepting
Theoretical	Practical
Thinker	Doer
Hope for the best	Plan for the worst
Easy to read	Not easy to read
Immediate	Reflective
Evaluative	Non-judgemental
Exciting	Safe

Table 2.3   Some helping styles

as the MBTI questionnaire. This may help you to appreciate how you prefer to work with others. Reflecting on your style can help you to understand your coaching and mentoring strengths, and your areas for development, as in this example:

> **Alex** prefers thinking about possibilities and the future, sometimes at the expense of noticing what's going on in the present. One of his coaching strengths is helping the client to consider possibilities, ways forward and 'what if' scenarios. However, he knows he must be careful not to rush ahead too quickly. He works hard to pay attention and understand how things are for the client at present.

Coach and mentor competence

The professional coaching and mentoring organizations are rightly concerned with establishing and maintaining standards of practice. Many of them, including the International Coaching Federation (ICF) and the European Mentoring and Coaching Council (EMCC) have developed competence frameworks which form the basis of their accreditation processes. The EMCC competence framework describes eight competence categories (see www.emccaccreditation.org) and these are listed in Chapter 6 on page 131.

Attached to each category are descriptors of behaviours, called capabilities, which are indicators of competence in that category. The EMCC offers four levels of accreditation, and there are indicators for each level – the higher the level, the higher the capability. So, for example, at the foundation level an indicator of the competence 'commitment to self-development' is 'practises and evaluates their coaching/mentoring skills'. At master practitioner level, an indicator is 'invites feedback from peers by demonstrating their practice before them'.

Whether or not you are interested in becoming accredited, competence frameworks are a useful backdrop against which to reflect on your practice. The safe and effective coach or mentor monitors their own competence and pays attention to developing their capabilities. The indicators offer accessible descriptions of good practice which can help ongoing reflection and development. We say more about supervision, accreditation and self-development in Chapters 4 and 6.

Summary

In this chapter we have:

- Helped you to clarify your motivation for coaching or mentoring.
- Described the core skills essential in coaching and mentoring.
- Considered how to establish and use a working agreement.
- Illustrated with checklists and examples how the coach or mentor develops the learning relationship and uses the core skills effectively.
- Discussed how to select a coaching or mentoring framework.
- Described some benefits of using tools and techniques.
- Invited you to assess your own coaching or mentoring style and qualities.
- Outlined how competence frameworks might support your development.

3 How can I be an effective client?

Introduction

The purpose of this chapter is to help you to get the most out of coaching and mentoring by knowing what you can do to be fully active in and between sessions. It should give you some insight into yourself, and into what the coach or mentor might expect of you. It also aims to inform you about what you can expect from your coach or mentor, and how to get it.

The chapter starts by helping you to clarify how to get the right coach or mentor for your particular needs and wants. Throughout the chapter we refer to you as 'client'. You may be an individual client, working with one coach or mentor, or you may be part of a team that is being coached. You will see how your personality preferences and learning style can affect the working relationship with a coach or mentor. Examples from coaching and mentoring are used to show differences as well as similarities. The importance of developing a clear working agreement is explained. Ways in which you can be proactive and make the most of the reflective space in sessions are outlined. There are examples of developing imagination, identifying resources, using skills, formulating goals and implementing action plans.

 Wherever you see this symbol there is an invitation for you to reflect upon how you can make the most of coaching and mentoring.

Getting the right coach or mentor

Box 3.1 What do I want from a coach or mentor?

You need to be aware that coaching and mentoring are described differently by different people and therefore, when choosing, do take care to read how the coach or mentor describes what they do, to see if it fits your purpose.

So what do you want, a coach or a mentor? You may even want both, for different needs in your life. Coaching at work is often about performance. It can be individual or team coaching. If you are being mentored or coached within the organization, it may be by your manager or leader, who may also be your appraiser or assessor. In this case, you will need to negotiate the agenda carefully, to ensure that it meets the expectations of both you and your coach or mentor. You may wish to benefit from the experience of a respected mentor who understands your profession or organization and who will share experience without expecting you to be a protégé. You may request 'off-line' mentoring or coaching either within the organization, or provided externally. This is particularly useful if it is an issue which is broader than a specific performance issue, or where there may be problems of confidentiality or conflicts of interest between you and your manager (see Table 3.1).

Executive coaching is often external to the organization. You may be paying an external coach or mentor yourself, or your organization may pay for your coaching or mentoring. In the latter case, it will be important to clarify and agree the expectations of all parties, the boundaries of confidentiality and the lines of communication.

Internal	External
Advantages	*Advantages*
Easy to meet together	Can be totally objective
Knows the organization	Easy to maintain confidentiality
Can network for you	Clear boundary: you and work
Understands the politics	Likely to be uninterrupted
Has personal experience of obstacles	You may prepare more carefully
May know people you talk about	Conflict of interest less likely
May be able to access resources	Knows other networks
Disadvantages	*Disadvantages*
Sessions may be interrupted	May cost more
People will know	Travel takes time
Confidentiality may be harder	Need to explain about your work
Boundaries may be blurred and you may be more casual and informal	The coach or mentor may not be monitored the way an 'insider' is

Table 3.1   Internal vs external coaching and mentoring

When you have decided whether you want a coach or a mentor, internal to your organization or external, you will need to find the right person for you. For this, you need to know something about yourself. The literature on coaching and mentoring emphasizes that the chemistry between the client and the coach or mentor is significant. Knowing about your personality and the way you react to the support and challenge that will be given in coaching and mentoring will help you to make the most of the learning relationship.

Knowing yourself

What is it that you need and want in a coach or mentor? How do you learn best? What sort of person can help you most to gain insight, explore possibilities, set goals and deliver results?

Think of a time when you were helped in the past with a work issue or with a career opportunity. What was it in you, and in the person helping you, that really made the difference? Think of a time when someone tried to help but it didn't work. What was it about the way that person tried to help that didn't work? Was it something in them, or something in you, or both?

Here is the example of Tim who has looked around until he has found the right mentor.

> **Tim teaches in an inner-city secondary school.** He was assigned an experienced senior colleague as his mentor. The mentor was generous with his time and in the way that he shared his considerable experience, but Tim found that the sessions were dominated by the mentor advising him what to do. What Tim really needed was some reflective space where he could talk over some of the concerns and opportunities arising in his new job. When he tried to raise issues, the mentor adopted a well-intentioned but nevertheless unhelpful 'if I were you' approach. Fortunately, Tim has now met another colleague, trained as a mentor, who is willing to act informally as a sounding board. He helps Tim to explore the issues on his mind, and reach his own conclusions. Tim continues to see the more experienced senior colleague from time to time, but uses those sessions to get advice on more practical aspects of lesson planning, marking and report writing.

So, what sort of person are you: what do you know about your personality preferences; what makes you put your trust in other people to whom you turn for help; what makes you respect them; what makes you feel safe with them?

The lists in Table 3.2 will help you to pick out your own personality preferences and clarify what sort of coach or mentor is best for you. Try ticking items that apply to you in the column 'I see myself as'. *There are no right or wrong answers, just preferences*. You may want to tick one of each pair in a row, or both in the pair, or neither may apply to you.

When you have done this, go to the column headed 'I want a coach or mentor who is' and repeat the exercise. You may find that you want someone like you, or that you would value someone who differs from you. If you have completed any psychometric questionnaires or inventories, they may give you additional information about your preferences.

I see myself as		I want a coach or mentor who is	
Reserved	Outgoing	Reserved	Outgoing
Objective	Subjective	Objective	Subjective
Sensitive	Robust	Sensitive	Robust
Challenging	Supportive	Challenging	Supportive
Involved	Detached	Involved	Detached
Cool	Warm	Cool	Warm
Active	Reflective	Active	Reflective
Intuitive	Evidence-based	Intuitive	Evidence-based
Practical	Conceptual	Practical	Conceptual
Problem-solver	Listener	Problem-solver	Listener
Controlling	Adaptable	Controlling	Adaptable
Humorous	Serious	Humorous	Serious
Imaginative	Realistic	Imaginative	Realistic
Empathic	Sympathetic	Empathic	Sympathetic
Directive	Non-directive	Directive	Non-directive
Open	Closed	Open	Closed
Fair	Just	Fair	Just
Spontaneous	Considered	Spontaneous	Considered
Transparent	Opaque	Transparent	Opaque

Table 3.2   Personality preferences when choosing a coach or mentor

Clients learn about themselves through dialogue with their coach or mentor. When this is effective it will increase your insight into issues, problems and opportunities. It will increase your motivation to make the changes that are really wanted and the actions that will deliver results. The effective coach or mentor understands how to help you to motivate yourself and to believe in yourself. In order for you to make the most of this learning *you need to be aware of how you like to learn.*

Do you know anything about your preferred ways of learning? There is a learning styles questionnaire (Honey and Mumford 2006) which suggests that each of us has preferences for learning. For example, when we started to write this book we talked about how we would approach the task of writing. For one of us, it was a case of sitting in front of the computer and starting to write. For the other, it was a case of going to read other books on the subject before feeling able to start. Kolb and Fry (1975) suggest that there are four main approaches to learning: reflection, theorizing, pragmatism and action. People should be able to move between these styles and this is called the 'learning cycle'. The descriptions below will help you to identify how you learn best and what type of coaching and mentoring will suit your learning style.

 Put these in your order of preference:

- Applying ideas in practice
- Observing and reflecting
- Experiencing and doing
- Thinking and conceptualizing

So, what will you want from your coach or mentor: exploration, discussion, practical targets, skill development or action?

Figures 3.1 and 3.2 show how different learning styles are used at different stages of the learning cycle, and will help you to establish which are your most and least preferred styles. When thinking about how we learn it is useful to remember that we do not learn from experience, but from reflection upon that experience.

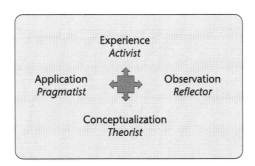

Figure 3.1 The learning cycle and learning styles (adapted from Honey and Mumford 1992)

PRAGMATIST	REFLECTOR
Keen to put ideas to the test	Careful and methodical
Loves practical activities	Doesn't jump to conclusions
May focus on task more than people	Doesn't like to be pushed into responses
Wants practical tips to use in real life	May appear unassertive
Needs time to practise and experiment	Needs time to think and consider options
ACTIVIST	THEORIST
Likes change	Likes logic and reason
Ready to experiment	Literal not lateral
Wants action	Asks challenging questions
Responds quickly	May not rate intuition
Likes fun	Prefers certainty and objectivity

Figure 3.2   Characteristics of the styles

When you are working with your coach or mentor there is an opportunity to move through these different ways of working and learning as you go through the process. However, you may find that if your coach or mentor has a different learning style from you it could affect your working relationship – the difference may be creative, or it may result in you feeling that you are not being understood or helped. There are two guidelines here. Firstly, know your own preferences. Secondly, talk openly with your coach or mentor about *their* preferences and talk about what you need from one another. Then make sure that you can review on a regular basis how well you work together.

Having realistic expectations

Coaching and mentoring are not the answer for all issues and problems. The coach or mentor is a *facilitator* but not a *fixer*. You may seek help with an issue, a problem or an opportunity and you probably have the resources within yourself to manage that. But for whatever reason you may become stuck and unable to access those resources, and so seek some coaching or mentoring. The process will help you to become unstuck, it will release your own potential to achieve the desired results. It will work only if the relationship between helper and helped is balanced, with each person taking responsibility. This can be difficult to manage if coaching has been imposed on you. But even if it is imposed, you can still choose how to make the most of it. The coach or mentor is responsible for managing the process and for providing specific skills within a framework of ethical practice. The client is responsible for setting the agenda and for taking action as a result of the coaching or mentoring.

Much of the really important work in coaching and mentoring takes place between sessions when you are either reflecting upon the previous session, acting as a result of it, or preparing for the next session. In order to be an effective client you will be proactive, not reactive. You will gradually become your own coach or mentor as you learn the skills and frameworks that have worked for you in the sessions.

> **Helen works in marketing.** She was sent for coaching by her line manager because of problems with team relationships during project work. She turned up expecting her coach to have all the answers. She was disappointed. The coach tried to get her to look at the problem from the perspective of the team as well as from her own point of view. But Helen was not ready to do this because she felt defensive at being 'told' that she needed some coaching. She attended two sessions but then went back to the manager and said that it had been a waste of time.

Helen's example is not uncommon. Readiness for coaching and mentoring is important. If it has been suggested by others it does not always work. But in the next case example it did.

> **Tony is a medical manager.** He had never heard of coaching when his boss suggested that a coach might help him to deal with his difficulties in meeting deadlines at work. Although Tony didn't understand what coaching was, he asked around and thought he would give it a try. He was recommended a coach who was outside his department but within the same organization. He arranged an introductory meeting where he negotiated how they might work together. By the time he arrived for his first proper session he had a clear idea of what to expect of himself and of his coach. They met on four occasions. This first session was mainly Tony talking and the coach listening as he revealed a lifelong problem with procrastination. They agreed some goals about charting his current tasks and prioritizing them. In the second session the coach presented some approaches that others had used successfully and Tony was able to evaluate which of these might fit for him. He then tried some out before the next session. The third session was a debriefing of the action taken, with the coach helping Tony to formulate some specific, realistic goals and

action plans. In the final session they evaluated the progress and talked about ending their working arrangement. Tony realized that he had a lifelong pattern of procrastination to change and that this would take time but he now had the confidence and skills to keep working at it.

In these two examples, both were referred for coaching but Tony was realistic, proactive and successful whereas Helen was passive and expected a magic wand instead of a coach!

Negotiating a working agreement

You have decided that you would like to start some coaching or mentoring. What next? You can find someone through personal recommendation or through coaching and mentoring networks and organizations. Before approaching someone, think through the type of working agreement you would like and have a look at a sample agreement in the previous chapter. Consider the questions shown in Figure 3.3. In our experience it is important to address these questions and issues right from the start and to make sure you work with a coach or mentor who encourages open and honest discussion of all these aspects.

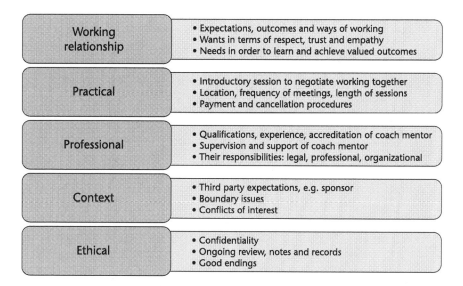

Figure 3.3   Aspects of a working agreement to be considered by the client

You will find useful information about these aspects in Chapters 2, 4, 5, 6, 10 and 11. These chapters tell you what to expect in terms of good ethical and professional practice.

Thinking ahead and being strategic

'Being strategic' means thinking ahead about your own working or professional life. It may mean developing a vision of what you want to be in one year, two years, five years or ten years from now. Having a coach or mentor helps to keep your focus on the now and on the future. It is the responsibility of the coach or mentor to help the client to keep scanning the horizon, rather than getting bogged down in the activity of everyday working life.

> Do you have a plan for your future?
>
> Do you have you a vision of where you want to be in five years' time?
>
> Have you worked with someone to clarify your values and goals?
>
> The most successful companies and organizations are constantly addressing these questions. The most successful people do it too, often accompanied by a coach or mentor.

To get the most out of coaching and mentoring it will be part of your overall strategy for personal and professional development. In this way, you become the leader in your own life, rather than allowing your work to lead you. Clients who prepare for coaching or mentoring sessions by reviewing what has happened between sessions maximize the benefits of the reflective space with the coach or mentor.

David has had a mentor for three years. He is a hospital consultant and wanted a mentor because he found the pressures of work at times overwhelming. There is constant change and never-ending targets to be met. As a senior doctor he did not want to confide in anyone within the hospital and so he joined an action learning set which provides the opportunity to work one-on-one with a mentor. Meetings are every three months. He decides on the agenda for each session. He ensures that only half of the two-hour mentoring session is spent on issues which need to be resolved immediately. The other hour is spent in exploring longer-range issues, what his ideal future would be and how he might achieve that in practice.

Being proactive

As a client, it helps if you set the agenda for your coaching or mentoring sessions and allow your coach or mentor to facilitate that agenda. If you need help with a specific issue or problem you may want your mentor or coach to be quite active in the process. Examples of this include helping you to role-play a particular scenario that has been problematic or practising a specific skill such as assertiveness. Decide what you want before you meet with your coach or mentor and then discuss how the session will address what you want. Make sure that the sort of working arrangement you have allows for constant evaluation of the process and of the dynamic in the working relationship, perhaps by spending the final few minutes of each session with both of you saying what you feel has been achieved, what helped and what hindered. You can then agree targets for the next meeting, and for your time between sessions. Here are some examples of ways in which clients have been proactive.

> **Sarah, an administrator in a telecoms company,** always arrives for her coaching session with a written list of things she wants help with, and she prioritizes them.

> **Bill, a sales manager in an oil company,** thinks of a couple of situations at work where he wants help and then uses the learning from dealing with these in order to inform his judgement and skill in other areas. So, when he leaves the session and gets into his car he always talks into a dictaphone to summarize the session before driving off. He wants to capture the learning before he gets swamped with the next round of sales.

> **Pat, a social worker,** keeps a reflective journal. She arrives in the session, opens the journal and picks from it some incident that has been especially significant.

> **Martin works in computers** and likes to bring written reports and documents to reflect upon. He always writes a summary of the sessions in bullet-point form, bringing this with him next time, to review any action taken.

> **Christine is a lecturer** and values just having space. She does not want to work from documents or reports, she has enough of those at

college. But she always gives herself 30 minutes of quiet time to prepare for the mentoring session she has with a senior colleague.

 Think of a time when you were helped by someone. Consider what worked well for you. Now think about your current situation. If you went for coaching or mentoring what would you do to be proactive? Try to think of three ways that would work for you. Consider: your time; your usual ways of reflecting; how you learn; how you might prepare for a session; how you would act between sessions.

Learning from support and challenge

Any effective learning relationship will have an appropriate balance of support and challenge. If you read the previous chapter you will know what the coach or mentor does in order to provide this potent mix in a way that empowers rather than overwhelms or overprotects. Everyone is different in the amount of support or challenge they want and need. Our needs vary at different points in our working life. Consider the example of Isaac.

> **Isaac has emigrated and is settling into a new job in engineering.** Mentoring was recommended to all newly-recruited staff from overseas and Isaac was pleased to be offered this support. When he started to see his mentor he was feeling very isolated, having left his family to come and work in a new country. Although he had been a high-flyer at home, he suddenly felt very much like the new kid on the block. He has a very understanding mentor who just gives him the space to talk about his feelings and who offers warm support. Isaac is relieved. He wants no more than this at first. Others are giving him the technical help he needs. He meets with his mentor on a monthly basis at first and after three months he says that he feels very supported and would now welcome some advice about whether to pursue a research opportunity to take his career to the next stage. His mentor becomes more active and helps Isaac to challenge himself about what he might achieve. This stage of mentoring is very powerful, but unnerving at times. Isaac says that he benefits greatly from this. He would have resisted too much challenge without support, and yet with too much support and not enough challenge he would not stretch himself to the next stage of his career.

Think about what you prefer in terms of support and challenge.

Do you want to be challenged or do you want the sort of support that will enable you to challenge yourself?

How would you ask for the sort of challenge that would work for you?

What would you do if your coach or mentor got the balance wrong?

Using reflective space

One of the most significant benefits of coaching and mentoring is the opportunity in busy working lives to take stock, in the reflective space provided by the coach or mentor. At first, this may make you feel uncomfortable because while your coach or mentor provides the silence you will search for thoughts, feelings and insights into the experiences that you have brought for discussion. You may try to avoid doing this because it is challenging and uncomfortable, even though it is very productive and helpful. A good coach or mentor will never expect you to talk about things that you do not wish to share. They will help you to decide what you really want to explore.

Some clients break the silence by changing the subject or using humour to distract their coach or mentor. However, if you can allow yourself to be psychologically 'held' by the attentive listening of your coach or mentor, then you will allow your inner voice to speak to you. Things which have been pushed down into your subconscious by the frenetic activity of everyday living can then slowly come up to the surface. You learn to listen to yourself. In terms of well-being, this is known to be very beneficial. It induces relaxation. You breathe more slowly and deeply, your pulse rate slows and you can then give voice to your wants, your needs, your problems, your issues, your opportunities and your dreams. Some people do this for 10 minutes every morning as a way of focusing on the day. If you are not used to doing this, then it may be worth trying to do it at some point in each day. You will then make more efficient use of the reflective space when you are with your coach or mentor. It is not just the time set aside that makes space 'reflective', it is the *quality of the session*.

 If you were to use a coach or mentor, how would you want to make most use of the time for reflection?

What do you already do in your life that is similar to this?

What difficulties might there be for you in working in this way?

What qualities and interventions would you want in your coach or mentor to help you (e.g. not having too much silence while you think about things, or asking your coach or mentor not to interrupt if you are thinking about something)?

Your coach or mentor will use skills of non-verbal and verbal communication to support you in your thinking and exploration. They will reflect back to you what you say, they will question and prompt and clarify, challenge and summarize. They will help you to explore fully your 'story' of the issues, problems or opportunities that you wish to discuss and they will help you to prioritize the ones which need more immediate attention. You can then focus upon these in order to draw up wish-lists of possible ways forward. In order to benefit from this part of the process you need to trust yourself and your coach or mentor. You also need to be open and straightforward so that your working relationship is one in which both of you take responsibility for the outcome. Undue dependency or indeed independence is not desirable. *Interdependence* and *mutuality* bring results.

> **Rosaleen, a PR consultant**, invariably arrives for her coaching session apologizing for being late yet again. She often sits down quite out of breath and explains that she has not had time to think about what she wants to talk about today. Topics of conversation have not been prioritized, and she tends to ramble. However, the skills of the coach in questioning, prompting and summarizing help her to become aware of the most important issue which needs change. She needs to be more strategic in marketing herself. The coach helps her to define specific goals and to make realistic plans for action. She could never have done this for herself because of her tendency to live for the moment and be constantly rushing from place to place. Having prearranged coaching sessions forces her to stop and reflect. It is this that brings change. Within six months of the first coaching session she has implemented her marketing strategy and the work is coming in at a steady pace.

Developing your imagination

Clients often want to see a coach or mentor because they are feeling a bit stuck. They may lack the imagination to discover possibilities for moving forward. Their potential is being stifled. The most effective clients are willing to engage in approaches and exercises which develop the imagination, the 'what if' scenarios. Some people are born with a preference for imagination and intuition but others find this more difficult. All can benefit from mentors and coaches who help to 'think out of the box' or 'engage in blue-sky thinking'.

> **Chan is a financial manager.** He has been in his current job for several years and is well respected and established. He applies for an exciting new opportunity in another region. He is offered the job but if he moves he will miss all that he has so carefully built up. He is given a week to decide whether he wants the job and he goes round in circles weighing up all the costs and benefits of going or staying. He cannot decide. Then he turns to a mentor for help. She knows his current job and she says (rather directively) 'You can take that job now or you can stay here and die slowly.' She is inviting him to use his imagination. The picture he paints in his head leaves him in no doubt that he should accept the job. He does. It is the best move of his life. The job he leaves is gradually eroded after a series of painful reorganizations.

> **Greg has just qualified as a teacher** and has one session with a mentor. He is about to take up his first teaching post but is not really sure that this is the career for him. He wants the mentor to help him to clarify his career ambitions. The other option he is considering is catering, because he has contacts in the restaurant business. After listening to his story and his doubts about teaching, his mentor asks him to close his eyes, try to breathe slowly and deeply, and to relax. He has to tell the mentor when he feels relaxed. This he does. The mentor then asks him to imagine himself in five years' time in a classroom in a school where he might have been teaching for that time. The mentor says, 'Tell me when you have a picture and describe to me what you see.' Greg says, 'I see an old man, bending over a desk, marking books.' The mentor helps Greg to fill in some details in the picture: what the old man is wearing; what he is thinking and feeling; what the pupils are doing. When the picture is complete the mentor carefully asks Greg to bring himself back to this room and then to open his eyes again. He reminds Greg that he is back in the office and that he is Greg, a newly-qualified teacher. The mentor notes how young and energetic he appears now and how different from the picture he painted of himself after five years of teaching. He asks Greg what he thought of the picture of himself that he had painted. He says, 'I'm horrified to think that could be me!' They then do the same exercise looking at the possible Greg five years down the line, working in a restaurant. A completely different picture emerges – of a vibrant, ambitious young man who is

going places. Insight dawns. Greg decides to take up his teaching post, but to leave after the probationary year and pursue his career in catering. In only one mentoring session, with skilful use of his own imagination, a career decision is made.

You will notice how powerful imagination can be! It is important that such exercises are used safely and ethically. You can check whether your coach or mentor is working safely and ethically by looking at Chapter 10. Brainstorming techniques are used to generate as many possible ideas as you can in the shortest possible time. These techniques are useful in coaching and mentoring. To be of most use you might need to practise using them on yourself – for example, 'If I won the lottery'. They work best if the client is relaxed, is focusing on what might be rather than what is, is not hindered by 'but' or 'ought' but focuses on 'want'. If you are a 'yes, but' sort of person you will benefit greatly from learning how to change it to 'yes, if'.

Do you have a good imagination?

Do you find it easy to imagine what might be, rather than just what is?

Do you tend to say 'yes, but' rather than 'yes, if'?

Which of these do you voice more: your 'wants' or your 'oughts'?

Identifying your resources and working smart

Coaching and mentoring are about releasing potential and delivering results. In order to do this you need to identify your resources. Easier said than done! The process of coaching or mentoring will help you to become more aware of underused or unused resources. Some of these will be in yourself, and some will be in the people you live and work with. Some resources will be organizational or structural ones.

Think about the personal resources you would bring to coaching or mentoring. For example: energy, passion, motivation, courage, stamina, persistence, resourcefulness, skills, knowledge, experience.

Now think of the resources that you could call upon in people around you. For example: their time, their know-how, their networks, their experience.

> Finally, reflect upon the resources in your place of work: the context, the structures and the processes. Don't forget that time is a resource that is often underused or misused.

If you can identify and exploit resources, within yourself and in others, you will work smart and become more effective. Hopefully, you will open up many more possibilities by engaging the help, knowledge and skills of others at work and at home, and therefore you will not be alone in achieving your objectives.

> **When Marian first started seeing her coach** it was because she wanted to become more visible with senior managers in the supermarket chain where she had worked for 10 years. She had watched male contemporaries leapfrog over her in the promotion stakes. What was she doing wrong? She wanted her coach to tell her what was stopping her from getting promoted. Coaching has provided her with the opportunity to challenge herself about unused resources. She realized that she was not being proactive about getting promotion. She was not using the skills and resources on herself that she used so well when developing projects for the supermarket. She remembered times when she had made herself more visible in a previous job. At that time she had networked with senior leaders in the organization; she had found ways of showcasing her work at committee level; she had published in a national retailing publication and regularly went to her immediate superiors to inform them about ideas for innovative projects which she volunteered to lead. As a result of the coaching Marian tries out some of these ideas again and brainstorms other strategies with her coach. The coach gives her some reading material on assertiveness and they practise together some presentation skills which she then tries out for real at work. She identifies some trusted colleagues and asks for feedback on her new, more visible style. She then takes the feedback to a coaching session and, after reviewing with her coach, she modifies what she has been doing and has another go. At last, she is positively impacting upon her future instead of being overwhelmed by day-to-day matters at work.

Setting goals and making action plans

Goals and action plans are part of the intentional activity that is coaching and mentoring. Some performance coaches expect clients to articulate the goal for each session, before the session begins. The work is then focused upon achieving that specific goal. In mentoring, where the focus is broader, there may not be such a specific focus for each session. However, it is always useful to clarify for oneself, 'What do I expect to get out of this session?' and 'How am I going to make sure I get it?' You will find examples of goal-setting and action planning in Chapters 7 and 8. We advise that you also think about having a goal or goals, as well as action plans, to take away from the session. These can relate to changes you want: in thinking, in feeling or in acting.

A goal is best expressed as a specific outcome, not a vague statement of intent. You may go away from a coaching or mentoring session saying 'I want a better work–life balance' but that, as a specific goal, would be 'In order to achieve a better balance I will leave work at a pre-planned time each day and I will spend one hour with my children each evening before they go to bed.' A specific goal is SMART: specific, measurable, appropriate, relevant and in a timeframe. Goals help to make changes and changes help to deliver results. Your coach or mentor will help you to formulate realistic and meaningful goals that are in keeping with your values. They will also help you to develop the skills you need in order to act more effectively.

Developing skills, making changes and delivering results

This chapter started by considering what to expect of coaching and mentoring. It then focused on how you could put your own personality, preferences and resources into making it work. The outcome of the coaching or mentoring will hopefully be change: small change or life-changing change. You will probably learn new skills and new ways of thinking, feeling and acting. These will enable you to turn your wish-lists and dreams into reality. The skills will deliver results for you. In order to learn these skills you will need to be open to learning, you will need to practise and get feedback, and you will need to monitor your progress – and all this in partnership with your coach or mentor.

Summary

In this chapter we have:

- Helped you to understand how to be proactive in order to get the most out of coaching and mentoring.
- Provided self-assessment questions to increase awareness of what you, as a client, want and need.

- Stimulated thinking about how to get the best fit between client and coach or mentor in terms of personality preferences, expectations, limits, knowledge, experience, resources and work context.
- Given an example of what an effective working agreement might contain and indicated how to discuss this with a new coach or mentor.
- Used several case examples of issues which may arise for clients, giving the opportunity to reflect on what to do in similar situations.

PART 2
Coach and Mentor Development

4   What is reflective practice and supervision?

- Introduction
- Development
- Experience
- Reflective practice
- Supervision
- Summary

Introduction

In Part 2 we focus on coach and mentor development, and in this chapter on the way in which experience, reflective practice and supervision contribute to the development of the mentor or coach. Chapter 5 is an interactive case study raising issues and questions for reflective practice, and Chapter 6 discusses training as part of development and considers the value of professional networking and accreditation.

Development

Development is at the heart of coaching and mentoring work. In order to help clients, the coach or mentor continuously reflects upon their own practice. By doing so, they develop a more accurate perception of their levels of competence, they develop their capability and they monitor their capacity.

Hawkins and Smith (2006: 123, 206) identify three important elements for effectiveness:

- *competencies:* the ability to utilize a skill or use a tool;
- *capability:* the ability to use the tool or skill at the right time, in the right way and in the right place;
- *capacity:* a human quality rather than a skill and more to do with how you are rather than what you do.

In order to develop these three elements you will need not only training, but also the experience of work with clients. It is important to reflect upon experience, not only afterwards, but also while it is happening. Reflection is valuable, particularly if you are not a full-time coach or mentor, but do use coaching or mentoring skills in your job. If this is the case, then formal supervision may not be appropriate. However, taking the time for reflection on the experience of using the skills – for example, in an action learning set or a co-mentoring or co-coaching arrangement – may well be useful. Development can take many forms. Here are two very different pathways. The mentor and coach have given permission for their names to be used.

> **Shelley** was asked to coach staff as part of her managerial role. She really enjoyed this aspect of her work but found difficulties with regard to confidentiality and experienced conflicts of interest in her role of both supporting the staff and yet ensuring that they achieved demanding performance targets. Some of her staff gave her feedback that the coaching was too hurried and too directive. She was upset by this and reflected on the situation. She decided that she needed to get some supervision for her work. She was amazed at how much this helped her to become more aware of herself and more confident in handling difficulties with staff. Her supervisor told her about some training opportunities and she has now started a certificate in coaching. She really enjoys meeting up with other coaches on a regular basis and is getting a much broader view of what coaching involves.

> **Gordon is a doctor** who attended a mentor development programme. He enjoyed the programme, started mentoring, and a year later attended a follow-up day, where he met other mentors and heard about mentoring schemes. He influenced key stakeholders to fund mentor training for hospital consultants in the hospital where he worked. He helped out on these courses as a facilitator. At the same time he undertook research into doctors' attitudes to mentoring. He was able to use the research to influence his hospital to endorse a mentoring scheme. Further mentoring training programmes were run and a group of trained mentors was established. These mentors, including Gordon, formed a support group, where they could practise skills and techniques and keep up to date.

 Read the list in Box 4.1, which elaborates on the six aspects of development shown in Figure 4.1.

In what ways are you currently developing?

What would enhance your development?

Figure 4.1   Six aspects of development

Box 4.1 Developing as a coach or mentor: a checklist

- *Experience:* what experience do you have of being a coach or mentor? Are there any ways in which you might extend this experience? Do you have experience of being a client? Do you get one-to-one support for yourself when you need it?
- *Reflective practice:* do you currently reflect on your practice both within and outside the sessions? Are you part of a coach or mentor support group? An action learning set?
- *Supervision:* do you have supervision? How regularly? Are you making the most of it?
- *Training:* what coaching or mentoring training have you attended? What future training would be useful to enhance your capabilities? Would you wish to pursue a course which had academic and/or professional accreditation?
- *Professional networking:* are you a member of a coaching or mentoring organization? Could you start up an interest group? Do you attend conferences and network to keep up to date with current trends?
- *Accreditation:* are you accredited or seeking accreditation by a national or international coaching and mentoring organization which promotes ethical codes of practice and/or which regulates standards in coaching and mentoring?

Experience

We say to trainees on coaching and mentoring courses, 'The most important thing that you bring to your client is yourself.' The 'self' you bring includes: innate skills and abilities; values; personality; attitudes; experience of different types of people and relationships; knowledge of different organizations; and work contexts. We argue that this unique mix of knowledge and experience is what you bring to coaching and mentoring right from the start. You may have been approached by colleagues at work, for informal help and guidance, or you may have a more formal coaching or mentoring role. Whatever the reason, it is useful to ask:

- Why do these people turn to me?
- What do I bring to them?
- In which of these situations do I feel most adequate or inadequate?
- What might help me to respond to them more effectively?
- Who could I trust to help me review my experiences?

Once you ask yourself these questions, and address the issues they raise, you have started to become a *reflective practitioner*.

> **Sue is a senior teacher** in a secondary school. In this role she was asked to mentor a junior colleague who was having difficulties managing particular pupils in his class. Sue spent a lot of time listening to stories of wilful and troublesome pupils but whenever she tried to help the teacher to focus on his own responses to these pupils, he would change the subject. She began to feel quite powerless with him, she didn't want to work with him any more and yet she knew it was part of her role as staff mentor to do so.

 In Sue's situation, what would you have done?

> Sue was fortunate that she was able to talk this situation over with a trusted colleague. She began to see that all the practical suggestions she had for improvement were falling on deaf ears and that she would need to take a step back and listen more empathically to his story before trying to move him towards action. This helped her to relax more in the session, and to listen to his anxieties and fears more fully before trying to work with action plans. She learned to be a mentor, rather than a teacher!

Reflective practice

Effective practice is reflective practice. Reflective practice involves an ongoing cycle of preparation, engagement/encounter with the client and then reflection on that coaching or mentoring work. The reflection may involve others, for example someone who offers informal feedback, a supervisor with whom you have a formal working agreement, or a peer supervision group (see Figure 4.2).

Preparation: reflection before action

Preparation may involve any of a number of activities including:

- *extending* your knowledge of coaching and mentoring approaches and models;
- *learning* about appropriate tools and techniques;
- *doing* a continuing professional development (CPD) workshop;
- *finding out* about the organization or work context of your client;
- *ensuring* that you have considered how to work ethically with this client;
- *thinking* through what this client may want and/or need from you;
- *developing* an awareness of where your own limits and vulnerabilities may be;
- *becoming* aware of your strengths and how you will utilize them for the client;
- *checking* what a sponsor or manager expects from your work with this client.

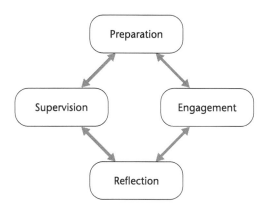

Figure 4.2 The four phases of reflective practice

Lara has realized how important it is to prepare before a coaching session. When she is meeting a client for the first time she prepares how she will introduce herself and how she will negotiate a productive working agreement with the client. If the client has been 'sent' by the organization she thinks through in advance of the first meeting with the client all the issues there could be concerning conflicts of expectation between the line manager, sponsor, client and herself as coach. She clarifies in her own mind what her stance is on confidentiality and rehearses how to discuss this with the client. She decides how to approach the issue of note-taking and records, and the practicalities of payment.

Ewan is mentor to a client in his own workplace. They have been meeting regularly for several months so that Ewan can share his experience of being a senior leader in the organization. He has got to the point of thinking that they are not making much progress and so he decides to attend a mentoring support group. In the group he rehearses some responses which he would like to use with his client. During the next session he uses creative questions to help the client shift the focus from problems to solutions. They both feel far more energized and positive at the end of the session.

Box 4.2 Some questions to address in preparation for work with a client

- What do I think the client wants and needs from me?
- What knowledge do I require for work with this client?
- What personal resources will I need?
- Will there be any boundary or confidentiality issues to address?
- What skills and tools will I need?
- What do I need to do before meeting my client?
- What would I like to achieve with and for this client?
- What will help and what will hinder, in me and in my client?

Engagement: reflection in action

At the heart of reflective practice is the encounter with the client, the capacity to be fully present with the client, and the ability to reflect on the session while it is happening. But what do you reflect upon within the session?

Let us start with *capacity* – in other words, 'how you are' with your client. We said earlier that the most important thing you bring to your client is yourself. The quality of your 'presence' with your client will make a significant impact. The more fully present you can be in the encounter, the greater the level of engagement with your client. Presence involves awareness of self, awareness of the client, awareness of the space between and awareness of the developing relationship. To be fully present you need to:

- be centred, grounded and alert throughout the session;
- focus all your attention on what your client is communicating both verbally and non-verbally;
- be aware of anything in yourself which is limiting you or distracting you from giving that full attention;
- notice what you are picking up and responding to, or conversely missing, from the client;
- spot patterns of thinking, feeling, and responding in both you and your client;
- notice what is happening in the dynamic of the relationship between you;
- reflect upon whether there are any parallels between the developing relationship in the session and the reports of the client about their other relationships;
- use immediacy to work appropriately with the parallels you have observed.

Your positive energy will enable you to meet, touch, influence, inspire and transform. A leading acting and voice coach talks about using energy to connect:

> Your energy is focused. It moves out toward the object of your attention, touches it and then receives energy back from it. You are living in a two-way street – you reach out and touch an energy outside your own, then receive energy back from it. You are giving to and responsive with that energy . . . You are in the moment – the zone – and moment to moment you give and take. Both giving and taking, in that moment, are equal to each other . . . You touch and influence another person rather than impress or impose your will on them. You influence them by allowing them to influence you.
>
> (Rodenburg 2007: 21)

In order to be present in this way Rodenburg (p. 22) recommends that you consciously:

- feel your body belongs to you and feel the earth beneath your feet;
- feel your breath is easy and complete;
- know you reach people and they hear you when you speak;

- notice details in others – their eyes, their moods, their anxieties;
- are curious and not judgemental.

> **Martha:** Before my client arrives I sit in my chair for 10 minutes to clear my mind of all that has gone before in my life that day, and to centre myself on the person whom I am about to meet. I close my eyes, take some deep breaths and listen to my body as I gradually unwind. I notice that my muscles relax and gradually the noise in my head subsides. The noise for example of unfinished business or of tasks in my in-tray. As the noise clears, I sense some space and at this point I start to focus upon my client: what will he bring today; what do I remember from last time; what do I think he wants and needs from me today; what can I give; how can I ensure that however difficult the client, or his material, we will connect, we will truly encounter one another.

Let us turn now to a couple of lived experiences of coaches and mentors reflecting on their ability to engage fully with their clients.

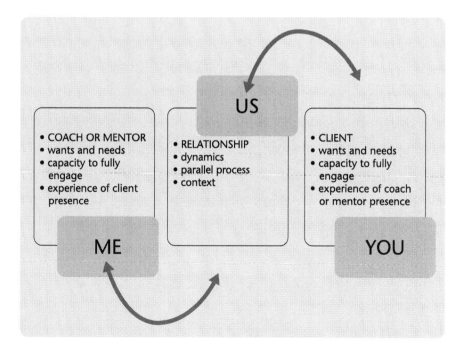

Figure 4.3   The dynamics of engagement

Hal is an experienced mentor. He knows his client well. They have been working together for some time now and they have a very productive working relationship. Hal usually emerges from the sessions energized by the capacity of his client to engage in their work together. The week before this session Hal had some bad news and wondered whether to cancel the session because he knew that his capacity to 'be with' his client would be affected. However, he decided to go ahead because he did not want to let his client down when the appointment had been agreed for some time. On the day, Hal was tired and found it difficult to concentrate. He noticed that this made him much more likely to be directive with his client, rather than really listening and allowing the client to arrive at his own conclusions. The atmosphere felt strained, as if the proverbial elephant was in the room without being acknowledged. As the session moved on he wondered whether to apologize and share with his client why he felt less useful than usual. But he decided against this so that he did not burden the client with his own problems. The session ended amicably enough, but the usual level of connectedness had not been achieved. The capacity of the client in the session had been significantly affected by the level of capacity of the mentor.

 How would you reflect on this session if you were Hal? What would you do as a result of your reflection? What principles do you use in order to decide whether to disclose personal details to clients?

Maya is an executive coach: I have always been very interested in the dynamics of the coaching relationship and I use knowledge and insights from psychodynamics and from transactional analysis to help me to understand what affects my level of connection and engagement with my client. These insights help me to notice when I start to experience something that has resonance with what the client has told me about their relationships in the workplace. For example, a client was talking about his boss wanting him to be more strategic in his leadership role at work. As the session developed I realized that I was feeling frustrated with him. He seemed to be flooding me with operational details, and was reluctant to get to grips with a wider picture. As I became aware of this I decided to share with him what I was experiencing: 'Trevor, I want to share with you something I have noticed that is happening between us. You mentioned that your boss was not completely happy about your ability to be strategic. Well I have noticed that in the session, whenever we get the opportunity to look at the wider picture and strategic direction for your unit, we seem to trail back again to discussing day-to-day operations. I have started to feel frustrated that we don't seem to be able to move forward. I wonder if what I have been experiencing here mirrors what happens between you and your boss?'

Maya has the knowledge and confidence to be aware of parallels between what happens in the coaching relationship and what happens in relationships at work. Rather than reflect on it later, she is able to respond to this insight immediately and as a result the level of engagement between the client and coach deepens. What would help you to be able to spot and respond to such insights?

Mel's mentor was so competent that on this particular day the session was transformed. It had started in a way that felt really heavy, yet it finished on an upbeat note. This energized Mel, who arrived that morning feeling pretty powerless, having been told that his job was to go in the next round of cuts. Somehow, this loss had triggered the memories of other losses, particularly the death of his father a couple of years previously. Mel poured out his story of loss, anger and abandonment. His mentor was aware that he could get sucked into the misery of all of this unless he kept his focus and energy directed at Mel. This he did and it was his ability to pick up metaphors such as 'hit on the head with a hammer' and 'black void' that made Mel feel that this mentor was completely alongside him. Gradually the trust built between these two people who had met for the first time that day. By the end of the session, there was a real sense of connection and energy between the two of them and Mel's powerlessness was transformed into the will to go back to work and actively secure the best possible deal to take him forward to his next job.

What would you have to be conscious of in yourself if a client came with issues such as Mel's? Would there be any memories of personal experiences which could distract you? Any difficulties staying positive when others are in pain? How would you keep the balance of energy in the room, between yourself and a client facing such loss and abandonment?

Box 4.3 Some questions for reflection during your encounter with a client

- What does my client want and need from me today?
- What do I notice about my client?
- What do I do with what I notice?
- What will the client be noticing about me?
- What positive or negative thoughts and feelings have I got towards the client?
- Are these telling me anything about how the client is with others outside of the session?
- What do I do with this awareness, if anything, in this session?
- Am I being too directive, forceful, laid back, critical, colluding?
- What can I do about that?
- What is my energy level today? What about energy from the client?
- What am I missing?
- Am I keeping my eye on time, boundaries and outcomes?
- How am I ensuring that my client will be leaving this session with plans for action?
- How am I helping my client to leave this session feeling supported, affirmed and sustained?

Reflection on action: after the session

Schön (1983) contributed greatly to our ideas about reflective learning and draws attention to the distinction between *reflection-in-action* and *reflection-on-action*. In the previous section we focused on ways in which the coach or mentor reflects upon what is going on in the encounter with the client, in the here and now, by trying to be fully present. But that is not enough. After the session the coach or mentor needs to reflect 'on the action' of the session: involving the client, the coach or mentor, and the relationship between the two. This can be done alone, perhaps with the aid of a reflective practice log and workbook, or with peers or a colleague as part of what Hay (2007) calls 'intervision'. It could also be done, most profitably, with a supervisor. We will consider the role of supervision more fully in the next section.

It helps to set aside some time immediately after a session to reflect on what happened. Some coaches and mentors make audio recordings of sessions, but they do this with permission from the client and with the awareness of issues of confidentiality. The first thing to do is to allow yourself to reflect upon the session in a broad way, noticing what aspects come most easily to mind. Then use some prompts to see what else might have been going on. To do this, our mnemonic, REFLECT, can be very helpful.

Box 4.4 Connor and Pokora's REFLECT mnemonic

Resources	*Competence, capability and capacity of both?*
Expectations	*What were the wants and needs of both?*
Flow	*What was going on in the relationship?*
Limitations	*What inhibits progress?*
Experience	*How was the session experienced by both?*
Content and context	*Was the session appropriate and manageable?*
Time, outcomes, action	*Were specific, valued, outcomes achieved?*

You may decide to use a more structured reflective practice log or brief. Box 4.5 gives an example of one used by some trainee coaches and mentors. Other examples of reflective practice logs and questionnaires can be found in resources such as Hay (2007).

Box 4.5 Example of a reflective practice log

Date of session: **Length of session:**

1   What did the client want and need from you?
2   What did you want and need from the client?
3   How did you begin?
4   What approach were you using?
5   What skills and/or tools did you try to use?
6   How did you end the session?
7   What do you think that you did well? How did the other person benefit?
8   What, in retrospect, would you like to have done differently?
9   What do you need to practise, research or brush up on now?
10 Now that you have reflected on this session, how would you describe your coaching/mentoring style?

At this point we shall look in more depth at the ways in which supervision closes the loop in our four-stage model of reflective practice. However insightful we are as coaches and mentors, we all have our blind spots and so reflective practice on our own will always be limited. We all need our resident 'internal supervisor' but we also need an external supervisor to ensure that our reflections lead to new learning with the help of different perspectives.

Supervision

Working as a coach or mentor can be stimulating, challenging and demanding. Supervision and support provide a confidential context for the coach or mentor to discuss their work and any problems associated with it. Importantly, the coach or mentor is the focus of the conversation, not the client. Hawkins and Smith (2010: 383) believe that there are three elements in coaching supervision:

1 Coaching the coach on their coaching.
2 Mentoring the coach on their development in the profession.
3 Providing an external perspective to ensure quality of practice.

They discuss supervision as *transformational* in the sense that the understanding which emerges from the process of sharing gives new insights and develops new perspectives on self, the client, self with client, work, and the context of work. The supervisor must be competent in enabling the coach or mentor in each of these areas. A knowledge of the psychology and dynamics of the coaching relationship is necessary, but so also is a knowledge of the organizational contexts, problems, issues and opportunities brought by the coach or mentor.

Not all writers assume that supervision is always beneficial. Rogers (2008: 215) argues that the jury is still out, because there has been so little research on coaching supervision to date. However, she discloses some of her own experience:

> I have worked with six different supervisors in my coaching career. All have contributed something different to my own development but what they have in common is that their impact on me was to increase my feelings of *prudent confidence* in relation to my own work. I have heard many other coaches describe the same thing and have heard it at first hand from my supervisees. But does a prudently confident coach do better work? We assume that this is so, but it is hard to prove.

Rogers draws attention to some of the problems of supervisors – for example, a supervisor with less knowledge, experience, wisdom or ability than the person they are supervising, or a supervisor with more blindspots, neediness, rigidity or blind adherence to particular coaching approaches than the person being supervised.

The alternative to individual supervision is peer co-supervision or group supervision. Terminology can be confusing, because the term 'supervision' is not used everywhere. Co-supervision and group supervision may be referred to as 'coach or mentor support'. However, they potentially offer the same benefits, helping mentors and coaches to work safely and effectively, to avoid burnout, to refer appropriately and to continue to develop skills and self-awareness.

Here are two stories of supervision, where there has been a good match between coach and supervisor. Leon is the coach and Ben is the supervisor.

Leon and Ben

My name is Leon and my supervisor is Ben. I run my own coaching business and I want to make the most of my supervision sessions, not least because I am paying for them myself. I always prepare for them by keeping a notebook of my work with clients. I don't write a lot, but I do like to pinpoint key things to bring to supervision, and I do this immediately after each session. Ben starts by asking what I want to talk about and I usually have three or four main things from two or three clients. We look at how to divide the time and then Ben keeps his eye on the clock so that we always have 10 minutes at the end to give each other feedback on the session. At the end of the session Ben asks me, 'What went well for you, what did you appreciate and what would you like me to have done differently or better?' At first Ben seemed to find it difficult to know when to stop me in my tracks and when to let me just continue telling a rather lengthy story. As we have got to know one another he seems more relaxed, realizing that I can actually do most of the work for myself, if he can just allow me the space to find the answers and solutions within me. What I have really valued in my supervision sessions is being helped to recognize when I have been vulnerable with a client in a way that I had not been able to admit before. He is so accepting that whatever thoughts and feelings get played out unwittingly with my clients, he will not only spot them, but do it in such a way that I am actually pleased to have realized what was really going on. That's what the books don't often tell you about supervision! That if you are using it properly, you lay yourself on the line and all sorts of things come to the surface. I have been surprised how often we talk about my current personal state, and patterns from my past, in relation to understanding me with my client. Ben works with the parallel processes he notices, things happening with us and between us, which seem to resonate with what I have told him about me and my clients. Those insights have helped me to be much sharper at noticing them when they happen with a client. I am even becoming skilled at how I then work with the insight in the here and now of a session.

As well as talking about work with clients, I get supervision on how I am managing the developments and changes in my business. You can't really do one without the other, because the whole context of my client work is the business. Ben doesn't want to advise me about it, but he helps me to see how relationships with business clients, fellow colleagues and sponsors impact on the resources I have and how they get allocated and distributed. Some of my 'clients' are groups or teams, and some are individuals. Often, I get supervision on how I can manage the confidentiality issues when coaching a team and then coaching them all individually as members of that team. Of course, another issue for me is when there has been a conflict of interest between the sponsor of a coaching intervention, and the individuals being coached.

My name is Ben and I supervise Leon. Leon knows what he wants and usually arrives, notebook in hand, with important issues highlighted for discussion. He knows how much time we have, and I encourage him to tell me how we will use our time on the different issues. Sometimes it will be a couple of quite separate client issues, sometimes something about his own development – for example, further training needs. Sometimes there are personal issues which he has noticed are impacting on his ability to 'be' with clients, whether these are health issues or unfinished business from past significant relationships. Sometimes the personal issues are about confidence and self-esteem. Leon drives our agenda and I help him to navigate his own choppy waters! Sometimes he is causing the waves himself, and sometimes the turbulence of his clients is causing a lack of equilibrium. Sometimes we notice patterns among issues presented by his current clients, or patterns in the way they are dealing with them and this can lead to important 'aha' moments in the session. Sometimes we notice that what Leon says is happening with clients starts happening in the room, with us. I always try to notice when this is occurring, and give us time to reflect on what's going on and what we may learn from that.

One of my issues as a supervisor is how much I should be intervening with someone who is so capable of learning from his own reflection. It feels like a balancing act most of the time, between allowing the space and encouraging focus. So at these moments when I'm not sure what to do, I say to myself, 'What would Leon benefit most from now?' Then I usually ask him! It sounds obvious doesn't it, but during a session as a supervisor I can get sucked into collusion with a supervisee without being conscious of what's going on, unless I stay really sharp and keep asking myself that key question, 'What is going on here?' If my supervisee is filling all the space with words so that I can't make a response, does that tell me how he or she is with clients? Are the words serving to keep a distance between us, or is it that my silence is unnerving him so he has to fill the space?

I have mentioned the importance of using my own 'internal supervisor' to reflect on the dynamics in the here and now of the supervision session, but we also do a number of more practical things as well. We talk about different approaches and tools that can be used with clients. We engage in role play and rehearse client situations where I take the role of the client so that Leon can try out new approaches and techniques in a safe place. We spend time looking at *his work with colleagues as well as with clients and we always have an eye on how the coaching business is developing. Some of the organizational issues we work on include how to manage conflicts of interest and confidentiality between organizations sponsoring the coaching and the individual clients whom Leon sees for coaching.*

The importance of supervision is well recognized in many helping professions, and it is mandatory in some. In coaching and mentoring, the EMCC *Code of Ethics* requires that all members have regular supervision and the APECS *Ethical Guidelines* (see Appendix for websites) refer to ongoing and regular supervision. In practice, the definition of 'regular' varies according to the nature and amount of coaching or mentoring work undertaken.

Approaches to supervision

Just as there are a wide variety of approaches and theories in coaching and mentoring, so there are in supervision. In fact the approaches to supervision often arise out of those that are used in coaching and mentoring. Some have more of a psychological base, whether more humanistic, as in the non-directive approaches, or with an emphasis on understanding the psychodynamics of the coaching and mentoring and supervisory relationship, as with Gestalt, NLP and TA. Others have more of an organizational and functional emphasis. But all approaches need to address the key competencies required by the professional and regulatory bodies for coaching and mentoring.

Perhaps one of the most widely used models is the 'seven-eyed process model' of Hawkins and Smith (2010: 159). For a very useful explanation of this model it is well worth referring directly to their work. They refer to 'seven modes' and these are illustrated as interconnecting circles:

1   *Client:* focus on the client and what and how they present.
2   *Supervisee:* exploration of strategies and interventions used.
3   *Relationship between client and supervisee:* conscious and unconscious.
4   *Supervisee:* focus on bringing self and client fully into awareness.
5   *Supervisory relationship:* focus on working alliance and parallel process.
6   *Supervisor:* focus on own process.
7   *Contexts:* focus on the wider contexts in which the work happens.

One way to approach supervision is to consider the main tasks required in order to help supervisees develop competence and confidence. These are listed in Box 4.6.

Box 4.6 Some tasks of supervision

- Clear contracting: safe boundaries and containment
- Providing supportive space for wide-ranging and deep reflection
- Working with the story
- Pushing the boundaries of the imagination
- Tapping into resources
- Developing the alliance
- Working with parallel processes
- Bringing the unconscious into awareness
- Challenging blindspots
- Offering new perspectives
- Using tools and techniques
- Working with 360-degree feedback
- Rehearsing new behaviours
- Supporting leaps of faith
- Transforming the capacity to function
- Learning about and learning from

APECS refers to supervision as 'the relationship between the coach and a qualified person who is not in any managerial relationship with the coach wherein the coaching work with particular clients may be discussed in strict confidence with the purpose of enhancing the quality of the coaching work and of ensuring client safety' (see www.apecs.org). The Association for Coaching (AC) notes that while supervision is a formal arrangement for maintaining adequate standards of coaching provision, 'it is also a supportive process. Supervision has sometimes been called "Super Vision" as a way of demonstrating that it is not restrictive or prescriptive but rather a process for increasing creativity' (see www.associationforcoaching.com). Both these definitions draw attention to the formal nature of supervision, as a planned, purposeful activity and something more than a casual chat. The EMCC *Guidelines on Supervision* (2004) list 12 criteria recommended for choosing a supervisor. Box 4.7 lists some questions in relation to making such a choice, derived from the EMCC criteria and adapted. Some of these questions may be more important to you than others, and this may give you some clues about who will be the right supervisor for you.

Julie works as a coach and mentor: I've known my supervisor for a long time. She taught on a coaching programme I attended, so I knew we both used the same coaching framework. I didn't think about asking which supervision framework she used. However, there was something about her quality of listening and attending that really impressed me even though she didn't know too much about the context in which I work. She just seemed like the right person and now that we have worked together I know that she is.

Box 4.7 Questions for choosing a supervisor

- Has the person been a coach, mentor or client?
- What coaching/mentoring framework do they use? Is this compatible with yours?
- Have they been supervised?
- How much/what type of experience do they have as a supervisor?
- Are they available for supervision at times/frequency to suit you?
- Have they been trained in supervision?
- What framework do they use for supervision?
- Do they communicate respect, empathy and genuineness to you?
- Can they be impartial as your supervisor (i.e. no conflicting roles)?
- Do they possess the qualities/skills which you are seeking in a supervisor?
- Do they subscribe to a code of ethics or belong to a professional body?
- Do they understand the context in which you work?

In a report published by the AC (2007: 6), based on an online survey of members to which there were 300 responses, the main reasons given for choice of supervisor were: someone from whom the coach would receive honest feedback about strengths and areas for development; someone who was qualified and experienced; someone who was a member of a professional body; someone with experience within an organizational context. The respondents in this survey put five benefits of supervision in rank order:

1 Provides a basis to learn and develop (95 per cent).
2 Provides a place to discuss ethical issues/concerns (93 per cent).
3 Offers a trusting and open relationship (78 per cent).
4 Offers maintenance and stability of practice (76 per cent).
5 Offers opportunities to increase our creativity (74 per cent).

This result concurs with our own experience. However, we would say that in supervision, offering a trusting and open relationship is the foundation upon which learning and development take place. This is the direct parallel with coaching and mentoring. This relationship then enables the supervisee to feel safe, to address ethical issues and concerns honestly, and to face difficulties with courage. By their nature, ethical issues are never straightforward. There are no easy answers. (See Chapter 10 for a more thorough discussion of these matters.) What appears to be an ethical issue with a client often takes the coach or mentor back to an examination of their own values, beliefs and attitudes, both conscious and unconscious. In order for this to happen in a productive and transformative way, the supervisor has to be a safe, trustworthy and respected person.

Supervision has been described as fulfilling several roles: normative, formative, restorative and perspective (Inskipp and Proctor 1989; Bond 1993). Applying these headings to coaching and mentoring, supervision may:

- help the coach or mentor to work safely, ethically and legally (normative);
- help the coach or mentor to learn and develop skills and understanding (formative);
- support the coach or mentor in dealing with the demands and stresses of the role (restorative);
- help the coach or mentor to maintain an overview of their work, and connections with other ways of helping (perspective).

 Box 4.8 provides a list of some of the benefits of supervision and support for the coach or mentor. How do they apply to you? Are some more important than others?

Box 4.8 Possible benefits of supervision and support

- Anticipating problems and avoiding/minimizing them
- Working as effectively as possible
- Responding to clients who are challenging
- Developing skills and confidence
- Getting support
- Maintaining perspective
- Staying connected with other approaches
- Maintaining boundaries and working ethically
- Developing self-insight
- Working fairly and valuing diversity
- Challenging assumptions about self and others

For more information on supervision, you may wish to refer to the guidelines produced by some of the professional bodies listed in the Appendix. In
the next chapter we invite you to take part in an interactive case study of
reflective practice.

Summary

In this chapter we have:

- Introduced aspects of coach and mentor development.
- Considered the value of learning from experience.
- Presented a four-stage model for reflective practice.
- Used several case examples to illustrate reflective practice.
- Discussed several aspects of supervision.
- Presented the perspectives of a supervisor and supervisee who work
  together.

5 How can I be reflective in practice?

> - Introduction
> - Your client: Paul
> - Session 1: building the relationship
> - Session 2: developing the relationship
> - Session 3: being resourceful
> - Summary

Introduction

This chapter is a case study to stimulate your thinking about some of the issues that arise when you are with a client. We hope it will help when you have to 'think on your feet', respond, and then reflect on your response both during the session and afterwards, perhaps in supervision. It is designed to help you to consider these questions:

- How do the key principles help me?
- What are some of the ethical and professional issues that may arise?
- What sorts of issues might I take to support and supervision?

Paul has asked you to be his mentor, and your first three sessions are explored in this chapter. You will have an introductory session with him and then two more sessions. There are interactive prompts and questions throughout the chapter, as well as explanations of how the principles of effective coaching and mentoring apply. You will find it useful to review the nine key principles for effective practice (see Chapter 1) before reading the case study. At various points you are asked to:

- reflect on what is happening;
- consider your response;
- decide how you will help the client.

When you see this sign, there is a summary of how the principles of effective coaching and mentoring are being used in practice.

 At the end of each session, when you see this symbol, it will indicate some issues that might be taken to mentor support or supervision.

Your client: Paul

Paul is a doctor. He has recently been appointed as medical director in a hospital. He has attended a leadership development programme which included coaching sessions. This has helped build his skills and confidence in working with managers and chairing meetings. He has asked for some regular mentoring to support development in his new role. In particular, a challenge for Paul is representing the interests of doctors in the hospital while also reflecting management interests, since sometimes these seem to be in conflict. He has chosen you because you work in the same organization and he respects you.

Session 1: building the relationship and negotiating a working agreement

 PRINCIPLES INTO PRACTICE

The context of the mentoring is Paul's development as a leader.

The agenda is his, and you facilitate the process.

You share **a model for change** and he decides whether to use it.

The outcome he wants is to become more skilful at managing and influencing in the organization.

The learning relationship is crucial because he has stated that he wants to learn from you as someone he respects.

The qualities of respect, empathy and honesty build rapport and trust.

The skills are active listening, appropriate sharing and negotiating.

Ethical issues include the possibility of blurring of boundaries because you work in the same organization.

You are the mentor. What do you want to achieve in your first session with Paul?

How would you negotiate a working agreement? Refer to Chapter 2 for an example of a working agreement. Are there any areas that may be particularly important?

How will you decide if you can work together or not?

This is the first meeting with Paul. It is for each of you to find out if you can work together. You start by asking him how he would like you to help. This gives you valuable insight into his expectations. You are able to clarify what you can offer in terms of time, commitment, experience and knowledge. He says that he needs help with leading and managing colleagues. He would like to meet for two or three sessions initially. You agree to this. You suggest that you put time aside at the end of each session to review how you are working together. You give him a copy of the working agreement and allow him time to look over it and ask any questions. You explain your approach, and again ask if there are any questions.

Looking at the working agreement immediately raises the question of confidentiality, and Paul asks if everything in the sessions will be confidential.

 Here are some responses to Paul's question about confidentiality. Which would you make? Or is there a better one?

- Oh, yes, definitely.
- I have some ideas about what the limits are. Would it be useful to talk about these?
- The sessions are completely in confidence unless there are legal or professional limits placed upon our confidentiality. We would both be bound by these. You can choose what you wish to disclose to me. If I was concerned about having to share some information with another person we would talk about it first, and I would help you, where possible, to take the initiative to disclose. How does that sound?

Another issue for clarification, because you work in the same organization, is about conflict of interest.

> *Paul:* Can I just check? You're a senior manager in this hospital. If I criticize one of your colleagues would that be difficult for you? If I told you that one of my projects was failing, what then?

 Would the response below adequately answer Paul's question. If not, what do you suggest?

> *Mentor:* When the mentoring system was set up we agreed that my first responsibility is to you, the client. So be assured that your interest comes first. If there is a problem I would be happy to help but I am not here as a mentor to get directly involved in managing it. I'm here to help you to do that!

Paul likes the fact that you have given him a working agreement for discussion. This echoes the transparency that he expects in his professional life. It makes him think that he can trust you. You agree to work together for another two sessions within the next month. Each session will be for two hours, with the final 15 minutes set aside for review. Paul is to set the agenda for each session and decide on relevant action between sessions.

 ## ISSUES FOR REFLECTION AND SUPERVISION

What issues has this session raised for you in your work as a mentor?

Reflecting on this session, what are your areas of strength and areas for development in an introductory session?

Having negotiated the working agreement and introduced your approach, would you do anything differently in future? Would you want to include anything else?

What might be potential ongoing issues concerning boundaries, confidentiality and conflict of interest in the relationship?

Session 2: developing the relationship and managing the agenda

 PRINCIPLES INTO PRACTICE

The **context** is Paul's role as a leader in dealing with colleagues, clinicians and managers.

The **mentoring objective** is to provide reflective space so that the story will unfold.

The mentor provides a balance of **support and challenge** so that new perspectives will develop and resources can be recognized and used. The first stage is to explore the story and find out which parts of it Paul would like to work on.

The **outcome** Paul wants is to be able to manage himself when dealing with difficult colleagues.

The **learning relationship** starts to develop and you use active and empathic listening to develop trust and rapport. Then the client asks if you would share your experiences.

The **qualities** that need to be communicated are respect for Paul, genuine interest in his story, empathic understanding and honest self-sharing. This will help to affirm and sustain him.

Ethical practice includes: responding appropriately to a request for shared experience; keeping to the time boundary; allowing enough time to end the session safely; and evaluation of the working relationship.

Before you start the session you remind yourself that Paul will set the agenda for each session and so you ask him what he wants to work on today. Paul says that there have been a couple of very difficult situations in his leadership role with colleagues. You ask him how he would like to use the time. He wants to divide the time between the problem he is having with a clinician, and the problem with the finance director. The final 15 minutes will be for review.

 You are aware that you need to keep an eye on the time if Paul is to deal with both the difficult situations. You also need to allow time for the review at the end of the session. How will you decide what to do next?

Paul starts to tell the story of his two 'difficult' colleagues. The first is a doctor, who is dismissive of management. He is highly regarded in his specialty, and much in demand at international conferences. He is often away and it falls increasingly to his colleagues to pick up his work. They are grumbling about this. Some managers are unhappy about his dismissive attitude. He is reluctant to comply with recently introduced protocols for appraisal and personal development plans. Paul, as medical director, has been asked to meet with this colleague and investigate.

After paraphrasing the story, you say, 'So you have been asked to meet with him?' and this repeating of key words helps Paul to continue.

> *Paul:* Yes, and I'm dreading it. He's such a powerful personality! It will be quite an achievement if I get him to the meeting at all. But how to handle it? That's the difficulty. I don't want to end up with us shouting at one another. If I'm going to do this job successfully, I need to keep people like him 'on board'. That brings me to my next problem with the other colleague. I suppose the problems are related really! The other one is the finance director who keeps hounding me because there is an overspend on the medical budget. He wants to manage the overspend by cutting the budget for the doctors' study leave and conference attendance. This means that I will not be able to approve study leave applications and the consultants will see me as the hard-arm of management, rather than as their champion. I feel as if I am between a rock and a hard place. This job is already making me feel exposed and isolated.

 Paul has fairly quickly presented two difficult situations. You want to keep the focus on him, rather than spending too much time talking about the other people involved.

Reflect back to Paul what he seems to be thinking and feeling.

> *Mentor:* Let me check that I understand. You're dreading the meeting with the doctor because he's such a powerful personality and you don't want to end up in a slanging match. On top of that you've also got a problem with the demands being made by the finance director. You're feeling 'between a rock and a hard place', exposed as well as isolated. You are caught between the pressures of the finance director and what your consultant colleagues want. Is that how it is?

Now that you have paraphrased what you have heard and checked your understanding with Paul, he is encouraged to continue. He talks about how he enjoys a challenge and this is why he accepted the job. He knew that leading clinicians would be difficult, but he hadn't realized how exposed and isolated he might feel, so soon into the job.

Paul is still telling his story, but you help him to clarify which part of it he wishes to pursue in this session. Your summary has identified that his feelings of isolation and powerlessness are an important part of the problem for him. You help him to focus, and prioritize an issue to take forward and work on. This may help him to move from feeling stuck to imagining how things could be better.

> *Mentor:* There is the difficult colleague, there is the finance director, and there are your feelings about the job. Which of these should we look at first?
>
> *Paul:* I suppose that if I looked at how I react to these situations it would help. Have you any advice you could give me from your experience?

You know that Paul chose you as mentor partly because of your experience in the organization. You want to respond to his request for advice, but you also want to keep the focus on Paul and his experiences so that he learns what is useful to him.

 How do you feel when Paul asks for advice? How would you respond?

How could you share your experience in a way that opens up discussion and invites Paul's ideas, rather than offering your solutions?

You start by sharing some experiences of similar situations and you finish by saying: 'Those are examples of what worked for me. The same things may not work for you. Is there anything that seems useful to you in what I have shared?'

Having shared briefly some of your own experiences, you ask about Paul's reactions to his own situation. You help him to challenge himself by developing new perspectives. You do this by asking him to reflect upon times in the past when he dealt with feelings of exposure and isolation, and what or who helped then. You help him to consider what resources might be available: friends, family, other clinicians and other medical directors in the wider network? Finally, you help him to get some insight into the perspectives of both the doctor and the finance director by asking, 'If they were here now, what would they be saying about you? About what they would want from you?'

Time moves on, and you are nearing the end of the session. You encourage Paul to identify something that would move him forward with this issue. He says that the most pressing thing is to get more ideas about how to manage the meeting with the clinician.

> Would you summarize what has been said, or would you ask Paul to summarize? What would you say in a concise but comprehensive summary?
>
> How would you help him to find something to work on between now and the next session?

Paul decides that, in the next two weeks, he will make contact with the previous medical director to talk over how he managed situations like these. He decides that he will postpone the meeting with the doctor until after the next mentoring session. At the next session he wants to look at specific strategies for not allowing himself to be intimidated in the meeting with his difficult colleague.

> Finally, you review how you have worked together.
>
> What might you include in the review of the session?
>
> What do you think of the question below, as a starting-point?

You say: 'Could we finish by saying what it was like to work together today? What seemed to help or hinder? What did we appreciate and what would we like to be different next time?' The session concludes with both of you agreeing what Paul will do between now and next time. He writes down his action points. Finally, you check diaries for the date of the next session.

In this session Paul has articulated his problems with colleagues and developed insight into their perspectives as well as his own. He has identified valuable resources in himself and in others. There has been appropriate sharing of experience from you, the mentor, with regard to the politics of the organization.

ISSUES FOR REFLECTION AND SUPERVISION

Did you deal adequately with Paul's feelings of exposure and isolation?

How did you feel when Paul asked for your advice? How do you normally respond to such a request?

Should you have offered to network for Paul?

How can you prepare for working with him next time, on specific strategies for not feeling intimidated?

Session 3: being resourceful and listening to your 'internal supervisor'

 PRINCIPLES INTO PRACTICE

The **context** is Paul's leadership role. He wants strategies for a meeting.

The **objective** is to develop his confidence by identifying a goal and planning realistic action.

The **outcome** is that Paul is arranging the meeting with the doctor after doing further preparation.

The **learning relationship** is tested twice in this session. Firstly when you, the mentor, experience 'resistance' from Paul in defining a specific goal. Secondly, when you need to manage a time issue.

You remain **facilitative** and client-centred even when planning action.

The **qualities** that are needed in the mentor are: affirmation of Paul; belief in his ability to make changes; and balance of support and challenge.

Ethical practice includes keeping time boundaries. As both you and Paul work in the same organization it will be essential to maintain confidentiality. Contingency planning is necessary to support action.

Paul is returning for his third mentoring session, and you remember that he described how isolated he felt in his new role. You wonder how things are. You check the notes you made together:

1   Paul was to meet with the previous medical director to find out how he managed difficult colleagues.

2   He wanted help with specific strategies for dealing with his feelings of intimidation when he meets with his difficult colleague.

How do you start the session?

Which of these introductions might you choose and why?

Would you have a better introduction?

- Hello Paul. How are you today?
- Paul, I've looked at the notes we made last time. We listed two things, they were . . . shall we start with the meeting you had with the previous medical director?
- Paul, I am wondering what you want to get out of the session today.

Paul says that things have moved on since last time. He tells you that he has met with the previous medical director. There has been a history of difficulty with both the doctor colleague and the finance director. The meeting made Paul realize that he wants to be more direct than his predecessor. It also confirmed that Paul's feelings of exposure and isolation did seem to come with the job, and confirmed that it was a wise decision to find a mentor.

> *Paul:* So, can you help me with some strategies for not allowing myself to be overwhelmed and intimidated, so that I can say in a meeting what needs to be said, even when I am being drowned out by the other person?
> *Mentor:* Well, let's start by looking at what you want to happen, in the ideal world. Let's take one of these colleagues, which should we work with first?
> *Paul:* The doctor.
> *Mentor:* Imagine the scenario now where you have asked him to come to see you about the complaints from colleagues and management. Imagine your ideal meeting with him. Take a minute to visualize this and let me know when you have a picture in mind.

You guide Paul in brainstorming what he ideally wants and needs from such a meeting. You prompt him to describe what he would and would not be doing, thinking and feeling, and ideally what the doctor would and would not be doing, thinking and feeling. You ask about the ideal outcome from the meeting, and encourage him to go for some wild ideas. When he completes the brainstorm, you ask him to choose which of the possibilities seem most important to him. (For more information about this technique and useful prompts to use, refer to Chapters 7 and 9.)

> *Paul:* I saw myself standing there, staying firm while a barrage of words was being fired at me. I didn't raise my voice, but I said clearly what had to be said. That's what I want. I felt powerful then, and certainly not intimidated.

You ask him how he might turn that picture into something specific that he wants to do: that is, a goal.

 You notice that Paul is very energized and hopeful during the brainstorm. As he considers what he needs to do, he becomes more thoughtful, and he seems reluctant to specify a goal. How does this make you feel? What are you thinking? What will you do? How would you remain non-directive and facilitative even though you are guiding the process of change?

Despite his initial reluctance to be specific, you help Paul to shape up his goal and he decides that: 'I'll meet with the doctor next week and I'll achieve my objectives for the meeting without being overwhelmed by his power and aggression.' You check with him whether this is realistic in the timeframe he has allowed himself, and how he will feel if he achieves this. He says that he will feel confident and reassured. You check with him the costs and benefits of being assertive. The personal costs almost outweigh the benefits, but Paul believes that the potential benefits for him as a leader are significant. If he can be assertive with this colleague, he will more confident in being assertive in other difficult situations, whether at meetings or with individuals.

Now that he has a specific goal you help him to look at all the possible ways he might achieve it. You encourage him to think of as many as possible, whether realistic or not. This helps him to open his mind to as many possibilities as he can. Paul begins to brainstorm strategies, which include: listening to the doctor; understanding the doctor's concerns; preparing by rehearsing for the meeting beforehand; identifying his own 'bottom line position'; deciding what is negotiable and what isn't; and trying out some arguments he might use with a friend as 'devil's advocate'. At this point you share with him some other strategies which he may not already be aware of: the CAN model of negotiation; using transactional analysis to examine his own reactions; doing some role-reversal to rehearse how to end a negotiation with both him and the doctor committed to the outcome (see Chapter 9 for more information on these strategies). You also mention a couple of useful books.

 You are aware that you are more than halfway through the session. You are also concerned about leaving Paul with unfinished preparation for the meeting. You feel worried that you are mismanaging the timing as well as Paul's expectations of what can realistically be achieved in this session.

What would you do? Consider the five ethical principles when making your decision: what does least harm; what does most good; what safeguards Paul's autonomy; what is fair; what is in keeping with what has been promised? Would you choose one of the options below, or do something else?

- Cut him short in his planning, saying that there are only a few minutes left for this part of the session if you are to spend 15 minutes on review at the end?
- Decide to drop the review this time as there won't be enough time?
- Wait for a suitable moment, summarize your understanding of the session so far and mention that there is not much time left, asking Paul what he would like to do now?
- Do nothing and see what he says, letting him use all the time for this issue if he says nothing?

You can't decide, so you do nothing. Paul continues talking and you are getting increasingly worried but you feel that you can't interrupt him. A few more minutes pass and then he suddenly looks at his watch and says:

> *Paul:* Oh! I didn't realize the time. We've only got 30 minutes left and I do need to be sure about what I'm going to do at this meeting.

You breathe a sigh of relief! Paul has solved the problem himself. But you are concerned that you hadn't been keeping a close eye on the clock. This could have led to Paul not achieving what he wanted from the session. In hindsight, you reflect that, whatever the problem or issue, the important thing is to have open discussion about it and allow Paul to be involved in any decisions about how to proceed. You now want to bring the discussion back to Paul's strategies for action and so you ask him to summarize the ones he mentioned before.

How will you now help Paul to firm up a strategy that would be 'best fit' for him?

How will you help him to explore what will help or hinder that strategy?

Of all the ideas mentioned Paul decides that the most useful would be to read and to practise the CAN model of negotiation. He will then rehearse the negotiation with a friend who will take the role of the clinician. Paul will rehearse three things: trying to express his interests clearly; communicating that he understands where the colleague is coming from; and remaining calm and positive in the face of aggressive behaviour. You ask him what might help and what might hinder this strategy.

> *Mentor:* This idea of preparing your case and then rehearsing with a friend – what will help that strategy to succeed?
> *Paul:* The fact that I can trust my friend to be honest and supportive, and also that I really am keen on trying this out now. My friend will tell me directly what I need to change or do. Also, he knows what I'm up against!
> *Mentor:* And what might get in the way? What might stop it from working?
> *Paul:* If neither of us can get our diaries together. It's such a short time till the meeting. Or if I bottle out!

You have used some questions about what will help or hinder the strategy. These help Paul to identify untapped resources in himself or others and also anything that may sabotage his attempts at rehearsing the meeting. Now he moves to the practicalities of a manageable plan. He decides on a time when he can do his reading and preparation and also that tomorrow he will approach his friend so that they can firm up a date in their diaries, within the next week.

What would you include in discussion about a manageable action plan?

What contingency plan might be necessary?

What support might you offer?

What about links into the next session?

You have helped Paul to firm up his action plan and now you turn to ending the session. In this session you realize that Paul has moved from feeling stuck with his problems to the hope that came from realizing possibilities for different ways of thinking, feeling and acting. From this he, somewhat reluctantly at first, found the courage to choose a realistic goal for change. You notice that the session felt energetic and active and you used models and techniques to keep it moving. There was a hiccup halfway through when you realized that time was short, but in the end you felt it worked out, with Paul's objectives met. Now it is time to find out what Paul thinks as you evaluate how you have worked together. As this is the last of the agreed sessions with Paul you also want to offer him the possibility of returning to review his progress.

Mentor: I notice we have 15 minutes left. We've done quite a bit of active work together today and I'm wondering how you're feeling now?

Paul: Exhausted! I didn't realize that mentoring was such hard work! It has given me plenty to think about, and to do. My most pressing problem is the meeting but I do feel more confident after our work today.

Mentor: I'm pleased that you're feeling more confident. Is there anything that I could have done, or not done, that would have made the session better for you? And do you feel you would like to come back for another session to review your progress?

Paul: Definitely. And maybe you need to make me keep more focused next time so that we cover more! I can ramble on a bit.

Mentor: What would you like me to do, to help you keep more focused?

Paul: Actually, I'd like you to be a bit more challenging.

Mentor: That's fine by me. We can start next time by agreeing the focus at the beginning. Then we can review again at the end of the session to see if we achieved what you wanted. I've enjoyed working together today and have noticed your resourcefulness and determination. I admire your resilience in the face of challenge and I look forward to hearing what happens in your meeting! We seem to have achieved what you wanted. But can I ask you, when we got to stating a goal, did you feel I was pushing too much?

Paul: Well, actually, I didn't really want to say something so definite as 'a goal' and I did feel myself pulling back at that stage. But you did give me enough space to decide for myself so, after my initial reluctance, I went for it.

You check if there is anything else that Paul wants to say, you ask him to summarize his action plan and how he feels at the end of the session.

 ISSUES FOR REFLECTION AND SUPERVISION

You reflect on the three sessions. Then you decide which issues you would like to take to supervision. In particular, you want to use some supervision to reflect on your own development, including the way you use your approach, skills, tools and techniques, within the learning relationship. You want to explore how to keep the balance between support and challenge, and how to remain client-centred at the problem-solving and action stages of mentoring. You have heard about 'parrallel process', where there is a resonance between issues the client brings to supervision and what the mentor experiences in the here-and-now relationship with the client. You are not sure whether that happened in these sessions, but you want to learn more about this, in supervision.

What did you do well in this case study?

What would you now like to be able to do differently?

Who will help you to develop as a coach or mentor?

Summary

In this chapter we have:

- Developed an interactive case study with Paul, over three sessions.
- Invited you to be the mentor during each session.
- Applied key principles for effective practice.
- Given extracts of dialogue so that you can reflect on what is happening in the session and choose appropriate responses.
- Highlighted, for reflection at the end of each session, some ethical and professional issues which could be taken to supervision.

6 What about training and accreditation?

- Introduction
- Choosing a training programme
- Key elements of training
- The learning climate
- Ethical and professional training
- Qualifications
- Competence and professionalism
- Accreditation
- Summary

Introduction

Effective coaching or mentoring will occur only if you are constantly updating knowledge of yourself, clients, and the contexts in which your clients live and work. Organizations and clients who employ coaches and mentors increasingly demand that they hold a relevant qualification and that they are accredited by one of the professional coaching or mentoring organizations. The 2009 CIPD survey, *Taking the Temperature of Coaching and Mentoring*, reported that about a third of respondent organizations required coaches to have coaching credentials. However, those who use coaching and mentoring as part of a leadership or management role at work may be looking for shorter training opportunities. Accreditation as a coach or mentor is linked to evidence of performance against specific competencies. There is now an expectation that to be accredited by major international coaching and mentoring bodies, there must also be evidence of successful ongoing supervision and CPD, as discussed in Chapter 4.

Choosing a training programme

In our experience, well-designed training is helpful for all those involved in coaching and mentoring, but should be regarded as essential by those considering a full-time coaching or mentoring role.

Currently, anyone may call themselves a coach or mentor, without any training or qualification. Both purchasers and providers of coaching and mentoring services have raised concerns that coaches and mentors who are not trained may do more harm than good. Moreover, individuals who are asked to take on a coaching or mentoring role without formal preparation and training can feel ill-equipped. The CIPD survey (2009: 3) revealed that only 36 per cent of respondents said that in-depth coaching training was provided in their organization.

In this chapter we explore important aspects of effective coach and mentor training and offer guidelines for choosing a training programme. Using material drawn from a variety of sources, including an established programme, the key components of training are described. This chapter will be of particular relevance if you want to:

- understand more about training;
- select the right training course;
- get the best out of a course you are on already;
- commission coach or mentor training for your organization or professional body;
- design or develop coach or mentor training for your organization or professional body.

Throughout the chapter, case examples illustrate key topics, and practical exercises will help you to design or choose the right training programme for you, and get the most out of training.

Assessing your training needs

In assessing your training needs, a good place to start is to ask yourself why you are interested in training at this time in your life and work. It may be that external factors are steering you. Perhaps you have been asked, or required, to work as a coach or mentor in your organization. It may be that personal interest is the major factor. Becoming a coach or mentor, whether full-time or part-time, may be part of your personal development plan. For many people, a mixture of motivations are involved. When participants are asked about their reasons for attending training programmes, typical replies include:

- I've been doing mentoring for several years . . . it's about time I found out if I was doing it right!
- Many junior staff approach me for help, and I want to feel more confident in having a framework and the right skills for working with them.
- I do coaching in my organization, but I think I'm often quite prescriptive and give people advice . . . I wonder if there is a better way.
- I want to set up a mentoring scheme in my company and need to find out what it's all about.
- I've been asked to take on a mentoring/coaching role, which I see as an opportunity, but also daunting. I've experienced it being done badly and I want to do it better.
- I don't think we get the best out of our managers at work, and I think coaching could support them and help to deliver better results.

 What is happening in your organization or professional environment that makes training important at this time?

A review of personal development planning in a large organization showed that many employees would benefit from individual support in addressing their training and development needs. The organization commissioned a coaching skills programme for managers, designed to increase their confidence and skill in supporting their staff, whether high flyers or those with performance problems.

 What is happening for you in your career or at work that makes training important at this time?

Examples of reasons why training might be important include a new or changed job role, increased responsibility for staff, an experience of handling a 'difficult' person, or a requirement to take on a formal coaching or mentoring role.

Kim, a manager, says: I've just joined an organization where staff development is a high priority, and I will have a large number of people reporting directly to me. I'm used to troubleshooting problems myself, but I'm not so experienced at delegating and developing others. I need some training to help me find out how to build good relationships and support staff while at the same time getting the work done.

In assessing your training needs, it is also helpful to think about your preferences in leading, working and learning. In previous chapters, the usefulness of inventories and questionnaires is described. You can use insight from these to consider your training needs.

> **Diane is senior teacher in a city school** and as a member of the leadership team she is outgoing and decisive and prefers to learn by doing, with the opportunity for experimentation and trial and error. She wants a mentor training programme which will allow her to capitalize on this strength, with plenty of practice, but that will also challenge her to work in different ways. She has a tendency to 'act first, think later', and knows that she may miss opportunities for learning. She wants to develop the capacity to be reflective, which will be important both while being trained and also while being a mentor to her staff colleagues.

Another exercise that may help to clarify your training needs is to focus on what you hope to achieve from coach or mentor training. Clarifying your ideal can highlight what is important to you. Here is an example:

> **A group of nurses** decided to set up a mentoring scheme for all staff working in local health centres, and asked for volunteers to be trained as mentors. The trainee mentors brainstormed their ideal for the mentoring scheme, and shared ideas about what it would be like if it were working really well. The brainstorming session created a sense of excitement and possibility among the would-be mentors about what they could achieve. Using the results of brainstorming, they set up specific goals for their training and for establishing the mentoring scheme.

 Thinking ahead, imagine that you have successfully completed or implemented a coach or mentor training programme, and it has gone very well, better than you could have hoped for.

What would be different in your organization?

What would be different for you personally?

What would you have achieved?

A final approach to exploring your training needs is based on a typology of learning. Pedler and Aspinwall (1996: 25) describe four types of learning, and we give an example of each:

1   **About** things (or *knowledge*) (e.g. I learn that coaching requires the skills of support and challenge).

2   **To do** things (or *skills, abilities, competencies*) (e.g. I learn to listen actively in coaching practice and coaching situations).

3   **To become ourselves**, to achieve our full potential (or *personal development*) (e.g. I find myself listening in this different way in many aspects of my life, which changes the nature of my interactions with others).

4   **To achieve things together** (or *collaborative enquiry*) (e.g. we reflect, in my leadership team, on the way in which we listen to each other, and hear, and check understanding. This has an impact on us, and on the decisions we make together).

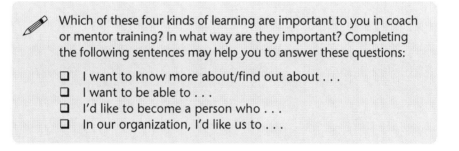

Which of these four kinds of learning are important to you in coach or mentor training? In what way are they important? Completing the following sentences may help you to answer these questions:

- ❏   I want to know more about/find out about . . .
- ❏   I want to be able to . . .
- ❏   I'd like to become a person who . . .
- ❏   In our organization, I'd like us to . . .

Selecting a training programme

Your assessment of training needs will influence your choice of coach or mentor training programme. The previous section helped you to clarify your training requirements. The next step is to choose the right programme for you. An obvious starting place is the training programme objectives. Are they clear and explicit? Is the programme flexible or fixed? Can it be tailored to your requirements or is it 'off the shelf'? How close is the match between your needs and the programme objectives?

Whatever your objectives, a training programme should describe in simple language the aims and learning outcomes. A training provider should be clear about what they are offering, and also indicate any topics not covered. If your aim is to find out more about coaching and mentoring, a short programme of a day or thereabouts may be sufficient. Such a programme is best considered as an introduction, and will probably include topics such as:

- definitions of coaching and mentoring;
- the benefits of coaching and mentoring – individual and organizational;

- approaches, frameworks and skills;
- implementing coaching or mentoring schemes;
- future trends in coaching and mentoring.

If you want to develop coaching and mentoring skills then a longer programme is essential. A development programme which targeted both knowledge and skills included outcomes whereby at the end of the programme participants:

- understood what coaching and mentoring is and how it differs from counselling or patronage;
- had been introduced to a framework for coaching and mentoring;
- had practised each stage of the framework and the associated skills, received feedback and reviewed their skills development;
- had considered the ethical and practical issues involved in being coaches and mentors and setting up coaching and mentoring schemes.

Timescale

If you are looking for a short course of initial training, our experience is that four days' training are needed, and five days are preferable, for those who are developing skills as coaches or mentors. These days are best spaced out over time to enable participants to assimilate learning and to practise skills. Training providers offer a range of courses with qualifications at different levels, from certificate to diploma and masters level. The timescale of these will vary from six months for a certificate to two or three years for the masters. Training is the start, not the end, of the coaching or mentoring journey. Completing a training programme is an important step in developing as a coach or mentor, but it is only the beginning.

Structure

When considering potential programmes, find out how the training time is structured. Will there be formal inputs on models, theories and approaches? Will there be practical demonstrations of skills being taught? Will there be the opportunity to practise skills and get feedback? When skills development is a key objective, our recommendation is that at least 50 per cent of the course time should be spent on skills practice and review of learning. Will there be the opportunity to discuss how the skills have been used at work, and any ethical and practical issues arising? A mixture of activities and learning methods is preferable.

A learning design might include:

- a variety of learning and teaching methods, including input, large-group discussion, demonstration of a framework and skills, small-group skills practice and small-group activity;
- a balance between learner-centred activity (e.g. discussing experiences of practising the skills at work) and theory-centred activity (e.g. taught input);
- a breadth of content, including a framework for coaching or mentoring, the skills, ethical and professional considerations, and coach or mentor self-development;
- a time gap between the programme days, to allow for assimilation of skills and practice in everyday settings;
- discussion of life after training, including ongoing support and supervision;
- opportunities for networking during and after the programme.

Trainers

A key resource on a training programme is the trainer or trainers. How many will there be and what is the ratio of staff to participants? For skills development, small-group work is essential and a workable ratio is one experienced facilitator or tutor for every three participants. What is the background and experience of the trainers? Do they have coaching or mentoring experience and relevant qualifications?

Participants

The participants themselves are another key learning resource. A training programme needs sufficient numbers for breadth and variety of style and experience, but not so many people as to make large-group dialogue difficult. If skills development is a priority, the ratio of tutors to participants is important. In addition, consider what other resources are available. These might include course materials, books, online materials, case studies, training follow-up days and trainer support back at work.

Ethical considerations

A discussion of ethical and professional issues is an important aspect of coach and mentor training. A training programme is frequently part of an organization's initiative to develop a coaching or mentoring scheme, or to create an organizational culture which fosters coaching and mentoring. It is therefore important to consider how a coaching or mentoring scheme would work in practice within the organizational culture and existing systems. Participants need to think about how their coaching or mentoring role will work in their organization or professional body, how it will fit in with their other roles and the ethical and professional dilemmas that might arise from coaching and mentoring in practice. In addition, participants need to plan how their support and supervision needs will be met.

Key elements of training

Having introduced the assessment of training needs and training programme selection, we now look at the key elements of training, which are usually linked to the competencies and capabilities required by professional coaching and mentoring organizations. These include:

- self-awareness and development of insight;
- the coaching and mentoring relationship;
- knowledge of different approaches and models;
- skill development;
- the context of coaching and mentoring;
- use of tools and techniques.

Self-awareness and development of insight

An effective training programme creates opportunities for self-insight and self-development at all stages of the learning process. Examples include use of a learning journal or learning log, doing a career lifeline (as illustrated in Chapter 9), and use of psychometric instruments and inventories such as the MBTI Questionnare and the Learning Styles Inventory (see Chapters 1 and 3).

> **Bruce:** I was pretty sceptical about keeping a journal and it took some doing at first! However, when I reviewed it with my learning partner, it underlined some key learning moments for me, and highlighted how I'd changed in my views, and also my skill development.

> **Ali:** On my training course we drew our own career lifelines and talked in small groups about ourselves, past, present and hopes for the future. It was a powerful exercise, which highlighted the high points and low points in my career to date and got me thinking about

what I really wanted for the future. I would consider offering this activity to a client, but only when we'd got to know each other and if I thought it would be helpful. It needs a supportive atmosphere and plenty of time to debrief it.

Krysia: On my course we did the MBTI questionnaire. It confirmed that I'm quite easy-going and relaxed. I like exploring options and gathering more information, rather than closing down on options too quickly. I do sometimes find it difficult to meet deadlines and finish things on time. I used to beat myself up about this, but now I understand that it is a natural preference and has its advantages. The questionnaire has helped me to be more accepting of myself, and more understanding of differences in clients.

Phil: By doing the Learning Styles Inventory I confirmed that my learning style is quite reflective and I need time to mull things over. I found the skills practice, where I just had to get on with it, quite difficult. I didn't feel as if I'd had enough time to prepare. I noticed too that as a coach I'm quite happy with silences, but some clients aren't!

The coaching and mentoring relationship

This is central to all other aspects of training and our definition of coaching and mentoring is that 'Coaching and mentoring are learning relationships which help people to take charge of their own development, to release their potential and to achieve results which they value.' On a training programme you will learn about different approaches to establishing and sustaining the learning relationship. You will review your strengths and areas for development in relation to core qualities, such as empathy, respect and integrity. Every time you engage in coaching and mentoring you should get feedback, from peers, tutors and facilitators on the way in which you initiate and develop the relationship (see Chapter 2 for more information on how to build an effective learning relationship). Some courses include personal development group work and this is a powerful way of testing out some of your relationship qualities and skills with other trainees, in a safe setting.

Knowledge of approaches and models

An important aspect of training is to extend your knowledge and understanding of a range of approaches, models and frameworks. If the training is short, then the focus is likely to be on understanding one or two approaches, but if it is part of training for a qualification then several will be introduced with the expectation that you will not only understand them, but also be able to use one or more of them, and critically evaluate them. Please refer to Chapters 1 and 7 for more information about some of these.

Skill development

However much you 'know about' coaching and mentoring, to be an effective practitioner you must 'be able to'. An effective training programme should address each of the following stages of skill development, so that participants have the opportunity to:

- *learn* about skills;
- *recognize* them when they are used;
- *practise* them in training conditions, with appropriate feedback;
- *use* the skills outside the training environment;
- *integrate* the skills into their personal and professional development.

This skills development sequence, with the emphasis on *doing* rather than *talking about*, has been described as rather like learning to ride a bike. At first, you are unaware of your lack of skill, because it is not something you have tried (this has been called 'unconscious incompetence'). Then you try, and fall off ('conscious incompetence'). Then, if you concentrate, you can stay upright, at first only for a few seconds, then for minutes ('conscious competence'). Finally, you just get on the bike and ride it, without thinking about it. The skill has become automatic ('unconscious competence'). On a training programme, you should expect to reach the level of conscious competence in basic skills, and if you are lucky you may reflect on moments of unconscious competence! Of course it is not always comfortable to move through this learning curve, which is why a supportive learning climate is so important.

> **Luke:** When I first tried to practise active listening, it was hopeless. I'm so used to asking closed questions in my job that it felt impossible not to try to solve the client's problem. I knew I wasn't supposed to do that, but I couldn't remember what to do instead. However, the trio I was working with were great, and they helped me out. We pressed an imaginary 'pause' button when I got stuck. Gradually, I found I could use the skills and was amazed at their impact. It has made me think about how I do my job. I still need my expert knowledge but I see a need for these skills as well.

> **Jenna is used to giving advice** in her job. She tends to use this approach when managing her staff and when coaching trainees, and

realizes it isn't always helpful. She wants to practise asking open questions when staff come to her with problems, rather than always giving advice and suggesting solutions. Helped by a learning partner on the training programme, she identified a few key phrases that she can try out back at work:

. . . tell me some more about that?
. . . let me check I've understood you . . .
. . . it's a problem for you because . . .?

The context of coaching and mentoring

In this book we focus on effective coaching and mentoring at work. Training programmes provide opportunities to explore the way in which contracts can be negotiated and managed, with the client, with an organization or with a sponsor. Participants will be expected to 'establish and maintain the expectations and boundaries of the coaching/mentoring contract with the client and, where appropriate, with sponsors' (EMCC 2009). So, on an effective training programme issues such as confidentiality and conflicts of interest will be explored. Differences between work with individuals and work with teams or groups will be highlighted. Topics explored will range from diversity and bullying in the workplace, to how to work with the reluctant client who is 'sent'. Another important area for discussion is how to use skills and frameworks in other contexts such as appraisal or personal development planning.

Use of tools and techniques

Chapter 9 describes some tools and techniques which can be used by coaches and mentors. An important aspect of training is to help coaches and mentors to have a working knowledge of a range of these to develop not only insight and awareness in the client, but also to stimulate outcome and action. Trainees will become aware that there is no place for 'one size fits all' and that whereas one client may be helped through working with metaphor, the next may be helped best by using role-play and role-reversal techniques. The effective coach or mentor will ensure that they have a wide range of tools and techniques at their disposal, which they are able to use both appropriately and confidently.

The learning climate

The training journey parallels the coaching or mentoring journey. In a safe and effective coaching or mentoring relationship, a working agreement and ground rules are established at the outset, in order to create the right conditions for learning – the learning climate. Similarly, in a safe and effective training programme, ground rules and working agreements are clearly established and agreed at the beginning. This enables participants to learn. They feel safe enough to take the risk of letting go of old behaviours and old assumptions, and trying out new ones. They know that confidences will be respected, and understand the appropriate boundaries for disclosure. They feel confident enough to challenge respectfully and be challenged. And, more prosaically, they arrive on time, and cancel only if absolutely unavoidable! Trainers should be explicit about these issues from day one, ensure that they themselves adhere to the ground rules and, by giving plenty of opportunity for review, catch any difficulties as they arise. When this is done well, a positive learning climate is created.

Here is a description of a learning climate, taken from *The Learning Company* (Pedler *et al.* 1991: 27):

- If something goes wrong around here, you can expect help, support and interest in learning lessons from it.
- People make time to question their own practice, to analyse, discuss and learn from what happens.
- There is a general attitude of continuous improvement – always trying to learn and do better.
- When you don't know something, it's normal to ask around until you get the required help or information.
- Differences of all sorts, between young and old, women and men, black and white etc. are recognized and positively valued as essential to learning and creativity.

On a training programme with a positive learning climate, you might expect to see some of the characteristics described in Box 6.1.

Box 6.1 A positive learning climate

- Participants are supported in trying out new skills and expanding their knowledge
- Participants receive constructive feedback
- Trainers get feedback from participants if something goes awry
- Trainers and participants are flexible and open to new ideas
- There is time to discuss and make explicit both individual and group learning
- People learn from each other, not just the trainers
- Training and development goals are appropriate and challenging
- Differences between people are valued
- No one is marginalized on account of difference – for example, gender, age, race.

Thinking back to a training programme that you have organized or attended, how would you describe the learning climate? What helped individual and group learning? What hindered it?

Thinking forward to coach or mentor training, what would be important for you in a training environment? What would you want to avoid? What could you do to help create the best learning climate?

Ethical and professional training

As we have said, the training experience parallels the coaching or mentoring experience. An effective training programme is based on a clear understanding about what is offered and required to make it successful. Ethical and professional standards are important in the training programme, and it is vital that trainers act with integrity, impartiality and respect (Connor 1994). These values are closely linked with the moral principles described in Chapter 10. The questions in Box 6.2, adapted from Connor, are prompts for assessing a training programme.

Box 6.2 Ethical and professional training

- Are the trainers open about their qualifications and experience?
- Do the trainers model the behaviour they expect from participants?
- Are training policies and procedures clearly communicated?
- Do the trainers adhere to a code of practice or ethics?
- Do the trainers treat all participants fairly?
- Is it clear what is/is not confidential to the programme?
- If participants are to be assessed, do they know when and how this will happen?
- Are the trainers sensitive to issues of race, gender, etc.?
- Do the trainers deliver the training programme as agreed?
- Are the trainers clear about any support offered outside the programme?
- How is the programme evaluated?

Qualifications

There are a large number of coaching and mentoring training programmes available, ranging from one-day workshops through to certificate, diploma and masters-level programmes and even doctorates. Providers include private organizations, professional bodies and universities. Whether you are an individual purchaser or acting on behalf of your organization, you will need to consider whether formal qualifications or accreditation are important to you.

Some programmes are accredited by universities, and some recognized by professional bodies and other organizations. Coaching and mentoring professional bodies offering accreditation of training programmes include the ICF and EMCC. In addition, purchasers may wish to know whether trainers are members of a professional body, and whether they adhere to a code of ethics and ethical guidelines. Evidence of completion of approved training may be part of the requirement for individual accreditation as a coach or mentor.

Courses which are designed to provide qualifications are usually mapped against the key competencies required by major national or international coaching and mentoring associations.

Most training programmes, with qualifications, will include the elements shown in Box 6.3.

Box 6.3 Elements of a typical training programme

1   Introduction to a range of coaching and mentoring models, theories and approaches
2   Knowledge and understanding of the work context
3   Understanding of individual differences in clients as they try to utilize the coaching or mentoring process – for example, learning styles and personality preferences
4   Development of skills that enable insight and action in the client
5   Development of self-awareness, self-reflexivity, confidence and competence in the coach or mentor
6   Proficiency in the use of relevant models and frameworks
7   Ability to use appropriate tools, techniques and psychometric inventories
8   Ability to learn from, and respond to, feedback from peers, tutors and supervisor
9   Evidence of all of the above using written accounts, audio- and video-recordings of practice, live demonstrations, reflective journals or logs, and case studies

---

Competence and professionalism

This section will be of particular interest to those who are working full-time as coaches or mentors and to those who may be considering purchasing coaching or mentoring services.

Competence, capability and capacity

In Chapters 2 and 4 we argued that the effective coach or mentor not only possesses specific skills or competencies, but is also reflective in their practice and aware of their ongoing learning and development needs.

The term 'competence' refers to the ability to perform to recognized standards. It implies successful performance against specific criteria – that, for example, a coach or mentor is 'fit for purpose'. While competence approaches have become popular in recent years, questions about their limitations have been raised, particularly in the context of management development. One of the issues highlighted by Burgoyne is 'whether performance can be divided into competencies and then re-integrated' (1990: 20), and the same question may be asked about coach and mentor competencies. The undoubted useful-ness of competence frameworks in coaching and mentoring must be weighed against the risks of reductionism through the adoption of a 'tick box' approach to professional competence. One way of addressing this concern is to ensure that accreditation processes assess capability and capacity as well as competencies.

Fraser and Greenhalgh (2001: 799) note the focus on competence in traditional approaches to education and training and assert that 'in today's complex world we must educate not merely for competence but for capability (the ability to adapt to change, generate new knowledge and continuously improve performance)'. This is a challenge for coach and mentor training, and accreditation. Robust training and accreditation procedures should reflect not only competence at a given moment, but also capability, including the individual's willingness to monitor their own performance and development, and to be self-reflective. In addition to competencies and capa-bility there is the importance of developing the *capacity* of each coach or mentor. This will vary according to individual resources at any given time. Supervision and support, alongside CPD, are the processes which enhance the ongoing capacity to learn, enabling the coach or mentor to maintain professional effectiveness:

> when competencies are assessed as observable behaviours or skills, successful performance depends on the capacity and capability of that coach or mentor to learn. This capacity develops continuously and so good accreditation procedures will require that the coach or mentor is not accredited on one occasion only, but that there will be evidence of ongoing learning and development in order for accreditation of professional registration to be valid.
>
> (Easterby-Smith *et al.* 1999: 150)

Competence frameworks

As noted in Chapter 2, some of the professional bodies concerned with coaching and mentoring have developed competence frameworks, and examples are listed below. Our nine key principles for effective practice reflect these competencies. We give examples from two international professional bodies which have been at the forefront of developing competence frameworks alongside codes of ethical practice, as a basis for sound credentialing (ICF) and accreditation (EMCC). The ICF has outlined four clusters of core competencies (see www.coachfederation.org), as follows:

A　Setting the foundation
1　Meeting ethical guidelines and professional standards
2　Establishing the coaching agreement

B　Co-creating the relationship
3　Establishing trust and intimacy with the client
4　Coaching presence

C　Communicating effectively
5　Active listening
6　Powerful questioning
7　Direct communication

D　Facilitating learning and results
8　Creating awareness
9　Designing actions
10　Planning and goal-setting
11　Managing progress and accountability

The EMCC highlights eight coaching or mentoring competence categories (see www.emccouncil.org), as follows:

1　Understanding self
2　Commitment to self-development
3　Managing the contract
4　Building the relationship
5　Enabling insight and learning
6　Outcome and action orientation
7　Use of models and techniques
8　Evaluation

Accreditation

There is currently considerable interest in the accreditation of both coach and mentor training programmes, and of individual coaches and mentors. This reflects a concern that those hiring or receiving coaching and mentoring services should know how to judge the competence and professionalism of the individual coach or mentor. In the UK, the CIPD (2008b) has produced guidance for organizations wishing to develop coaching and mentoring and wanting to know what to look for when hiring coaches or mentors.

An example of training accreditation is the EMCC European Quality Award (EQA) (EMCC 2009) for coach and mentor training, which has four award categories. Capability indicators (CIs) are used to assess competence in each of the eight competencies listed earlier and they are mapped against the four award categories, which are: foundation, practitioner, senior practitioner and master. 'The progression principles used are: at each "higher" level, the CIs should describe the greater breadth and depth of knowledge; greater synthesis of ideas; ability to evoke more significant insights; working effectively with increasingly complex issues and contexts; and, at the higher levels, the creation of a coherent personal approach to coach/mentoring' (EMCC 2009: 14).

The foundation level requires a minimum of 20 study hours, whereas the master practitioner level requires a minimum of 1,800 study hours and within this the coaching practice varies from 6 hours at foundation level to 252 hours at master practitioner level.

An example of individual accreditation is the ICF credentialing programme, with three designations: associate certified coach, professional certified coach and master certified coach. Each designation requires a set amount of coach-specific training, minimum coaching experience hours and minimum number of clients. These vary from 100 coaching hours at associate level, to 2,500 coaching hours at master level. The number of clients required varies from at least 8 at associate level to at least 35 at master level (see www.coachfederation.org for more information).

The advantages of professional accreditation are not just in the outcome, but also in the learning that takes place during what can be quite a lengthy journey. Many people admit that their main reason for gaining accreditation is so that the stamp of approval will enhance their reputation and career prospects. It will be increasingly important to be accredited as purchasing organizations become more knowledgeable about the standards that can be expected from a coach or mentor, and as the number of available coaches and mentors increases. There is evidence that this is already happening. Our view is that the learning journey which will take you towards accreditation, though long and hard, can be a unique opportunity for CPD and networking.

Joss explains his experience of 'going for accreditation'.

I had been a mentor for several years in my own organization and eventually I decided to go part-time so that I could do some training with a view to becoming a full-time coach and mentor. I chose the course carefully, it was one that was accredited academically by my local college but it was also accredited by the EMCC with the EQA. I was able to fit in the main workshops for the part-time course, but I did find it difficult at first to have enough clients for the mentoring practice sessions that we had to do and write up. I almost got panicky about this after the first few months but others on the course helped me to work out how to extend my hours of experience. We each had a course supervisor and we had to tape our sessions and play extracts back within an action learning set of four course members. I learnt so much from this. It was amazing to hear how other people mentor and coach, some so different from me.

We also had to keep a portfolio of all our learning. This was quite onerous to keep up to date. It included a reflective log of all practice sessions both on and outside of the course. We were told that some of these could count towards individual accreditation hours, if we decided to go for that. When I read over my reflective practice log and journal I realize how difficult it all was at the beginning, and how I nearly gave up. But I stuck it out with plenty of support and guidance from my tutor and also from my wonderful action learning set. The theory of coaching was very interesting but I did find it hard doing the written assignments and I needed a lot of help with these. Well, after an unsuccessful first try at the certificate I resubmitted my supervised practice file and passed!

I am now enrolled on the diploma and I am working up my hours so that I can apply for individual accreditation soon after finishing the diploma. I wanted this so that my clients (individuals and organizations) would know that I am professionally qualified for the job. But, you know what, the reason I want it now is not so much to satisfy my clients as to satisfy me. It gives me some sort of assurance that what I am doing is on the right lines. Yes, I will make mistakes, but I know what to do and how best to proceed if things get difficult with a client. I have regular supervision, both group and individual. It is challenging, but very valuable. I am confident that I am up to date with developments in the profession of coaching and mentoring, and I have developed my own awareness to the point of being confident that I will be a 'good enough mentor'. I intend to move through the accreditation levels to master practitioner and I know that will take quite some time. But during that time I will be part of a stimulating, challenging and supportive network of coaches and mentors helping one another for the benefit of our clients.

Summary

In this chapter we have:

- Used interactive prompts to help you to assess individual and organizational training needs.
- Highlighted key aspects of coaching and mentoring training.
- Described how you might recognize a positive learning climate and assess ethical and professional aspects of training.
- Discussed the range of qualifications in coaching and mentoring.
- Introduced the competencies required for accreditation by professional coaching and mentoring organizations.

PART 3
Model, Tools and Techniques

7 What is The Skilled Helper model?

Introduction

In this chapter we present one model in detail, but we begin by evaluating the advantages and disadvantages of models or frameworks in general in relation to coaching and mentoring. An overview of The Skilled Helper model is then given, followed by a detailed explanation of how to use each of its three stages. We then work through an example of using The Skilled Helper in practice.

The Skilled Helper model is used worldwide, and has been developed over the past 35 years by Professor Gerard Egan. For two decades we have been training coaches and mentors who consistently tell us that the model is robust and enabling. They find that the model and its associated skills are easily transferable to other professional, leadership, management and work roles. In this chapter we discuss their experiences, as well as our own, to identify hints and tips for using each of the three stages with clients.

Why have a model?

Coaching and mentoring are intentional helping activities. Listening is not enough. Time is precious. Coaching and mentoring cost money. In our working lives we often use frameworks and models, in the form of policies, procedures and protocols – for example, those used for appraisals or for presenting a business case. We carry these around in our heads and refer to them as necessary. We also use our personal and professional judgement to decide when a particular model does not serve our purpose and then we turn to something else that helps us to achieve our objectives.

In coaching and mentoring we help people to articulate and achieve their objectives. We guide. We facilitate. We enable learning about self and about opportunity. We motivate for change. We encourage action that delivers results. The professional associations and bodies for coaching and mentoring are concerned about regulating these activities, to ensure that coaches and mentors are properly equipped and fit for purpose. Using tried and tested frameworks or models is one way of ensuring quality, and we outline some of these approaches in Chapter 1.

Advantages and disadvantages

Models or frameworks are of value only if they are client-centred, not model-centred. The message is: start with wherever the client is, and let the model follow the client, using the parts of the model that are appropriate. A model can guide the coach or mentor when mapping out an intentional process for helping the client to gain insight, decide upon goals and develop strategies for action. However, the map is not the territory (Korzybski 1994). The client decides what is needed and wanted, and so any model should be used to help the client, not to constrain them. We pinpoint other advantages of using a model in the next section. Here are some disadvantages:

- focus on skills and process instead of fully tuning in to the client;
- relationship may be affected by too close adherence to model;
- client issue may not fit with the model in use;
- client may not like the model chosen by the coach or mentor;
- distinctive style of the coach or mentor may be cramped by the model;
- coach or mentor may overlook valuable hunches and intuition;
- coach or mentor may not stay with the significance of the moment;
- important leads may not be followed up because they do not fit the model;

- the coach or mentor may be too conscious of where they are in the model, rather than going with the flow, and following the client.

Why use The Skilled Helper?

Coaching and mentoring provide the opportunity to change and develop, through working in a learning relationship with a coach or mentor. The client talks about an issue or opportunity and in the process of coaching or mentoring they become more hopeful about possibilities, and they develop the courage to act, to make changes and to deliver results. The Skilled Helper is a well-grounded, practical model for coaching and mentoring. Like all models, it is not 'one size fits all' and must be tailored to the individual requirements of each client.

We value the fact that The Skilled Helper has been updated and refined over 35 years, with constant feedback from users. It is informed by humanistic, cognitive and behavioural approaches to the understanding of the person, applying these to knowledge from social psychology about people in contexts and systems. The result is a pragmatic approach, which turns theory into practical application. The advantages of using The Skilled Helper are:

- clients readily understand it and can easily use it;
- users find it robust and enabling;
- developed and refined over 35 years, now published in its ninth edition (Egan 2010);
- Professor Egan consults to organizations worldwide;
- an integrative model;
- emphasis on change, leading to valued outcomes;
- applicable across cultures;
- applicable for a variety of helping situations;
- positive and systematic;
- a framework that can be shared with the client;
- a framework that can be used by the client between sessions;
- maps the process of coaching or mentoring sessions;
- utilizes skills of support and challenge to achieve change;
- coaches, mentors and clients find the skills transferable to life and work.

Using The Skilled Helper within a learning relationship

Egan (2010) states that there are three goals of helping. The first is to help clients manage their problems more effectively and develop underused or unused resources and opportunities more fully. The second goal is to help clients

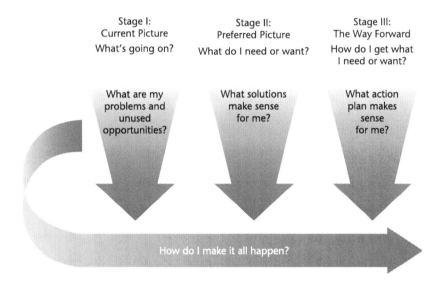

Stage I:
Current Picture
What's going on?

Stage II:
Preferred Picture
What do I need or want?

Stage III:
The Way Forward
How do I get what
I need or want?

What are my
problems and
unused
opportunities?

What solutions
make sense
for me?

What action
plan makes
sense
for me?

How do I make it all happen?

Figure 7.1 The Skilled Helper model (Egan 2010: 70)
From G. Egan, *The Skilled Helper*, International Edition, 9th edn. © 2010 Wadsworth, a part of Cengage Learning, Inc. Reproduced by permission. www.cengage.com/permissions

become better at helping themselves. The third goal is to help clients develop an action-oriented prevention mentality. The Skilled Helper model helps clients to achieve these goals. There are three stages of the model, shown in Figure 7.1.

This practical model may appear to be rational and linear because it is presented in stages, but it is intended to be used flexibly according to the needs of the client. Egan has often stated that the model is for the client, not the client for the model. The Skilled Helper is used within a coaching or mentoring relationship characterized by respect, genuineness and empathy. This respect ensures that the model, used well, always starts with where the client is. It focuses upon how the client is at the present moment and how the client would like to be. In that sense, coaching and mentoring are intentional activities. Underlying the helping process are basic communication skills which enhance the effectiveness of the coach or mentor. Consciously developed listening, responding and challenging skills are important throughout the process. The effective coach or mentor tries to maintain the right balance of support and challenge throughout.

How do the stages of The Skilled Helper achieve change?

The interactive stages and tasks of The Skilled Helper model are shown in Figure 7.2. Each of the three stages has three tasks. The three stages are designed

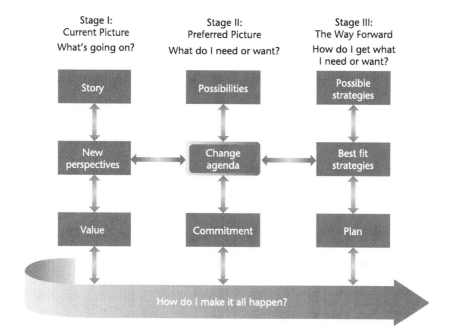

Figure 7.2 The helping model showing interactive stages and steps (Egan 2010: 81) From G. Egan, *The Skilled Helper*, International Edition, 9th edn. © 2010 Wadsworth, a part of Cengage Learning, Inc. Reproduced by permission. www.cengage.com/permissions

to move the client forward towards change and action. In order for the client to be able to change, the coach or mentor must communicate genuine interest, respect and empathy. Coaching or mentoring will then develop into an effective working alliance. Reviewing the working alliance openly and honestly through frequent evaluation can be a direct source of learning and change.

The first stage

The first stage helps the client to clarify the key issues calling for change. The three tasks which work towards this exploration are: the telling of the story; the development of new perspectives; and the focusing upon issues that will make a difference and add value. The first stage helps the client to elaborate their issue, concern or opportunity, making sure that all aspects have been fully explored. The skills of the coach or mentor are used to help move from an overall 'story' to exploring any new perspectives, and then to focusing and prioritizing something to work on. This then leads to the next stage which focuses upon the future and goals.

The second stage

The second stage helps the client to identify what they need or want in relation to the aspect they have chosen to work on. In the first task, the client is encouraged to engage creatively in imagining the possibilities of a better future. The psychological importance of this key stage is significant because by identifying 'wants' rather than 'oughts' the client is more likely to develop hope and motivation to create a better future. The second task involves the client in finding a SMART goal from all the wants and possibilities. In fact, goal-setting is at the heart of this model. Egan calls this the 'change agenda'. The third task helps the client to test their own commitment to change and explore whether specific goals are realistic and valued. The *hope for change* can now develop into the *courage to change*. This leads into the third and final stage of the model, which deals with how to achieve the chosen goal.

The third stage

The third stage helps the client discover how to get what they need or want by developing strategies for action. In the first task, the stated goal gets tested through brainstorming all the possible strategies for action. In the second task, the client decides which of these strategies fits best with their particular resources. Forcefield analysis can be used to examine the helpful and unhelpful factors which could influence the implementation of strategies. The third task in this final stage is formulating and implementing an action plan.

Underlying all stages is the challenge of constant incremental change on the part of the client. Egan reminds us that talking about change is not the same as doing it. The coach or mentor can ensure that action permeates the helping process. Action does not always mean 'doing'. It can also, very profitably, entail thinking and reflecting. Work between sessions can help to achieve this sense of continuous growth and development.

We will now describe in detail The Skilled Helper process, highlighting the tasks of the coach or mentor in each stage. We will use a case example, Steve, to track the main tasks of each stage.

Stage 1: What's going on?

Overview of the stage

The client usually comes to see a coach or mentor because they feel stuck over a problem, issue or opportunity. So, the coach or mentor gives the person space to talk about what is going on. In this first stage of the process, rapport will be developed through the support that is offered while the client 'tells their story'. Attending, listening, paraphrasing, reflecting feelings, summarizing, probing and clarifying are skills that are needed throughout this process. In addition, empathic challenge is essential in order to identify areas that have been overlooked or avoided. These areas could be inaccuracies or deficiencies in perception of the problem situation, or underused resources and opportunities. New perspectives are developed from this exploration. Finally, in the first stage, the coach or mentor uses the skills of focusing and prioritizing to help the client choose which aspect of the story to work on. They are helped to choose the aspect that would make a difference and add value to their life. Once this is identified the client can move on. The key questions in this stage are shown in Figure 7.3. Each task will now be described in detail.

Telling the story

The first task of the coaching and mentoring process is used whenever a client comes to talk about an issue, problem or opportunity that they want to work on. So, it may be at the initial visit, or it may be at any point in longer-term work where an issue needs to be explored.

The coach or mentor is first and foremost trying to build rapport to help the client tell their story. At this time the client needs space in order to reflect on what it is they want to say. Skills of support and challenge are used

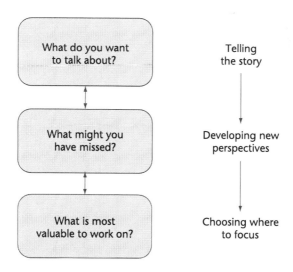

Figure 7.3   Key questions in Stage 1 (adapted from Egan 2010)

to help the client open up all aspects of the issue that are relevant. Basic listening skills are essential here. What is needed is attentive listening rather than diagnostic listening. Attentive listening includes observation of non-verbal communication as well as listening to the words used. The coach or mentor:

- ✓ *Notes non-verbal communication:* eye contact, facial expression, posture, smiling or frowning, voice tone.
- ✓ *Notes any discrepancy* between non-verbal signs and words spoken.
- ✓ *Listens carefully* to thoughts, feelings and actions.
- ✓ *Uses silence*, when appropriate, to give the client time to think and to encourage them to elaborate.
- ✓ *Reflects back* succinctly and tentatively what has been said by the client so that the client can hear it clearly.
- ✓ *Summarizes and paraphrases* to let the client know that they have been understood.
- ✓ *Uses open questions and probes* to clarify, challenge or check understanding.
- ✓ *Repeats key words* from the client with a non-verbal question mark: 'angry?'; 'stressed?'; 'excited?'

Figure 7.4 Lists some of the things that a coach or mentor might say in order to help the client tell their story.

Active listening skills and prompts will help the client to relax and open up. They will also communicate interest, concern and empathy. These qualities in helpers are known to influence rapport between helper and helped (Rogers 1961). Once the client has perceived these qualities in the coach or

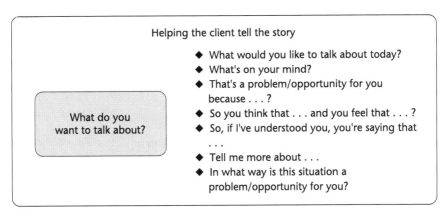

Helping the client tell the story

What do you want to talk about?

- ◆ What would you like to talk about today?
- ◆ What's on your mind?
- ◆ That's a problem/opportunity for you because . . . ?
- ◆ So you think that . . . and you feel that . . . ?
- ◆ So, if I've understood you, you're saying that . . .
- ◆ Tell me more about . . .
- ◆ In what way is this situation a problem/opportunity for you?

Figure 7.4 Prompts for Stage 1, Task 1

mentor, then trust develops. Trust makes challenge possible and more likely to be effective. Throughout the relationship the coach or mentor is trying to establish the right balance of support and challenge. Too much support may provide comfort, but no change. Challenge has the power to make a difference, but if too strong, or too early, it may be rejected. If the coach or mentor challenges with empathy and with the intention of facilitating self-challenge in the client, then there is the likelihood that the right balance of support and challenge will be achieved.

Developing new perspectives

This is the second task of Stage 1. The coach or mentor continues to use active listening skills and prompts to help the client to elaborate all parts of their story. In order to move forward it is important to check that no significant perspective had been overlooked. The coach or mentor:

✓ *Enables client self-challenge* by actively reflecting the story and any key words.
✓ *Explores blindspots* by listening and asking focused questions.
✓ *Draws attention to client strengths and resources.*
✓ *Encourages the client to consider the views of others.*
✓ *Highlights any discrepancies* by reflecting and paraphrasing.
✓ *Invites the client to look at the situation in different ways.*
✓ *Checks that nothing has been overlooked.*

Helping the client develop new perspectives

What might you have missed?

◆ Is there anything you may have missed?
◆ If X were here now, what might they be saying?
◆ When you have faced situations like this before, what, or who, has helped you? Could you use any of those resources now?
◆ Do you recognize any patterns of thoughts, feelings or actions that have occurred before in your life? Do you want to repeat them? Or change them?
◆ What personal and professional strengths do you have which you could bring to this situation?

Figure 7.5 Prompts for Stage 1, Task 2

This second task in Stage 1 gives something of a reality check on the story and a review of the possible resources that could be used by the client to move it forward. Blindspots are explored and the client is encouraged to notice self-defeating patterns of thinking, feeling and acting. The coach or mentor also helps the client to identify strengths and strategies which have worked well in the past and which could be applied in the current situation. Figure 7.5 lists some prompts that the coach or mentor might use in helping the client to explore new perspectives.

One technique that is useful at this stage is outlined by two coaches writing from an NLP background (neuro-linguistic progamming: see Chapter 1). Eaton and Johnson (2001) say that creative people use frames to look at things from different angles. Table 7.1 shows how problem perspectives, or 'limiting frames', can be changed to productive ones.

The coach or mentor can use these frames. For example, if the client seems to be bogged down with detail, the coach or mentor can ask them a question about 'the big picture'. This is one way of helping the client to develop new perspectives. Other ways are to get them to imagine the situation from the point of view of another person. A role reversal exercise can be helpful here and there is an explanation of this technique in Chapter 9.

Limiting frame	Productive frame
Everything seen as a problem	Everything seen as a learning opportunity
Focusing on one element of an issue	Focusing on the issue as a whole
Noticing only your own perspective	Noticing how events affect others
Focus is on points of disagreement	Focus is on resolving differences

Table 7.1 Changing limiting frames to productive frames (Eaton and Johnson 2001: 39)

Egan (2006: 192) gives a useful list of things that clients are able to say when they have been helped to develop new perspectives:

- Here's a new angle . . .
- Here's something I've not thought of . . .
- Here's something I've overlooked . . .
- To be completely honest . . .
- Here's one way I've been fooling myself . . .

- Here's an important piece of the puzzle . . .
- Here's the real story . . .
- Here's the complete story . . .
- Oh, now I see that . . .

Choosing where to focus

The first task of Stage 1 helps the client to have a full picture of the issue or opportunity: it is about 'putting all the pieces of the jigsaw out on the table'. The second task ensures that none of the important pieces is missing. The third task is to decide which are the really important pieces. Egan describes this as the 'search for value' and it leads to the point of value for the client – i.e. working on something that will make a difference. The third task enables the client to focus and prioritize, and to find the aspect of the issue or opportunity that they want to work on.

Value is the part of the issue or opportunity which, if worked on, would have the most impact. In order to arrive at this point, the coach or mentor helps the client to:

✓ *summarize* all the parts of the story;
✓ *focus* on the most important aspects needing immediate attention;
✓ *prioritize* which part or parts to take forward.

Egan (2006: 193, 2010: 262) gives some principles for helping the client to decide which issues to choose to work on. We have adapted these as follows:

1 Check whether coaching or mentoring is the right kind of help.
2 If there is a crisis, help the client to manage the crisis.
3 Begin with the aspect that seems to be causing the most concern.
4 Begin with issues the client sees as important.
5 Begin with some manageable part of a larger situation.
6 Begin with a part that, if handled, will lead to some kind of general improvement.
7 Focus on a part of the issue for which the benefits outweigh the costs.

Figure 7.6 lists some prompts that the coach or mentor might use in this task.

So, at the end of Stage 1 the client has identified something that they can work on, and they can now more forward to Stage 2, to think about what that aspect would be like if it were much better; if it were ideal.

Helping the client choose where to focus

What is most valuable to work on?

- So, if I can try to summarize the key aspects of this situation . . .
- What seems most important to you out of all the things we've talked about?
- Which part of this have you got energy for tackling first?
- Is there something we could work on that would make a real difference to you?
- What feels like a manageable bit to work on?
- If you wanted to change one aspect of things, where would you start?
- Out of all of this, is there something we can take forward to work on?

Figure 7.6   Prompts for Stage, 1 Task 3

Box 7.1 At the end of Stage 1

The client has:
- ✓ Explored the story
- ✓ Developed new perspectives
- ✓ Chosen something to focus on and take forward

The coach or mentor has:
- ✓ Attended to the client's non-verbal and verbal communication
- ✓ Listened actively
- ✓ Responded empathically using reflecting, paraphrasing and summarizing
- ✓ Repeated key words
- ✓ Used silence to provide reflective space
- ✓ Used open questions to clarify, challenge and check understanding
- ✓ Provided a balance of support and challenge
- ✓ Encouraged self-challenge in the client
- ✓ Stimulated the client to reframe perspectives
- ✓ Enabled the client to focus and prioritize
- ✓ Helped the client to identify what aspect is most valuable to work on

Hints and tips for Stage 1

These are some hints and tips from coaches and mentors to help you in Stage 1:

- Attentive listening, with few closed questions and plenty of reflecting, paraphrasing and summarizing, will be most helpful in order to build rapport and enable the client to tell their story. Resist the temptation to start diagnostic listening and to ask questions which help *you* solve the problem.
- If you find yourself asking lots of questions to which the client already knows the answer, stop! Don't assume you need to know all the details of everything that led up to the situation presented by the client.
- If this stage has become a question and answer interview, rather than 'telling the story', pause and start to paraphrase and echo key words or phrases. A useful tip is to stay with recent and current events and keep focused on 'what is and what might be', rather than 'what was'.
- When this stage is going well, you should feel as if you are following the content of the story, rather than leading it.
- In the second task of this stage, there may be many new perspectives to be discovered or very few or even none. Sometimes new perspectives emerge as the story is told, and the coach or mentor can then move straight to asking the client which aspect will be of most value to work on.
- In helping the client to identify the *value issue*, the following question has often proved useful: 'Out of everything that you have talked about so far, is there one thing we could take forward to work on, that would make a real difference?'

Example of Stage 1 in action

Steve is the client. His issue is 'work seems to be dominating my life'. He is helped to explore this issue and to unravel various aspects of the way in which it is a problem for him. He talks about increasing pressure at work, his concern that standards are maintained, longer hours, less time with family and friends, and a general feeling that he is being driven by events, rather than being in the driving seat. He is helped to see that putting work first is a pattern in his life, which has reaped rewards but also had some costs. He is asked, 'What would your colleagues say about you if they were here now?' and he is surprised when he replies that they'd say, 'Good old Steve, you can always count on him to get things done.' He realizes that although this is a compliment, such a perception may be contributing to his problem. He is asked about his strengths and resources, and realizes that since he is the manager of his department, he has some power to organize the work differently. Perhaps he is not currently using this power. He also realizes that as work has taken over his life, he is spending less time with family and friends and has also got out of the habit of taking exercise, which used to 'recharge my batteries'. He is asked, 'Out of all of the things we've talked about, is there one thing that we could take forward to work on that would really make a difference?' and he identifies that 'What I need now is to get a healthier balance back into my life.' This is his 'value' issue.

Stage 2: What do I need or want?

Overview of Stage 2

The second stage moves the client from the stuckness which they may have experienced when they arrived for coaching or mentoring to the hope which arises from describing their wants and needs. In order to begin work in the second stage the coach or mentor reminds the client of their chosen value issue. This becomes the focus for brainstorming an ideal scenario in relation to that issue. If the coaching and mentoring has been done well in the first stage the client has removed any blinkers, and so in the second stage they can explore all sorts of exciting possibilities 'in the ideal scenario'. The client is invited to imagine possibilities, then to choose from these possibilities some aspect/s which they can shape into a specific goal. This leads to the choice of a *wanted goal*. The choice of a wanted goal is powerful in psychological terms. The driver for change is intrinsic, not extrinsic. The goal that is chosen is really wanted, and so is more likely to be acted upon. Finally in this stage, the client checks their commitment to the goal. Commitment moves the client from hope to courage, and from courage to action. This final task helps the client to follow the goal through to action and results. Figure 7.7 shows the tasks and key questions in Stage 2.

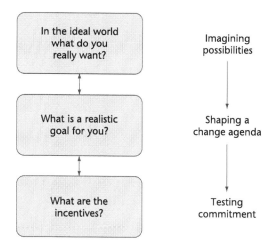

Figure 7.7   Key questions in Stage 2 (adapted from Egan 2010)

Imagining possibilities

The first task of Stage 2 is to help the client to access their creativity and to imagine their ideal scenario. The coach or mentor can invite the client to use methods that stimulate their creativity: for example, drawing, sculpting or writing. Such methods may also include visualization or brainstorming (see Chapter 9). The purpose of this task is to open out possibilities, to encourage the client, in a positive sense, to 'think the unthinkable', because within the seeds of wild ideas may be the germ of a realistic possibility. In the first task of Stage 2, the client is helped to access their valued 'wants' and to minimize the constraining effect of 'oughts'.

In this task the coach or mentor is trying to encourage the client to produce as many ideas as possible in the shortest possible time. They help the client to:

✓ *Let go of their current reality and feeling of being stuck.*
✓ *Imagine the ideal future.*
✓ *Stay future-oriented.*
✓ *Focus on 'what' not how.*
✓ *Generate a large quantity of ideas.*
✓ *Create hope in the possibilities.*
✓ *Have fun and avoid self-censure.*
✓ *Give themselves permission to 'dream with their eyes open'.*

Figure 7.8 lists some brainstorming prompts the coach or mentor can use.

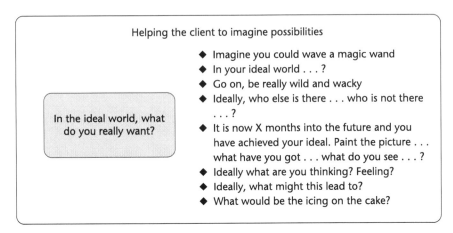

Figure 7.8 Some prompts for Stage 2, Task 1

Some coaches or mentors find brainstorming difficult, and some clients do too. When listening to the story, during the first stage, it is possible to note whether the client finds it easy to imagine things in picture form, or do this through artwork. Two things are important, whichever format is preferred. Firstly, the focus is future, not present. Secondly, the focus is '*What* do you want or need?' not '*How* can you get it?' The 'how' question is not asked until the third stage of the model.

Shaping a change agenda

Having helped the client to brainstorm as many 'wants' as possible, the coach or mentor then helps them to choose the most realistic of these to take forward as a specific goal. The process moves the client from *wanting* to *choosing* (see Figure 7.9). The skills of selecting important 'wants' and shaping these into workable goals are important in this task. The coach or mentor helps the client to:

✓ *Critique their list of wants.*
✓ *Choose those that are most important to them.*
✓ *Consider what is realistic.*
✓ *Move from aims to outcomes.*
✓ *Identify a specific goal and timeframe.*
✓ *Shape a SMART goal.*
✓ *Check the goal against their values.*

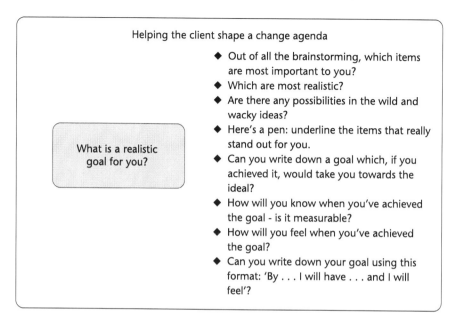

Figure 7.9 Prompts for Stage 2, Task 2

Eaton and Johnson (2001) have drawn up a useful list of questions for coaches to elicit SMART goals (see Table 7.2).

Elements of SMART	Useful questions
SPECIFIC Ensure everyone knows the aim	What will you be doing when you have achieved the goal? What do you want to do next?
MEASURED Define standards to work towards	How will you measure the achievement of the goal? What will you feel when the goal is reached?
ACHIEVABLE Ensure that the goal is realistic	What might hinder you as you progress towards the goal? What resources can you call upon?
RELEVANT Make sure the goal is worthwhile	What do you, and others, get out of this? Have other parties involved agreed to it?
TIMED Agree a timeframe	When will you achieve the goal? What will be your first step?

Table 7.2 Questions to elicit SMART goals (Eaton and Johnson 2001: 31)

Testing commitment

The final task in this stage is to check how the client will feel if they achieve the goal. The coach or mentor asks: 'How committed are you to this goal?' If the client is not really committed, then the chances are that the goal will not be achieved. The coach or mentor can use *cost–benefit analysis* as a way of helping the client to evaluate the factors affecting their commitment. (There is a fuller explanation of this technique in Chapter 9.) The client is helped to identify both costs and benefits. Forewarned is forearmed. There will always be costs, but the client can learn how to manage these and not allow them to subvert the wanted goal. They may also become aware of reasons why this goal has not been pursued before or not been achieved before. On the plus side, becoming more aware of the payoffs and rewards helps to strengthen resolve. This increases the motivation to succeed and inspires the sort of courage which hopefully will propel the client to act and get results. The coach or mentor helps the client to:

✓ *Identify incentives.*
✓ *Identify costs.*
✓ *Decide if it is worth the effort.*
✓ *Check whether incentives and payoffs outweigh costs.*
✓ *Consider who or what might help or hinder.*
✓ *Consider what has stopped them until now.*
✓ *Move from hope to courage and action.*

Figure 7.10 lists some prompts that the coach or mentor can use in this task.

Once the client has been helped to commit to a specific goal, coaching or mentoring can move to the third and final stage. Up to now the focus has been on 'what': 'What is the present situation?' (Stage 1) and 'What ideally do you need and want in the future?' (Stage 2). Now that a goal has been articulated the client can move on to Stage 3, 'How'. They are helped to plan 'How can you achieve that goal?'. At the end of Stage 2, some coaches or mentors think that the most important work is now done and that the client can do the 'action' bit for themselves. Not so. There is still important work to do in the final stage as we will see in the next section.

Helping the client to test commitment

What are the incentives?

◆ For you, what are the benefits of achieving this goal?
◆ Are there any benefits for other people or for your organization?
◆ What are the incentives?
◆ Are there any costs for you in achieving this goal?
◆ Are there any costs for others or for your organization?
◆ What has stopped you until now?
◆ What are the advantages of acting now?
◆ Will achieving this goal really improve your situation?
◆ On balance, do you want to pursue this goal?

Figure 7.10　Prompts for Stage 2, Task 3

Box 7.2 At the end of Stage 2

The client has:
✓　Brainstormed possibilities in relation to their value issue
✓　Chosen a specific goal as the agenda for change
✓　Tested their commitment to achieving the goal

The coach or mentor has:
✓　Encouraged visioning
✓　Used prompts to brainstorm
✓　Given permission to suspend reality and 'dream out loud'
✓　Kept up a fast and fun pace
✓　Shaped up a SMART goal
✓　Identified important client values
✓　Used cost–benefit analysis to test commitment
✓　Checked how the client feels about accomplishing the goal

Hints and tips for Stage 2

- Make sure that both you and the client are clear about the value issue. Being clear about this issue will help to get started in imagining the ideal future.
- Be aware that the pace is very different from the previous stage. In this stage the coach or mentor models energy, imagination, creativity, hope and optimism. It is more upbeat and energetic. For some coaches and mentors, and clients, this is liberating. For others, it can be more of an effort.
- If brainstorming is used, it can be useful to write down the ideas as they are spoken by the client. Check whether they wish to write or whether they would like you to write for them. Either way, the output of the brainstorm is theirs and should be given to them at the end of the session. Ideas should be written down verbatim, without judgement or discussion. In order to produce as many ideas as possible in the shortest time the coach or mentor encourages a fast pace.
- The best ideas often emerge right at the end of the brainstorm. Encourage the client to keep going with the brainstorm – a useful prompt is 'Give me three more things that are there in your ideal'.
- Some clients are very grounded and realistic, and find it difficult to imagine the ideal. Encourage them: 'In your wildest dreams' or 'If you were being really selfish'. Quote Einstein, who said that imagination is more important than knowledge. He said that imagination embraces the entire world and all that there will ever be to know and understand, whereas knowledge is limited to what we currently know and understand. Imagining possibilities liberates the mind. It is often from one of these seemingly implausible possibilities that new hope dawns.
- If you have written down the possibilities generated in imagining the ideal, give the client the pen for the critique task. Let them decide whether they prefer to tick off the brainstormed ideas one by one, or whether they want to scan the list and pick out those that seem most significant.
- When helping the client to set a SMART goal, listen carefully to them. It is not necessary to laboriously go through each element of the SMART criteria but rather to highlight any areas of SMART that have been missed. This should lead naturally into the final task of Stage 2: testing commitment.
- When looking at costs and benefits, include values and feelings as well as more tangible costs and benefits.

At the end of Stage 1, we saw how Steve, our case example, was helped to clarify the key issue that he wanted to work on. In this stage, Stage 2, Steve is helped to imagine his ideal in relation to the issue, to shape a smart goal, and to test his commitment to that goal.

Steve's work in Stage 2

Steve's chosen value issue is 'I need to work on getting a healthier balance back into my life'. He is encouraged, by the skilful use of the prompts, to think about what that would be like if he had actually achieved it. He is asked to imagine a future time when he has the ideal healthier balance and to describe what that is like. He is asked about what he is doing, ideally, and what he has stopped doing. He is asked to describe his ideal day, what he is thinking and feeling, and ideally what others – colleagues, friends and family – are saying about him. There are a great many items on his brainstorm list – here are just a few:

- *Feel more energetic*
- *Let go of work at the end of the day*
- *Others say, 'Steve is conscientious but not a pushover'*
- *Arrive home with batteries recharged not depleted*
- *Reconnect with friends and social life*
- *Reorganize work and it gets done better*

Steve is helped to review his list and underline the items that are most important to him. From these items, he generates a goal: 'By the beginning of next month I will be doing 30 minutes' exercise each evening after work. I will see my director within the next two weeks to agree the allocation of some of my work to other members of the team. I will feel healthier and I will be pleased that I have regained control of my life. I may also miss some of the work I have delegated.' This is a SMART goal. It is specific, Steve thinks it is realistic and he will know when it has been achieved. He can meet the director within two weeks and thinks that 30 minutes' exercise each day is manageable, sometimes by walking home from work or maybe at the gym. Steve is asked about the incentives for achieving this goal – what are benefits for him and others, and what might be the costs? He weighs up the pros and cons and decides that on balance this goal is right for him and will be a significant step towards a healthier life balance.

Stage 3: How do I get what I need or want?

Overview of Stage 3

This is the final stage of the coaching or mentoring process in relation to a specific issue or opportunity. A realistic goal has been set by the client, and the coach or mentor has checked whether it is really valued and wanted. Now is the time to see how it may be achieved. The coach or mentor helps the client to move from 'what' to 'how'.

The three tasks in the final stage help the client to open up a range of different possible strategies, to evaluate which of these makes most sense for them and then finally to develop a plan of action. In this stage hope and courage are transferred into practical action. The coach or mentor remains client-centred and does not become directive. All the preparatory work of the first two stages will come to nothing if this stage is done too hurriedly. Active listening and empathy go alongside active planning for results.

When the action plan is agreed, the coach or mentor discusses contingency plans in case the plan does not succeed. This is the responsibility of the coach or mentor. Because action takes place within a learning relationship, failure can be viewed as a learning opportunity, not a disaster. The client can come back to report on action and results. At that point, the cyclical nature of this model becomes evident, as the client returns to 'tell their story'. The key questions in Stage 3 are shown in Figure 7.11.

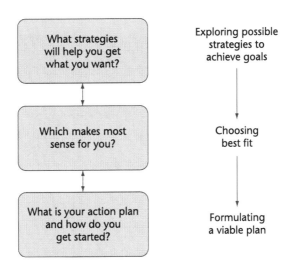

Figure 7.11   Key questions in Stage 3 (adapted from Egan 2010)

Exploring possible strategies to achieve the goal

The first task in this stage is to open up possible strategies for achieving the goal. Egan (2010) reminds us that there are more than just one or two ways to achieve our goals – there are many ways. The aim is to help the client get in touch with as many possible strategies as can be thought of, whether or not they might seem feasible. In this task, 'off the wall' ideas are encouraged. Helping the client to 'think out of the box' may generate strategies that might otherwise not have surfaced. The client can include strategies used by others even if they have not yet been used by the client. This helps to broaden the canvas. The coach or mentor uses prompts appropriately, but does not tell the client what to do. Rather, they help the client to:

✓ *Restate the goal.*
✓ *Brainstorm possible ways to achieve that goal.*
✓ *Be creative* by using a range of prompts.
✓ *Have fun.*
✓ *Keep going and generate lots of ideas.*
✓ *Suspend any evaluation or judgement*
✓ *Piggyback on ideas* by summarizing and reflecting frequently.

Some prompts which can help the client to explore new or overlooked strategies are listed in Figure 7.12. You may notice that these prompts are not directive. The client supplies their own answers. The effective coach or mentor steers clear of becoming directive and making suggestions. Beware of prompts such as 'Why don't you?' or 'This worked for me so you should try it'.

When this task is successfully accomplished, the skilful coach or mentor has helped the client to generate ideas about strategies, and to develop these ideas. The client's resources and energy have been tapped. The client begins to see routes to their goals and so they are more likely to believe in themselves and in their capacity to get what they want or need. They develop a 'can-do' attitude which will sustain them during the action phase. Clients who are stuck with a 'can't-do' attitude are more likely to lose motivation when they encounter the inevitable obstacles on the way. When this task is done well, the client has been helped to maximise the use of their resources, both internal and external, and to increase the probability that they will achieve their goal.

Helping the client brainstorm strategies

What strategies will help
you get what you want?

- ◆ Can you think of any strategies that have worked for others?
- ◆ Who could help you?
- ◆ Who ideally would you like to help you?
- ◆ What places or organizations could be useful?
- ◆ Are there any precedents that you know of?
- ◆ What would you really like to do?
- ◆ What has worked well for you in the past?
- ◆ How might technology – for example the internet – help you?
- ◆ What's the wildest idea you can think of?

Figure 7.12   Some prompts for Stage 3, Task 1

Choosing best fit

The next task is to help the client to decide which of the brainstormed strategies would be the best fit for them. The client reviews all the possible strategies which have been brainstormed. They are invited to pick out those which are most attractive and which best fit with their resources. This increases the likelihood that the strategies will work for them. It is important that the coach or mentor does not presume to know which strategies will be most powerful or effective. The coach or mentor works with the client to:

✓   *Identify the most attractive strategies.*
✓   *Select those that match the client's resources.*
✓   *Look for helpful and hindering factors.*
✓   *Plan how to enhance positives and reduce negatives.*
✓   *Check for any unintended or unhelpful consequences.*
✓   *Consider whether the chosen strategies will achieve the goal.*
✓   *Check that strategies fit with the client's values.*

Egan lists some questions that can be asked at this stage (2010: 372) and we have adapted these in Figure 7.13.

Techniques such as forcefield analysis or SWOT analysis can enable the client to become aware of what may hinder and what may help in achieving the goal. In forcefield analysis the client identifies factors in self, others and the working, home and social contexts which could help or hinder. Having identified these, the client can look at ways of minimizing the power of the unhelpful factors and maximizing the power of the helpful factors. There is a description

Helping the client choose best fit strategies

Which makes most sense for you?

◆ Which strategies are most appealing to you?
◆ Which fit best with your resources?
◆ Which will be most powerful in producing an outcome?
◆ Which seem best for your goal?
◆ Which fit with your preferred way of doing things?
◆ Which seem manageable and do-able for you?
◆ Which fit with your values?
◆ Which have the fewest unwanted consequences?

Figure 7.13   Some prompts for Stage 3, Task 2

of this technique in Chapter 9. In SWOT analysis, the client draws a four-box diagram and charts their strengths and weaknesses, and the opportunities and threats which could affect the successful outcome of a chosen strategy.

Formulating a viable plan

In this final task of the model, the client is helped to draw up an action plan within a timeframe. Critical path analysis can be used to plot milestones and key actions. There is a description of this technique in Chapter 9. It is important that the realism of the intended actions is tested. Contingency plans need to be discussed so that the client has a 'plan B' if obstacles get in the way. Evaluation follows implementation and so the client can use a follow-up session to review what succeeded, what failed, why, and what can be learned for the future. So, in this task, the coach or mentor works with the client to:

✓ *Identify the chosen strategy.*
✓ *Develop a workable plan of action.*
✓ *Use critical plan analysis to plot activity on a timeline.*
✓ *Build in awareness of intrinsic and extrinsic rewards that will sustain momentum.*
✓ *Maximize the use of client resources.*
✓ *Develop a contingency plan.*
✓ *Consider whether a follow-up session is appropriate.*

The coach or mentor will be aware of the way that inertia or entropy can prevent action from starting or prevent it being completed (Egan 2006).

Inertia bedevils those who procrastinate. Entropy bedevils those who get started but 'fall apart' before completion. One of the responsibilities of the coach or mentor is to help the client to recognize whether either of these could come into play, and how to prevent this from happening.

The real test of whether the coaching or mentoring is successful is whether the client acts, makes changes and delivers the results that they want and need. So, specific and detailed action plans are important. During this task, some skill deficits may be apparent and may prevent successful action. The coach or mentor will want to talk about these and help to develop whatever is needed. Figure 7.14 lists some prompts that the coach or mentor might use in this task.

It can be very satisfying to complete the cycle of The Skilled Helper in this way and then there is a natural feedback into debriefing the results of the action in a future session. The effective coach or mentor will realize that work goes on not just in the sessions but, most importantly, between sessions as well. The work that the client and coach or mentor do together is preparation for the action that takes place in everyday life and work.

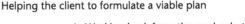

Helping the client to formulate a viable plan

What is your action plan and how do you get started?

◆ Working back from the goal, what are the key milestones?
◆ What are the main tasks that you need to complete? By when?
◆ What are you going to do first? Next?
◆ Who else needs to be involved? How?
◆ What/who could stop this plan from succeeding?
◆ What/who could help this plan to succeed?
◆ How committed are you to this plan?
◆ Will inertia or entropy affect you? What can you do about this?
◆ Is there anything we could do now to increase your commitment?
◆ How does this plan relate to the story that we originally discussed?
◆ What is your strongest incentive to implement this plan?
◆ What if plans go awry - what is your 'plan B'?

Figure 7.14 Some prompts for Stage 3, Task 3

Box 7.4 At the end of Stage 3

The client has:
✓ Brainstormed several possible strategies for achieving the goal
✓ Decided which of these best fit their values and resources
✓ Evaluated what may help or hinder the chosen strategy
✓ Worked on a specific action plan
✓ Developed a contingency plan

The coach or mentor has:
✓ Facilitated a brainstorm of strategies, using relevant prompts
✓ Evaluated possibilities to find best fit
✓ Used forcefield analysis, SWOT analysis or cost–benefit analysis
✓ Ensured that there is a specific action plan in a timeframe
✓ Supported the development of a contingency plan
✓ Checked with the client about how they feel about the plans
✓ Considered the possibility of a session to evaluate action

Hints and tips for Stage 3

- When helping the client to generate ideas for how to achieve the goal, aim to get some new ideas, not just a re-hash of previously thought-through ones. The prompt, 'What would you ideally like to do?' can be powerful in liberating the client's creativity.
- Take time over critiquing the brainstorm. There needs to be a full critique, leading to a choice of strategies for action.
- Forcefield analysis, if done well, can identify important factors which will affect whether the action succeeds. Once again, it should not be hurried.
- Stay client-centred while in the active stage of action planning, and resist the temptation to start directing.
- The timeline is a very useful and visual way of helping the client check whether their plan is do-able in the time they have. Invite the client to draw the line – after all, this is *their* action plan. Marking key milestones will help them to ensure that important details are included and so the plan is more likely to be successful.
- If the client asks directly for your experiences then you might share them, with the proviso that 'This worked for me, but how do you think it would be for you?' When you give back to the client the responsibility for evaluating the shared experience, this ensures that the helping process remains client-centred.

- It may be useful at the end of this stage to ask the client 'On a 1–10 scale, how committed are you to your action plan? What helps you to be committed? Is there anything that we can do now to increase your commitment?'

Steve's work in Stage 3

Steve's goal is: 'By the beginning of next month I will be doing 30 minutes' exercise each evening after work. I will see my director within the next two weeks to agree the allocation of some of my work to other members of the team. I will feel healthier and I will be pleased that I have regained control of my life. I may also miss some of the work I have delegated!' His brainstorm of possible strategies to achieve the goal includes:

- *Rejoin a gym*
- *Have a gym extension added to the house*
- *Hire a personal trainer to come to my home*
- *Buy an exercise bike for home*
- *Walk home from work instead of using the car*
- *Leave office at 5.00 p.m. each day*
- *Start working from home on two days each week*
- *Meet with director in my office not his, so he can see work pressures*
- *Be well prepared with statistics of hours worked*
- *Give him plans for who and what to delegate*
- *Rehearse this meeting with coach or mentor and feel confident*
- *Plan beforehand what my 'walk away position' with director will be*

Steve identifies four strategies that appeal to him, and underlines these. Two address the part of his goal that was to do with having 30 minutes' exercise each day. The other two address the pressures at work. He then looks at what will help and what will hinder his four chosen strategies, using forcefield analysis (see Figure 7.15)

Steve considers how he can enhance the power of the helpful factors and decrease the power of the unhelpful ones. He is then able to consider his action plan. Steve draws a timeline, and describes his action plan as follows:

'I will start walking home from work three nights each week for the first month and then review that part of my plan. I will begin walking home from next Monday. In bad weather I will use the exercise bike instead. I will start arranging the meeting with my director, in my office, for two weeks' time. In the meantime I will have another session with you to rehearse the meeting. If I arrange that for next week, I will be able to come to the meeting

Force Field Analysis of Chosen Strategies

Goal: 30 minutes of exercise each evening after work

1 Walk home from work instead of using the car
2 Buy exercise bike
3 Meet with director
4 Rehearse this meeting with coach or mentor

GOAL

Enabling forces	Restraining forces
Want to feel healthier	May feel too tired to take exercise
Will buy exercise bike	Cost of bike
Walking makes me feel good	Cold, damp weather may stop me
Could refocus job	Not good at delegating
Capable of planning ahead	Director not pleased
My partner will encourage me	Promotion prospects could be affected

Figure 7.15   Force field analysis

having prepared what I think would be my position and what I think might be his.'

Steve's contingency plan is:

'If I find after the first week that I haven't kept to the exercise routine I will talk to my partner and ask for support. Even if the walking home from work doesn't seem manageable I will ride the bike instead. If I have problems with arranging the meeting with my director, or if I start getting very stressed before we are due to meet again, I will contact you, as you suggested.'

Staying client-centred

As stated earlier, frameworks are of value only if they are client-centred, not model-centred. Our message here is: start wherever the client is. Let the framework follow the client. Use only the parts of the framework that are appropriate within that coaching or mentoring session. It could be that simply attending and listening is appropriate for a whole session because the client can use the reflective space to self-challenge and to decide upon action. Alternatively, it may be that all the client needs from the coach or mentor is some help with visioning the ideal future.

If the client has a clearly articulated goal they do not want to be dragged back through Stage 1 and Stage 2 simply in order to use a model or framework. The wise coach or mentor will listen carefully and will check that the client's goal is SMART. If it is, then they can proceed to the next stage. However, if during the discussion about the goal it becomes apparent that it is not so clear or SMART after all, then the client may be ready to tell more of the story about why this was chosen as a goal. It may be that the goal was not chosen by the client, but by a line manager or close friend, partner or colleague. If so, it may be in the category of 'ought' not 'want'. Until a goal is wanted it is unlikely that the benefits outweigh the costs and this is why action fails. Of course, sometimes in organizations we are told what goals we will pursue, whether we like it or not. In that case the coach or mentor has a more difficult job of helping the client to find the part that is meaningful to them within a larger goal which is not.

Reviewing skills are needed throughout the process, as the coach or mentor monitors carefully the progress of the client and encourages them to use the framework for action between sessions. At any point in the process the client can return to the first stage to 'tell the story' of how it has been between sessions. The skills of being able to go spontaneously with the flow of where the client is and apply the framework flexibly in the service of the client are perhaps the most advanced required of a coach or mentor. The Skilled Helper model is then used with integrity and wisdom, not mechanistically in the way a more inexperienced person may use it. It is used most effectively when it is known so well that it is in the background, with the client in the foreground. At this stage the coach or mentor has moved through the stage of 'conscious competence', to a level of proficiency that is characterized by 'unconscious competence'.

In the next chapter a case study is presented. You are invited to put yourself in the position of a coach using The Skilled Helper to work with a client, Anna.

Summary

In this chapter we have:

- Discussed the advantages and disadvantages of using models in coaching and mentoring.
- Presented one model in detail: The Skilled Helper.
- Illustrated how the three stages of The Skilled Helper can be used to help clients to release potential and achieve results they value.
- Explained each stage and task in detail, giving examples of coach and mentor questions, prompts and interventions and using a case study to track client progress through the stages.
- Identified useful hints and tips for each stage.

8 How is The Skilled Helper used in practice?

> - Introduction
> - Using The Skilled Helper
> - The first session
> - The second session
> - Summary

Introduction

This chapter demonstrates the way in which The Skilled Helper model can be used in practice. A case study, with commentary, forms the major part of the chapter, and illustrates how the skills of effective coaching and mentoring are used intentionally within the model. In the case study, you are the coach and you use the model stage by stage.

You are the coach for Anna, who has recently taken up a leadership role. The case study is designed to help you to reflect on the following.

- How do I use the skills of effective coaching and mentoring with The Skilled Helper model?
- How do the key principles help me to work effectively?

The case study explores the development of your learning relationship over the first two of four sessions. In each session you work with Anna using all three stages of The Skilled Helper. The stages and tasks are highlighted **in bold** in the text as they are used in the session. At the end of each stage, there is a summary of how the model and principles have been applied.

The Skilled Helper is described in detail in the previous chapter. There are three stages, each with three tasks. In the first stage, the client is helped to tell their story, to develop new perspectives and to choose an issue to work on that will make a difference. In the second stage, the client imagines a better future, chooses a realistic goal and then balances the incentives of the goal against the costs. In the third stage, the client looks at all the different strategies to achieve their goal, chooses those that fit best for them and then creates an action plan. The key principles of coaching and mentoring are described in Chapter 1.

In the case study there are interactive prompts and questions. At various points you are asked to:

- reflect on what is happening;
- consider your response;
- decide how you will help the client.

 When you see this sign, there is a summary of how the principles of effective coaching and mentoring and The Skilled Helper model are being used in practice.

Using The Skilled Helper

Anna has recently been promoted to her first leadership role. She is bright and has no difficulty in grasping the technical aspects of complex assignments. Her previous boss described her as talented and impressive. The organization has recently conducted a 360-degree feedback exercise as part of a leadership development initiative. Feedback to Anna indicated that staff sometimes find her 'difficult'. Her boss has discussed the feedback with Anna and, as part of her personal development plan, talked about the option of some coaching support. You are the coach and you have met Anna and her boss. You have agreed to work with Anna, initially for four two-hour sessions, meeting monthly. You have also clarified the working agreement and discussed how you and Anna might use The Skilled Helper model to structure and support your work together.

The first session

You are Anna's coach. This is your first session, and you are wondering how things will go.

 What are your hopes and aims for this first meeting? Any concerns?

Stage 1: What's going on? The story – new perspectives – value

The story: At the first session, you ask Anna to describe how things are at work. She starts talking animatedly about her new job, and as you listen and paraphrase, she tells you how happy she was until the 360-degree feedback exercise. Now, she says in a rather disgruntled manner, 'There is clearly a problem in the way people see me.'

 How might you respond? You could:

- Ask a question: how do they see you?
- Make a statement: yes, the feedback indicates that . . .
- Reflect her words in the form of a question: the way people see you?

You decide that the first two options run the risk of being too challenging at this early stage, so you choose the third.

Anna says, in a rather abrupt way, 'Well, they certainly don't like me.' She begins to talk about how surprised she was by the feedback and how she is always 100 per cent successful in delivering on time and on budget, whatever it takes. Her job, she tells you, is extremely demanding and there isn't always time for 'handling everyone with kid gloves'.

 You say?

- I know the job's tough, but don't you think you're being a bit defensive?
- So it's tough delivering on time all the time, and it's been a surprise to hear that you may have ruffled a few feathers?
- I imagine anyone would be stressed in your role.

The first option lacks empathy, and the third is rather more sympathetic than empathic, so you choose the second.

New perspectives: Anna looks a little taken aback by your response, as if she was expecting more of a challenge, but slowly she relaxes and begins to tell you how difficult it is being a newly-appointed manager, being under scrutiny and anxious to do well. She talks about the constant pressure of deadlines, and how everything seems to rest on her shoulders. You notice that her demeanour has changed and the vivacious person has become quieter; the word that comes into your mind is 'smaller'.

You say?

- Rest on your shoulders . . . that sounds like a burden . . . is it?
- How does it feel to be under such pressure?
- And if your staff were here now, and heard you talking, what would they be saying?
- In the past, how have you handled being under pressure?

All of these responses could be helpful, and you use them in turn to help Anna to elaborate her story. She tells you how, under pressure, she becomes rather bossy, both with herself and with others. She talks about the way her management style changes from 'how I try to be – calm and even tempered' into 'the gorgon'. As she says the words, she laughs at herself. You encourage Anna to tell you about 'the gorgon' and she paints a verbal picture that has you both smiling, describing a gorgon prowling around a cave terrifying all who dare approach!

You sense that Anna is now more willing to reflect on her behaviour, and challenge herself, so you risk a challenge:

- So, if you met 'the gorgon' in a cave what would you do?

Anna says immediately, 'Oh, I'd run like crazy and get away as fast as I could, and make sure I kept away!' She pauses for a moment, and then says, 'But of course staff can't actually run away.' She seems more reflective now, and she talks about how abrupt she can be with staff. In fact she is finding the new role much tougher than she anticipated. She is even wondering whether this is the right job for her. She thinks that the technical aspects of work are much more satisfying than the people management aspects. This is why, she says, she would rather talk to you than her boss, because 'I wanted to talk completely off-line.'

 You are wondering what to say next in order to summarize Anna's problems. Try to complete this sentence: 'Anna, the current situation seems to be a problem for you in several ways . . .'

Compare your answer with the suggestions below, all of which describe ways in which the situation may be a problem for Anna. Did your answer include one or more of these points?

- The feedback has come as a surprise
- You are hurt by the feedback

- You are finding the new job harder than you expected
- You are wondering whether you are on the right career path
- You feel under constant pressure
- You are aware that your management style can be less than perfect!
- Perhaps you don't feel appreciated for always delivering on time?

Having explored the situation with Anna, you ask her whether there is anything that you or she might have overlooked. She can't think of anything. You ask if she has any strengths or resources that might help in what is obviously a difficult situation for her. Anna replies that she is very determined and will do whatever it takes to improve things.

Value: You are not sure what is the most pressing or important aspect of the situation for Anna, and you are also aware that you have a limited number of sessions with her. You are wondering whether her question 'Is this the right job for me?' is within your remit, and whether it might be more than you can deal with in a limited time.

 What do you say next? Which of the options below do you prefer?

- So, out of all the things we've talked about, what seems the right bit for you to work on now?
- I wonder if you need to attend a stress management workshop?
- Perhaps you need to sort out your career issues first.

You select the first option because it offers Anna choice, whereas with the other two options you are making suggestions.

She says, 'Well, the career thing is a big issue, but maybe I need to see if I can get on top of this job first of all. That's what I want to work on, getting on top of this job and losing "the gorgon".'

At this point, you have reached the end of Stage 1, although not the end of the session.

SESSION 1: USING STAGE 1 AND APPLYING THE PRINCIPLES

You have worked through each of the three tasks of Stage 1 of The Skilled Helper. The model has enabled you to work intentionally.

Anna began by talking about the negative 360-degree feedback. You've helped her to explore the ways in which this a problem for her, and she has talked about her job and her career.

You've worked to establish a safe, trusting relationship with Anna, who was quite 'prickly' to begin with. At one point you thought that she anticipated critical challenge from you, but when she received support and empathic challenge, she began to relax.

You've challenged her and enabled her to challenge herself in exploring new perspectives.

She has been supported in identifying something manageable to take forward and work on.

You noticed that she is willing to laugh at herself, and you've been able to share humour together.

You've tried to ensure that Anna has autonomy in creating the coaching agenda. While you have steered the process, she has made the decisions about which issue to tackle.

You have helped Anna to focus on what she wants to work on now, while at the same time acknowledging that in the future she may explore broader career issues. You wonder whether it might be more appropriate for her to be mentored by a director if she decides to explore these issues.

The session continues.

Stage 2: What do I need or want? Possibilities – change agenda – commitment

Possibilities: Anna has identified something that would be valuable to work on: getting on top of her job and losing 'the gorgon'. You suggest that, rather than working on *how* she can get on top of the job and lose the 'gorgon', which may seem like an obvious place to begin, she could start by painting a picture in words of *what* would be happening in her ideal situation. You ask her to think forward in time, and picture herself 'on top of the job and losing the gorgon'. What would it be like for her if things were going really well? You've noticed that Anna uses visual imagery in the way she talks, so you decide to include some prompts which might appeal to the visual sense.

 What brainstorming prompts might you use? Try to add five to those below.

- So, imagine it's going really well . . . describe your day . . .
- Paint a picture of what are you doing?
- In your ideal, what are you thinking? Feeling?
- Ideally, what are people saying about you? About your team?

There are more prompts in Figure 7.8, page 152.

Anna comes up with lots of ideas, however many of them seem to be quite realistic. You encourage her to 'suspend reality for a moment and picture your absolute ideal, if there were no constraints'. Your prompt helps her to be more imaginative and Anna's brainstorm list is several pages long. You struggle to keep up with writing each item down verbatim, but you manage. You wonder how on earth she'll be able to sort through all the items, and so you ask her how she wants to select the important points. You suggest going through the list item by item, but Anna is intuitive and prefers to scan the list. She underlines three items that seem most important to her:

- not losing my cool;
- we're all one team, not just me the boss;
- feeling calmer, happier.

Change agenda: You hope that by identifying the important elements of what she *wants*, Anna can now *choose* a goal. The items that she has selected are aspects of the ideal which are particularly important to her. She now needs to choose something that she can achieve, a goal which will take her towards those important aspects.

 Can you think of a question that might help Anna to formulate a goal?

You ask a question; 'Anna, is there a goal emerging from the items that you underlined; something you can achieve, and want to achieve?' Anna says yes, her goal is that within three months her group will be functioning as a team, and she will be part of the team and not, as she currently feels, apart from them. You ask her to phrase this as a SMART goal. Anna says, 'Within three months, the team will be working better with me, and I will feel more relaxed.'

 While this is a useful first attempt at getting a goal statement, there are some difficulties with it. Can you spot them?

With your help, Anna refines the goal statement. She makes two important changes. Firstly, she focuses on achievements within her control, changing the goal from 'the team will' to 'I will'. Secondly, she tries to make the goal more specific and measurable. This is her revised goal statement:

> By the end of June, I will be acting calmly at work in all situations, and involving my team in responding to demands and deadlines, and I will feel happier.

 If you wanted to review this goal against the SMART checklist in Table 7.2 on page 153, what additional questions might you ask Anna at this stage?

Commitment: Before you start working on how Anna can achieve this goal, you want to check that it is the right goal for her. You ask her about the advantages and disadvantages of achieving the goal, the costs and benefits, both for herself and others. (There is a description of this technique in Chapter 9.) She thinks the advantages are pretty obvious: both she and the team would be happier and hopefully working more effectively. The disadvantages are less obvious; however, she notices that her goal is to *behave* calmly. She wonders if she will always *feel* calm. Maybe a disadvantage for her will be coping with how she feels and having to manage 'the gorgon'. She also wonders whether the team's work will get done, or whether standards will suffer.

 How would you paraphrase what you've heard, and check if this is the right goal for Anna?

You ask Anna whether, considering both potential costs and benefits, this is the right goal for her. Anna decides that the goal is fine, and now she wants to work on how she can achieve it. You have reached the end of Stage 2.

SESSION 1: USING STAGE 2 AND APPLYING THE PRINCIPLES

Stage 2 has enabled Anna to take one part of the problem which she can work on, and picture how that would be if things were much improved.

Anna found it easy to brainstorm. She was energized in this stage – it played to her strengths, and you mentally noted that brainstorming may be a useful technique to use again.

You noticed how Anna's values became apparent as she described her ideal. While you weren't sure how you would move from the ideal to the practical goal, the process seemed to flow.

You steered the process, and with plenty of reflecting and active listening, as well as using the framework, you helped her move forward and identify this goal. You found that being clear in your own mind about a format for a goal statement helped Anna to avoid the pitfall of setting a goal which wasn't really hers to achieve. The format 'by . . . I will have . . . and I will feel' enabled her to set a goal that was within her control.

When you tested her commitment to the goal, she mentioned that work standards might suffer. You remembered that earlier on she had talked about getting the work done 'whatever it takes'. You wondered how important this was to her and whether you might have asked her. Maybe it would have been helpful to return to Stage 1 and explore this? However, the moment passed and you mentally 'logged' it, and noted that perhaps it would crop up again.

Stage 3: How do I get what I need or want? Possible strategies – best fit strategies – plan

Possible strategies: There are 30 minutes until the end of the session. You wonder what would be a good outcome from this session for Anna. You are rather concerned. You don't want to leave matters in mid-air, but neither do you want to force the pace.

 What might you say to Anna now?

You say: 'Anna, I see we have 30 minutes left. You've identified a goal. Do you want to use the time to talk about how you might achieve your goal, or is there something else more useful that we could do?' Anna tells you that she thinks that a lot has been achieved already. She has focused on something which is manageable, after initially feeling rather overwhelmed by the 360-degree feedback. She says that in this last part of the session it would be useful to identify some actions for her to take between now and the next time you meet. You ask her to restate the goal, and then describe all the ways in which she might achieve it, including some wild and wacky ideas. She restates her goal: 'By the end of June, I will be acting calmly at work in all situations, and involving my team in responding to demands and deadlines, and I will feel happier.'

 What prompts might you use to help Anna to brainstorm all the different ways that she could achieve her goal? There are some in Figure 7.12 on page 160.

In response to your prompts, here are some items from Anna's list:

101 ways to achieve my goal
- identify role models . . . other colleagues who stay calm . . . talk to them
- talk to my team more . . . involve them at the front end
- take more notice of my own behaviour . . . notice what I do
- take five, take time out to think before I start rushing around issuing orders
- challenge deadlines . . . do I always have to respond instantly?
- read a book . . . . find some techniques on how to manage stress
- join a relaxation class
- take a holiday, have a break

Best fit strategies: You ask Anna which of these she wants to do, which would fit with her values and resources, and which have the fewest unwanted consequences. Anna says, 'That certainly rules out taking a holiday, because I'd have a mountain of tasks to return to.' You agree that it's important that she chooses a strategy which doesn't add more stress at work and make the goal less likely to be achieved.

Anna decides that a good starting point would be to keep a record of her reactions in times of stress at work, and what happens to her when work pressures build. She says that this start point appeals to her. You ask, 'Because?' and she tells you that it appeals because it's something that she can do every day, it's under her control, and she will generate her own data.

Plan: Anna has identified a strategy, and you are wondering what would help her to put it into action.

 What do you do next? What questions will help Anna firm up her actions? Help her to plan for contingencies? Help her to check that the actions will achieve her goal? There are some prompts in Figure 7.14 on page 162.

Anna commits to the following actions, which she writes down:

- At the end of each day, I will note down any incidents where I have been under pressure. I will use three columns: what I was thinking at the time, what I was feeling and what I actually did.
- When I notice myself about to go into 'gorgon mode', I will 'take five', by getting a coffee or going for a walk around the block or finding some other distraction.
- When we meet again in a month, I will bring my notes and discuss with you what has happened.

You have reached the end of Stage 3 and of the first session.

 SESSION 1: USING STAGE 3 AND APPLYING THE PRINCIPLES

In Stage 3, you enabled Anna to identify manageable actions she could take. Anna was supported in choosing actions which would not increase her stress levels too much – for example, by being too difficult to achieve or by having negative consequences. What she has chosen, however, does require her to reflect and notice her own behaviour, thoughts and feelings.

You were aware that, as the session progressed, you were feeling under time pressure. You remember that Anna's team members have said they often feel under pressure, and indeed so does Anna. You wonder whether you might have shared this observation with Anna and asked to what extent you and she were recreating in the session what happens at work.

However, you were pleased that, despite feeling concerned, you did offer choices to Anna about how to use the time.

You realize that you forgot to leave space at the end of the session to review with Anna how you have worked together. This would have been useful, especially since it was your first session. You make a mental note to ensure that you leave sufficient space for review at the end of the next session, which takes place, as planned, a month later.

The second session

Stage 1: What's going on?

You are wondering how to start the second session. You consider saying:

- Hello Anna, how are things?
- Hello Anna, let's start by looking at how you got on with your action plans.

Which option do you prefer? Why?

You decide that it's better not to make any assumptions about what's been happening, so you ask the more general question 'How are things?'. Anna tells you that the past month has been 'an eye-opener' for her. As planned, she has kept notes, and has been surprised by what she has found. Firstly, she noticed how often she gets stressed at work. Secondly, she noticed her feelings: annoyance at requests, anxiety about her team's ability (and her own ability) to respond, and impatience with others. In these situations, she has tried to take time out and avoid getting irritated with those around her.

What do you notice about Anna's reaction to this data compared with her reaction to the 360-degree feedback? Why do you think that is? Reflect this to Anna, balancing support and challenge.

You say, 'You know Anna, when you talked about the staff feedback it was as though you didn't really want to believe it, maybe it was a bit difficult to take in. Today it's different – you are challenging yourself, and sounding quite energized.' Anna agrees, yes, this is her data and something she can work with. She says, 'I want to get on and make some changes. I can see now what I need to stop doing. I'm just not sure what to do instead!' It seems as if Anna is firing on all cylinders, so you match her pace. You say, 'OK, let's try this. Choose three behaviours you'd be happy to lose, three gorgon behaviours, and three you want to substitute.' She says, 'I want to stop issuing orders, taking charge and demanding. I want to start listening, involving others more but not [she laughs] lose control.'

At this point, you share with Anna some research about the skills of effective influencers, which describes specific skills that they use. In fact, they do a lot of active listening and involving others, and yet they are certainly not people who have lost control! She is interested in this, and says that she's keen to 'give it a go', to try out some of these skills and new behaviours, and see what happens.

You have reached the end of Stage 1, although not the end of the session.

SESSION 2: USING STAGE 1 AND APPLYING THE PRINCIPLES

You trod cautiously at the beginning of the session. Anna is a client who has a lot of pressure at work and you didn't want to recreate that pressure in the coaching session.

You invited Anna to tell her story of what had happened since your first session. It was clear that in carrying out her action plans she had generated some new perspectives for herself since last time.

Since she was enthusiastic, it seemed appropriate for you to offer some challenges and suggest some additional new perspectives in the session. You talked about the research on communication skills, and asked focused questions. Your questions helped her to identify the value issue, which was 'developing new behaviours'.

As she described these behaviours, she talked about how she wanted things to be in the future, and so she began to move into Stage 2, talking about the ideal and possibilities.

The session continues.

Stage 2: What do I need or want?

What do you do now? Which part of this stage will be most useful?

You say, 'Anna, remembering what we talked about last time, and putting that together with what you've said today, it sounds as though you have some ideas for a new goal, and now you want to get going with it?' Anna agrees. She wants to ask her team for suggestions, not assume that ideas have to come from her, talk less and not always jump in first. Her goal is: 'By the next time we meet, I will have spoken less and made fewer suggestions in our weekly meetings and elsewhere. Instead, I will ask for suggestions. I will feel pleased that I am doing this, and interested in whether I feel sufficiently in control!'

You are at the end of Stage 2, and midway through the session.

 SESSION 2: USING STAGE 2 AND APPLYING THE PRINCIPLES

Given the work that you and Anna had done, your hunch was that you could quite quickly firm up a goal. Anna began to describe her ideal behaviour, and the goal – i.e. the change agenda, evolved from her description. It did not seem necessary to use an intentional brainstorming process, as you did in the first session.

You did not specifically ask Anna about the costs and benefits of achieving this goal, but you noticed that she was concerned about losing control, a potential cost of this goal. You have an idea about how to help her with this. However, you wonder whether you might have reflected this concern back to her, to give her the opportunity to talk more about it.

The session continues.

Stage 3: How do I get what I need or want?

An hour of your session remains. You suggest to Anna that one way of exploring possible actions would be to use the remainder of the time to practise some of the new behaviours. She could rehearse them, and notice how the words sound and how she feels as she says them, in particular how 'in control' she feels. You explain the process and some options: perhaps you could take the part of a team member responding to her, or perhaps she could play both parts, physically moving between two chairs as she does so. (There is a description of this technique, role-reversal, in Chapter 9.) Anna is enthusiastic to try this out and asks you to play the part of a team member. She tries out different scenarios and forms of words, and is quite heartened. 'When I hear myself, it doesn't sound like losing control at all, in fact it sounds better, more responsive, not just reactive.'

Anna writes down some specific actions she will try out between now and next time you meet. These are:

- I will do less telling and ask more questions.
- When feeling anxious I will let my team know, not by being aggressive but rather by saying something such as 'I'm concerned that . . .'.
- Under pressure, I will continue to 'take five' and give myself time to calm down.
- I will read the article which you have recommended to me.

You check with Anna whether all these actions are do-able, and whether they fit with her goal.

As coach, in what ways have you influenced this part of the session? What are the potential advantages and disadvantages of the way you've worked?

In the time remaining, you suggest to Anna that you review together how you have worked over the two sessions, what has been achieved and what has been helpful or less helpful.

What questions might you ask Anna? Compare them with the checklist of questions in Box 2.4 on page 53. How do you think the sessions have gone?

SESSION 2: USING STAGE 3 AND APPLYING THE PRINCIPLES

You have helped Anna to move from setting a goal to exploring different ways of achieving the goal, and finally to identifying specific actions that she will take.

You've used role-reversal as a way of exploring possible actions that might work for Anna and finding the ones that suit her best. You followed your hunch that working in this more immediate way – i.e. trying out some new behaviour rather than simply talking about it, would be useful for Anna. She seems to have enjoyed this different learning method, and it has built the rapport between you.

Anna has written some specific action plans which she is confident are achievable.

You got rather carried away with how well the session was going, and realized afterwards that you forgot to help Anna to plan for contingencies and what she might do if things didn't go according to plan.

However, you did remember to make time to review with Anna how you have worked together in this session and the previous one.

A learning relationship has been established. You have established trust, worked with Anna, and enabled her to gain new perspectives and set achievable goals for herself.

Postscript

In the remaining two sessions, you continue this work. Anna builds her skills as she practises and refines the new behaviours. As her confidence grows, she plans an awayday with her team to reflect on how they are working together. She begins to try out skills with colleagues, so that she does less reacting and more clarifying what's wanted and needed. As her confidence increases, she finds she can negotiate deadlines and reduce some of the pressure on her and her team.

Summary

In this chapter we have:

- Invited you to use The Skilled Helper model with a client, Anna, in a case study.
- Used interactive prompts and questions to help you consider how you would work with Anna over two sessions.
- Described the stages and tasks of the model and summarized how these occur in the case study.
- Highlighted how you can use the model and principles to support and guide the sessions.

9   What are some useful tools and techniques?

Introduction

This chapter describes some tried and tested techniques in coaching and mentoring. We have used all of these in our own work and found them to be valuable. We present them in the order in which you might use them if working with a framework which starts with helping a client to tell their story, then proceeds to ways of helping them to explore possibilities and set goals, and finally develops and manages action plans.

These tools and techniques can be powerful. The less experienced coach or mentor would be advised to familiarize themselves with the techniques in a safe and appropriate context before using them with clients. Each technique or approach is presented by addressing these questions:

- What is it?
- When should it be used?
- How does it work?
- What skills does the coach or mentor need?
- What are the advantages?
- What are the disadvantages?
- Are there any useful references?

Johari Window

What is it?

The Johari Window (Luft 1970) is a tool for increasing a person's self-awareness and understanding of how they interact with others. 'Johari' is an abbreviation of the first names of its inventors, Joseph Luft and Harry Ingham. The Window, which represents a person, has four panes or quadrants, as illustrated in Figure 9.1. Each quadrant represents an element of personal awareness:

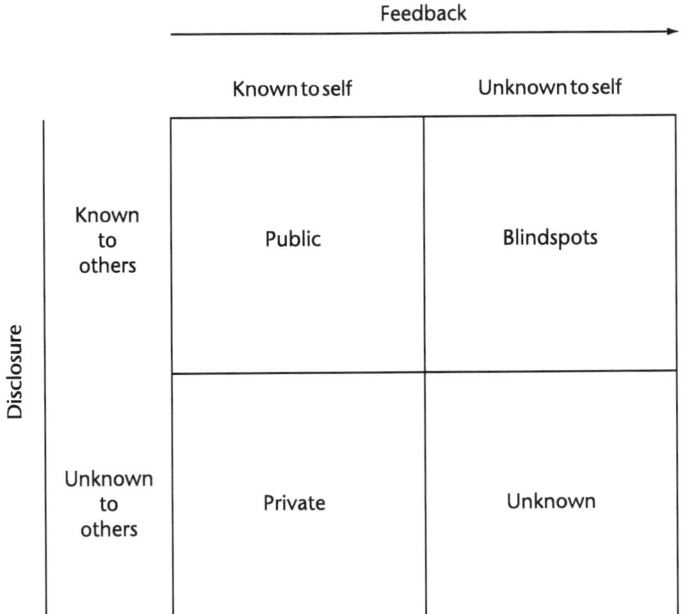

Figure 9.1 Johari Window

- The public quadrant represents what is known by a person about themselves and which others also know about them.
- The blindspots quadrant represents things a person is not aware of about themselves, although these things are known to others.
- The private quadrant refers to things a person knows about themselves which they do not reveal to others.
- The unknown quadrant represents things about a person that are unknown both to themselves and to others.

A person can draw their own window, reflecting the relative sizes of each panel. Quadrants can change over time and in different situations. When a person seeks information – for example, by asking for feedback, the size of their public quadrant increases and so their blindspot quadrant decreases. When a person discloses information about themselves, the size of their public quadrant increases and their private quadrant decreases. Notice how change in the size of one quadrant affects the others.

When should it be used?

The Johari Window can help clients to reflect upon how they see themselves in relation to others, and how they communicate with others. It can encourage the client to consider, for example:

- The blindspots quadrant: is there any mismatch between their view of themselves and how others see them? How could this be reduced?
- The private quadrant: how much do they share of what they are thinking and feeling? Could more (or less) disclosure improve trust and relationships?
- The hidden quadrant: do they have hidden talents or potential that is currently undeveloped?

How does it work?

The client is invited to draw their window and talk in as much detail as they wish about each quadrant and the relationship between quadrants. They can discuss any changes they would like to make in the relative sizes of the quadrants.

What skills does the coach or mentor need?

The coach or mentor needs to explain the Johari Window and prompt the client to consider the relative sizes of each quadrant, and their contents. For example, looking at the private quadrant they might ask the client, either in relation to a particular context (e.g. a work team), or more generally:

- How much about your background and history do you tell others? About your personal and your professional life?
- How clear are you with others about what you are thinking? About what you are feeling? About your expectations of others? About what you want?
- What is the impact on relationships of what you tell others, and what you don't tell them?
- Is there anything you would like to change? How would this improve your relationships and effectiveness?

What are the advantages?

The Johari Window can help a client to increase their self-awareness. They can review their assumptions about what information they can disclose or ask for, and whether they are getting useful feedback from others. They can gain insight into how others see them, and how their behaviour may affect the impression they make on others.

What are the disadvantages?

A client may feel that they 'ought' to disclose more about themselves or 'ought' to ask for feedback. There are risks in inappropriate disclosure and feedback, and clients should be encouraged to evaluate for themselves what might be safe and appropriate. The coach or mentor should avoid creating the impression that feedback and disclosure are always helpful, regardless of circumstances.

Are there any useful references?

Covey, S.R. (1989) *The Seven Habits of Highly Effective People*. London: Simon & Schuster.

Goleman, D. (1998) *Working with Emotional Intelligence*. London: Bloomsbury.

Luft, J. (1969) *Of Human Interaction*. Palo Alto, CA: National Press Books.

Luft, J. (1970) *Group Processes: An Introduction to Group Dynamics*. Palo Alto, CA: National Press Books.

Transactional Analysis

What is it?

Transactional Analysis, often abbreviated to TA, is a way of understanding a relationship by looking at the transactions between people (Berne 1972). The theory states that in any communication with another person we may operate from any of three ego states: parent, adult or child. Sometimes we get stuck and can only operate from one of these. Ideally, we can flex between them as the occasion demands.

When should it be used?

The coach or mentor can use TA to help the client understand why certain relationships are not working. Either the client is stuck, or the person with whom they are having difficulty is stuck. Self-limiting patterns of relating to another person can be perpetuated. TA can be used to highlight these and to practise different responses which make both parties feel better about each other. It gives the client new perspectives and resources.

How does it work?

In some situations with certain people, we may have a tendency to revert to certain patterns of behaviour and ways of thinking. These tendencies can be triggered by the way the other person is acting. To change our behaviour, we need insight into these patterns and we need to want to change them.

In Figure 9.2 you will notice that each person is able to operate, or indeed move between, any of the ego states in any transaction. If person A is operating from parent state it may well induce in person B the child state. In parent state, the person can be either critical or nurturing. Either way, they are not allowing for the autonomy of an 'adult' transaction in the other person. They could produce in person B a 'child' response, either overly adaptive and conforming, or rebellious. Sometimes such transactions can be useful and creative. Often, they are counterproductive.

Sometimes a comment or a situation can trigger a certain reaction. A bullying manager may trigger 'rebellious child' in a colleague. A difficult employee may trigger 'critical parent' in a manager. The task is to help the client to be aware of what is happening and to practise some different responses.

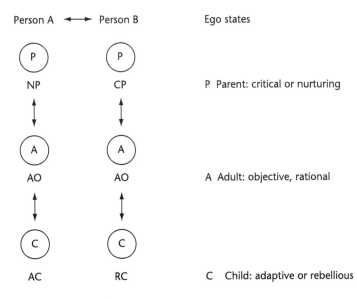

Figure 9.2   Transactions and ego states

What skills does the coach or mentor need?

These skills are all useful:

- listening to the story of the transactions;
- identifying themes or patterns;
- reflecting these back to the client;
- explaining parent, adult and child ego states with an accompanying diagram;
- giving examples of these that relate to the transaction described;
- asking the client to practise from different ego states.

This is how statements and responses could be reframed:

Bullying or harassment
You will finish that work by tomorrow or I will report you to the manager. (critical parent)

No, you won't. It is up to me when I finish it. (rebellious child)

I will be doing my best to get it finished. (adult)

Underperformance
These departmental meetings are a complete waste of time. Nobody ever has any good ideas. I don't want to waste my time attending any more. (rebellious child)

You don't have any choice in the matter. (critical parent)

Would you like to tell us what, specifically, would make them work better for you? (adult)

What are the advantages?

TA is a quick way of helping people to make small changes in behaviour that can produce very different ways of communicating. The insights can be used in individual interactions, group work, meetings and socially. The insight can stop problem situations from escalating and improve relationships.

What are the disadvantages?

The main disadvantage is that a client may develop insight into their patterns of interaction but be unable, in the short term, to change the way they respond to others. This client may need help beyond coaching or mentoring, for example counselling.

Are there any useful references?

Berne, E. (1972) *What Do You Say After You Say Hello*? London: Corgi Books.
Berne, E. (1976) *Beyond Games and Scripts*. New York: Ballantine.
Harris, A. and Harris, T. (1985) *Staying OK*. London: Pan Books.
Hay, J. (2007) *Reflective Practice and Supervision for Coaches*. Maidenhead: Open University Press.
Steiner, C. (1974) *Scripts People Live*. New York: Bantam Books.
www.ericberne.com/transactional_analysis

Karpmann Triangle

What is it?

The Karpmann Triangle (Karpmann 1968) is a way of looking at interactions between people. Sometimes people are stuck in unhelpful patterns of behaviour and they are unaware of these. When they recognize a pattern, they can make choices about changing it and relating to others in ways which make them more productive and fulfilled. The Karpmann Triangle describes one set of unhelpful patterns or 'scripts'. There are three roles, persecutor, rescuer and victim (see Figure 9.3). These roles refer to states of mind. The persecutor role

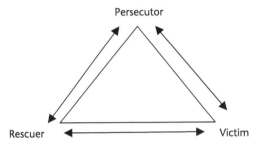

Figure 9.3   The Karpmann Triangle

is 'it's all your fault'. The victim role is 'poor me'. The rescuer role is 'let me help you'. The roles are interdependent, so when one person breaks out of the 'script', or changes their role, the other two roles will change.

When should it be used?

The Karpmann Triangle can help the client to become aware of patterns of interaction that they may unwittingly fall into, and which limit their behaviour and their potential. This can enable the client to change their behaviour; to think, feel and act differently. It can also give the client useful insight into dysfunctional dynamics between others.

How does it work?

The client may notice that, in a particular context which is proving troublesome, they are habitually stuck in a role, and respond to others in a predictable way. They may find that they interpret experiences through the role, so it becomes a self-fulfilling prophecy. For example, a client may have a pattern of feeling helpless or powerless ('victim') and looking for someone to help them ('rescuer'). They may see themselves as left out of important events and decisions or blamed by the 'persecutor' when things go wrong. Challenging the 'victim' mentality may help the client to reclaim their personal power, to become more assertive, and to take responsibility for their actions. Similarly, the 'rescuer' may realize that others may not want or need rescuing. They can stop feeling guilty if they don't rescue others. The 'persecutor' may see that they do not always have to take charge and take responsibility for others and their actions.

   A person can find themselves in one of these roles as a reaction to the behaviour of another. The Karpmann Triangle illustrates how the victim needs both an oppressor and a rescuer. The dynamic can go round and round with people caught in it, not realizing how they are being influenced to behave in particular ways, and Karpmann called this the 'Drama Triangle', with predictable dramatic encounters. So, for example, the 'rescuer' finds themselves blamed by the victim for not 'rescuing' successfully: the 'rescuer' has become the victim, and the 'victim' has become the 'persecutor'.

The client may be able to change the dynamic by noticing it, by re-framing their self-image and choosing to respond to others in a different way. For example:

> I must take care of everyone ('rescuer')
> becomes
> Sometimes people need help and sometimes they can take care of themselves

> I am hopeless and inadequate ('victim')
> becomes
> I have both power and also vulnerabilities

What skills does the coach or mentor need?

Skills of sensitivity as well as careful timing are needed. It can be challenging for a client to alter their view of themselves and their place in the world, especially if such role choices have affected much of their life. However, each client is different. Some clients change perceptions fairly readily. It may be that their role choices affect only a particular situation or group of people. A balance of support and challenge is needed and an awareness of the impact of trying out new behaviour. Suggesting further reading could be helpful to the client.

What are the advantages?

It can be liberating for the client to be freed from old, internalized 'scripts'. Also, it can make the client aware of ways in which colleagues, friends and family may also be 'stuck'. This can help the client to try out different strategies with them. Powerful life changes can result.

What are the disadvantages?

Some clients may find it challenging to rewrite long-established 'scripts'. When a client tries out new behaviour, colleagues and friends may be pleased, or may be upset. Support may be needed to help clients work through the realization that long-established scripts may have held them back. And finally, the coach or mentor (who, after all, may have their own scripts) should be mindful that scripts can play out in the coaching or mentoring session, with either party as persecutor, rescuer or victim.

Are there any useful references?

James, M. and Jongeward, D. (1971) *Born to Win*. Reading, MA: Addison-Wesley.
Karpmann, S. (1968) Fairy tales and script drama analysis, *Transactional Analysis Bulletin*, 7(26): 39–43.
www.karpmanndramatriangle.com

Career Lifeline

What is it?

The career lifeline is a method of helping the client to look back at the development of their career in relation to other significant factors in their life. Having drawn a lifeline, they can then use this information to inform the discussion of future career plans.

When should it be used?

It can be used either as a start to a new coaching or mentoring relationship, perhaps in preparation for a first session, or as the occasion arises, for example when a client is thinking of making a significant career move. It helps clients to:

- raise awareness;
- identify 'choicepoints';
- spot external influences and internal drivers;
- note themes, patterns or trends;
- get a sense of 'the right time' for decisions and moves;
- see the factors which influence choices and decisions;
- identify threats;
- clarify values;
- link past to present;
- link present to future;
- identify resources and strategies.

How does it work?

The client is asked to make a pictorial representation of their career to date. They may choose to draw a graph in a timeframe, or a picture or other visual representation. If the lifeline is drawn as a timeline on a graph, the horizontal axis represents age in years and the vertical axis represents level of satisfaction (see Figure 9.4). One line may be drawn to represent career development and another superimposed to represent significant life events which may have affected the career lifeline.

In the example shown the dotted line signifies the career journey through the years from age 15 to age 70. The solid line is the personal journey which sometimes intersects the career path, sometimes runs in parallel and sometimes overlaps. In this example the dips in levels of career and life satisfaction in the earlier years are far more marked. Some clients find the relationship between life events and career development very interesting. Others prefer to focus on a career lifeline, without a personal one. It is interesting to look at the obvious turning points and to explore what decisions were made at those times, what resources were available to the client, what influenced decisions, and what learning there may be now, from reflecting on these events.

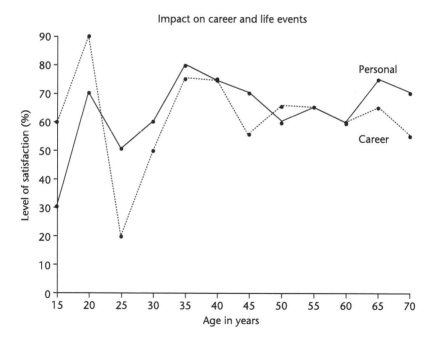

Figure 9.4   A career lifeline showing highs and lows across life stages

After the lifeline has been drawn the client is prompted to reflect on it. The coach or mentor may offer the client a list of questions, and the client can choose which they would find useful to explore:

- What do you notice about the line or about your drawing?
- Any patterns or themes about your career?
- How have you made educational and career decisions?
- Who/what has helped you in making decisions?
- Looking at high points, what inner strengths were evident?
- Looking at high points, what external conditions helped?
- Looking at low points, what would have helped?
- Looking at low points, what might you have done differently, if anything?
- What seem to be underlying values: the most important things to you?
- Identify three strengths that carry you through the hard times.
- What are the three most important features of a job for you now?
- What are your priorities for work–life balance?
- Where would you like to be in your career in X years' time?

Some people find graphs too limiting and prefer to be invited to draw a picture of the development of their career. The picture would still need to have some sense of development through time and possible linkages with significant life events.

What skills does the coach or mentor need?

This exercise needs plenty of time. It must be handled with sensitivity. The coach or mentor needs to leave enough time for adequate debriefing. The skills of active listening, open questioning, reflecting feeling, paraphrasing and summarizing are all essential. In addition some supportive challenging may be helpful, leading to brainstorming possibilities for the future. At least one hour should be allowed for the exercise.

What are the advantages?

A career lifeline can be a way of accessing strengths, resources and values. It provides a creative way of looking at career development. It also provides a useful structure for a coaching or mentoring session.

What are the disadvantages?

It may trigger memories which need careful handling. Asking someone to reflect on their past may trigger memories of, for example, difficult life events. The coach should be ready to suggest further help and support if necessary.

Are there any useful references?

Bolles, R.N. (2002) *What Color is Your Parachute? A Practical Guide for Job Hunters and Career Changers*. Berkeley, CA: Ten Speed Press.

Schein, E. (1990) *Career Anchors: Discovering Your Real Values*. San Francisco, CA: Jossey-Bass/Pfeiffer.

Brainstorming

What is it?

Brainstorming is a technique that encourages creativity and lateral thinking by stimulating the creative right hemisphere of the brain. Hope, ideas, possibilities and optimism are encouraged, while critique and evaluation are discouraged. Brainstorming focuses on the future and possibilities, rather than the present situation and current facts.

When should it be used?

Brainstorming can help the client to describe their ideal future in relation to some aspect of the current situation. It can help them to respond creatively to questions such as 'How would you like things to be, ideally? What do you want instead of what you've got?' It can also be helpful in prompting the client to think creatively about different ways to achieve a goal: 'What are 101 ways to achieve X?'

How does it work?

The coach or mentor sets the scene and briefly explains the process, thus creating the conditions for successful brainstorming. They encourage the client to think forward in time, rather than staying in the present. The coach or mentor emphasizes that the client can:

- think about their ideal;
- take themselves to the future and imagine they are there;
- focus on what is happening in the ideal;
- generate as many ideas as possible, as quickly as possible;
- have fun: 'anything goes' (i.e. wild or seemingly implausible ideas).

The client is asked to imagine, in relation to the issue they have selected, what would be happening if things were much better, if they were ideal. They are asked to paint a verbal picture of their preferred future, as if they were already there. They are helped by prompts from the coach or mentor, who writes down verbatim all responses. The aim of the brainstorming session is to generate as many ideas as possible, regardless of apparent quality, and to encourage ideas even when the client is stuck, or has 'dried up'. Some possible prompts include:

- Where are you?
- What are you doing/thinking/feeling?
- What have you achieved?
- What have you got rid of?
- What have you gained?
- In your wildest dreams . . .?
- Ideally, what might this lead to?
- If you could wave a magic wand . . .?
- Ideally, what are others saying about you?

At the end of the brainstorming session, the client reviews the ideas and is helped to identify the most important ones and to formulate realistic goals. Brainstorming can also be used to identify possible strategies for achieving a goal. It follows a similar process, with the important difference that the client is asked to think about how they might ideally achieve their goal. The responses to the brainstorm are then used to identify realistic change strategies which will work well for the client.

What skills does the coach or mentor need?

Brainstorming is a fast-paced, upbeat process and the style of the coach should model hope and optimism. They must stay focused, energetic and positive, encouraging the client to produce as many responses as possible, since quantity rather than quality is what counts here. They need to encourage the client to stay future-oriented and think wild and wacky, since it is in seemingly implausible ideas that the seeds of possibility are sown. Some clients prefer to draw rather than use words, so coloured pens may be needed.

What are the advantages?

Brainstorming can be an effective way of encouraging clients to overcome problems and blocks, to reframe their ideas and think laterally, and to access the elements of the future that are really important to them. Brainstorming is powerful in helping people to identify what they really want, rather than what others say they should have, or what they think is achievable. It can tap into the values of the client and help them to establish goals and realistic action strategies which will work for them.

What are the disadvantages?

Brainstorming is a powerful process, with potential for harm as well as good. The client should not be left 'high and dry' in the face of a gap between their ideal and their reality, because this might leave them feeling hopeless or helpless. If this is likely, time must be allowed to help the client to identify realistic or feasible elements or actions from the brainstorming output. In this way, they can link the future with the present. In addition, clients can be surprised by their unexpected responses to brainstorming prompts, and it is important to explain clearly the brainstorming process in advance and check that they are ready to 'have a go'. They may need time after the brainstorm to discuss their reactions to what they have produced and any surprises. Also, some people find brainstorming difficult. The sensitive coach or mentor will 'stretch' the client without becoming too challenging or insisting on using a technique which is not helpful for that client.

Are there any useful references?

De Bono, E. (1992) *Serious Creativity*. New York: Harper Business.
Rawlinson, J.G. (1986) *Creative Thinking and Brainstorming*. Aldershot: Gower.
Rich, J.R. (2003) *Brainstorm: Tap Into Your Creativity to Generate Awesome Ideas and Tremendous Results*. Franklin Lakes, NJ: Career Press.
Rickards, T. (1997) *Creativity and Problem Solving at Work*. Aldershot: Gower.

Visualization

What is it?

Visualization is a way of helping a client to imagine an ideal future. This could be an aspect of a current job that they want to improve, a new job, career, or any plan into the future.

When should it be used?

Whenever seems appropriate in trying to envisage a different or better future. It can be used as an alternative to brainstorming to develop wants and needs in a preferred scenario. It can be used whenever the client seems to be stuck and needs help in opening up possibilities. It can also be used to compare and contrast two or more different scenarios if each is visualized and debriefed in turn.

How does it work?

1   Explain the process to the client and ask if they would find it helpful.
2   Invite the client to make sure that they are comfortable and then to close their eyes and relax. They are then guided into relaxation, reminding them not to fall asleep! You can slowly remind them to relax their facial muscles, jaw, neck, shoulders, arms, hands and fingers. Then remind them to breathe slowly and deeply and gradually to relax their chest, abdomen, hips, legs, feet and toes.
3   Invite them to imagine their ideal. Let us take as an example a future job opportunity. The coach or mentor would ask the client to imagine their ideal job, perhaps that it is now X months ahead and they have been in the job for a while. Ask them to spend a few moments just getting into that picture, imagining what they are doing, whom they are with, where this ideal job is and how they are feeling.
4   When they have built up a full picture, ask them to keep their eyes closed and, when they are ready, ask what they see. Prompt, if necessary, to get details.
5   When they have given you the picture, the full picture, you can then gently bring them out of the visualization by saying: 'Now you are going to leave that picture and slowly and gradually you can open your eyes and come back to this room, with me, on X date, in X location.'
6   When the client has opened their eyes check they are OK.
7   Now debrief the visualization by helping the client to summarize what they found in their ideal picture that they want in their future job. They will also have probably clarified what they don't want!
8   Finally, the visualization exercise should lead to a critique of what will be realistic now to shape into some sort of goal.

What skills does the coach or mentor need?

This exercise can be a creative way of accessing ideas. The coach or mentor needs to appear relaxed and calm. It is best used by the experienced coach or mentor who has familiarized themselves with the technique in a safe and appropriate context before using it with clients. The process should be explained clearly and the client asked whether they would like to do this. While the client is visualizing, the coach or mentor needs to observe the client to check that they are relaxed. If there are any non-verbal signs of discomfort the exercise should be reviewed immediately to see if the client wishes to stop. Appropriate prompts are used to guide the visualization (see the brainstorming section in this chapter for examples). Careful timing and debriefing are essential for safe practice.

What are the advantages?

Visualization frees up the imagination. It can feel very positive for the client. It helps them to access new and exciting possibilities. It can be a powerful way of comparing different scenarios.

What are the disadvantages?

Some clients may not like relaxation exercises or may find imaginative work difficult. It is important to check. It is possible that the gap between current reality and future dreams is so great as to make a client despondent. This would need to be addressed and time allowed for good debriefing. However, most clients are likely to find the exercise energizing and motivating. The coach or mentor needs to ensure that the client is well 'grounded' after the visualization experience and so it should take place well in advance of the ending of a session.

Are there any useful references?

McKay, M., Davis, M. and Fanning, P. (1981) *Thoughts and Feelings*. Richmond, CA: New Harbinger Publications.

Vickers, A. and Bavister, S. (2005) *Teach Yourself Coaching*. London: Hodder Arnold.

Whitworth, L., Kimsey-House, H. and Sandahl, P. (1998) *Co-active Coaching*. Mountain View, CA: Davies Black Publishing.

Role-Reversal

What is it?

Role-reversal is an opportunity for the client to develop new perspectives on a problem by role-playing. It developed from the 'empty chair' technique used in Gestalt therapy.

When should it be used?

It is useful when the client is telling their story, in order to develop new perspectives and to challenge blindspots. It can also be useful when testing out new ways of negotiating or being assertive.

How does it work?

1   The coach or mentor asks the client to describe a typical scenario with person X, where there has been some difficulty or where the client wants to rehearse an interview or a meeting. They are asked to say exactly what X is like, what they might say, how they might feel and what they might do.
2   The coach or mentor then role-plays the scenario, with the client as themselves and with the coach or mentor playing the difficult person X. The scenario can be quite short, but enough time needs to be given for typical responses to be voiced.
3   There is then a debrief of what happened, asking the client to say whether X was portrayed accurately and, if so, what the client learned about both parties in the role-play.
4   It may be appropriate to then re-run that same scenario with the client trying out some different responses.
5   In addition, the client can be invited to be X while the coach or mentor takes the part of the client. This helps the client to empathize with X.
6   At the end of the exercise the debriefing should make clear what is role-play and what is reality.

What skills does the coach or mentor need?

The skills of role-playing. This requires clear instructions and the ability to flex between roles as the occasion demands. The skills of debriefing are needed to ensure that the client does not end up confused. Sensitivity is required because role-play can be a way of accessing previously unacknowledged ideas, feelings and actions.

What are the advantages?

It can bring a session alive. It is a quick way of finding out exactly what goes on in a difficult interaction. Skills of empathy, assertion and negotiation can be practised in a safe setting.

What are the disadvantages?

None, if it is done carefully, allowing enough time for debriefing. However, the coach or mentor should not assume that a client will want to use role-play. Some people do not like it at all. Some find it difficult to engage in a way that may seem artificial to them. Others engage readily but then find that the exercise touches a raw nerve. The wise and safe coach or mentor goes carefully and is ready to adapt at any stage in the process.

Are there any useful references?

Blatner, A. (1996) *Acting-In: Practical Applications of Psychodramatic Methods*, 3rd edn. New York: Springer.
Fritchie, R. and Leary, M. (1998) *Resolving Conflicts in Organisations*. London: Lemos & Crane.
www.mindtools.com has a section on role-playing.

Cost–Benefit Analysis

What is it?

Cost–benefit analysis is a technique for comparing the expected costs with the expected benefits of a course of action, in order to decide whether to proceed. It can also be used to compare several possible options in order to choose the best one. A simplified version of cost–benefit analysis can help the client to evaluate their goal and decide whether to proceed, or whether the goal needs to be reconsidered.

When should it be used?

When the client needs to test their commitment to a goal or evaluate a proposed course of action.

How does it work?

The client clarifies their goal statement, and is then asked to list all the potential advantages of achieving their goal: for themselves, for other people and for their wider context – for example, department, organization or family. They then list all the disadvantages for themselves and others and the wider

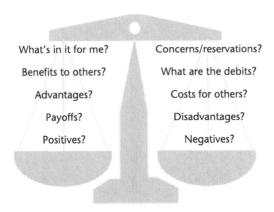

Figure 9.5   Cost–benefit analysis

context. The two lists can be thought of as balances on a set of weighing scales, and the client assesses whether the benefits outweigh the costs (see Figure 9.5).

What skills does the coach or mentor need?

The coach or mentor needs to use prompting questions to help the client identify all costs and benefits, some of which may have been overlooked.

What are the advantages?

The technique identifies the advantages of the chosen goal and thereby strengthens commitment to it. It also identifies disadvantages and can help the client to consider whether the gain is worth the pain, or whether any disadvantages could be minimized. It ensures that the client is really committed to a goal or course of action that is realistic for them.

What are the disadvantages?

The client may discover that the goal or action is unrealistic or not right for them. They may need to pause and reflect on how to proceed, or whether there is more exploration of issues needed. This may be seen as failure, and the client may become disheartened. If this is the case, the coach or mentor needs to be appropriately supportive.

Are there any useful references?

Egan, G. (2010) *The Skilled Helper*, 9th edn. Belmont, CA: Brooks/Cole.
www.mindtools.com describes this and other evaluation techniques.

Wheel of Work/Life

What is it?

The wheel of work and wheel of life pinpoint life and work activities and allow for exploration of areas of satisfaction and dissatisfaction. They also help to manage issues of work–life balance.

When should it be used?

Whenever the client is trying to prioritize and make decisions about work, career or work–life balance. It can also be used to help to understand why a client is feeling stressed, demotivated or demoralized at work or generally in life.

How does it work?

This tool is widely used by coaches and mentors. For the wheel of work, a blank template is provided, showing 10 possible hubs. Figure 9.6 gives an example of the 10 aspects identified by a client showing the least valued (1) as 'writing reports' and the most valued (10) as 'leading'.

1   Clients are invited to make a list of 10 aspects of their work. They write these on a blank template of the wheel of work, below.
2   They are then given 10 stickers each with a number 1–10.
3   They are invited to place one of these on each spoke of the wheel according to how much they value that part of their work at present: 1 would indicate the lowest area of satisfaction and 10 would indicate the highest.
4   They are then asked to think about the proportion of time spent on each activity. For example, the client may put the '10' sticker on leading, indicating the highest value for that aspect of work, but the percentage of time given to leading is only 20 per cent of total work time.

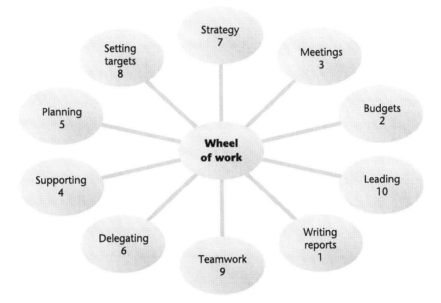

Figure 9.6 A wheel of work

The client can instantly see where the areas of satisfaction and dissatisfaction are. They may become clearer about what they value in work. They can also see the difference between what they want and need and what they have actually got. If this is the current situation with their job they can then be invited to repeat the same exercise for their ideal job, and to compare and contrast the two wheels.

Another version of this is a wheel of life. This helps clients who have problems with work–life balance. The client can be invited to suggest their own categories for what they value in life. They may include areas such as partner, money, health, leisure, personal growth, spirituality, family, friends and career.

When areas on either of these wheels have been identified and prioritized, the client can move to goal-setting around, for example, delegation, time management, career development, work–life balance, health, fitness and relationships. These exercises help clients to become clearer about what they value in work and life.

What skills does the coach or mentor need?

The skills of eliciting information from the client about the important categories in their life and work. The skills of open questioning and clarifying, as well as clearly presenting the techniques and instructing the client how to use them.

What are the advantages?

The wheels are a visual way of accessing important priorities and of noticing imbalances. They are something that can be done either in a coaching or mentoring session, or partly done between sessions.

What are the disadvantages?

The awareness of gaps between what the client wants and what they have got may require further support from the coach or mentor. This may not be a disadvantage, but is certainly something to consider.

Are there any useful references?

Francis, D. (1994) *Managing Your Own Career*. London: HarperCollins.
Robbins, A. (2004) *Awaken the Giant Within*. Riverside, NJ: Simon & Schuster.
Schein, E. (1990) *Career Anchors: Discovering Your Real Values*. San Francisco, CA: Jossey-Bass/Pfeiffer.
Vickers, A. and Bavister, S. (2005) *Teach Yourself Coaching*. London: Hodder Arnold.
Zeus, P. and Skiffington, S. (2000) *The Complete Guide to Coaching At Work*. North Ryde, NSW: McGraw-Hill.

Force Field Analysis

What is it?

Force field analysis is a technique derived from the ideas of the psychologist Kurt Lewin (1951). He said that all the forces and influences on a situation need to be taken into account in understanding that situation. If a person wants to change their behaviour, or change a situation, they need to look at the forces which might help move things in the desired direction, and the forces that are holding back change.

When should it be used?

Force field analysis can be useful at different stages in coaching or mentoring to:

- Look at the forces which are holding a problem in place and those pushing for change. This analysis can help the client to identify blindspots, new perspectives and a point of leverage.
- Test the realism of a goal and commitment to it. Force field analysis can help to identify the forces which support goal achievement and those that are restraining it.
- Test the feasibility of an action plan.

How does it work?

The following example illustrates how force field analysis can be applied to identify what will help or hinder goal achievement. In this example the client's goal is physical fitness.

1   The client is asked to write down their goal statement with a vertical line drawn beneath it, as in Figure 9.7. Next, they draw horizontal arrows showing all the factors or forces which will support and assist the goal achievement – i.e. the *helping forces*.
2   The client is prompted to think about: forces under *their* control: things about themselves; forces dependent upon *others*: colleagues/ friends/family; forces *within the organization and wider context*: events, policies, norms.
3   The forces can be drawn in graphically, ideally in green, with bold arrows for large forces, and smaller, finer ones for less powerful forces.

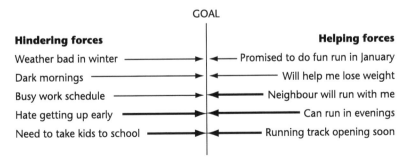

Force field analysis

By 31 December I will run three miles in 20 minutes
at least twice a week

GOAL

Hindering forces	Helping forces
Weather bad in winter	Promised to do fun run in January
Dark mornings	Will help me lose weight
Busy work schedule	Neighbour will run with me
Hate getting up early	Can run in evenings
Need to take kids to school	Running track opening soon

Figure 9.7   Force field analysis

4   The client then draws, ideally in red, all the *hindering forces* that will prevent them achieving the goal. As in Step 2, they consider forces under their control, forces dependent upon others and forces in the organization or wider context.

5   The final step is to consider which forces can be increased, diminished or diverted, to increase the likelihood of success.

This method could also be used to map the enabling and restraining forces impacting on a proposed action strategy. The action strategy would be drawn as the vertical line and the forces enabling or restraining successful implementation would be mapped.

What skills does the coach or mentor need?

The coach or mentor needs to prompt the client to identify the key helping or hindering forces. They then need to offer support and challenge to encourage the client to consider ways of shifting the balance of forces to increase the overall helping effect. The coach or mentor can use prompts, for example:

- Can you reduce/divert any hindering forces?
- Can you find new helping forces?
- Will reducing any enabling forces also reduce resistance?
- Can you increase any helping forces?

What are the advantages?

Force field analysis can make visible the positive and negative forces which have been previously overlooked. It can help the client reflect on their motivation, strengths and weaknesses, and also to reflect on the factors in their situation or context which will help or hinder them. Having identified these factors, the client selects manageable ones to work on and thus increases their probability of success.

What are the disadvantages?

No obvious ones, except that force field analysis is a visual representation, but not a science. A client may choose, even in the face of large restraining forces, to pursue a goal that is important to them.

Are there any useful references?

Lewin, K. (1951) *Field Theory in Social Science: Selected Theoretical Papers.* New York: Harper & Row.
Pedler, M., Burgoyne, J. and Boydell, T. (1994) *A Manager's Guide to Self Development.* Maidenhead: McGraw-Hill.

CAN model: conflict, assertiveness, negotiation

What is it?

There are many situations at work which require skilled negotiation in order to prevent or resolve conflict. CAN is a three-stage model which we have developed for understanding the processes of conflict management and for developing the skills of assertiveness and negotiation (Connor and Pokora 2007).

When should it be used?

Whenever the need arises. It can improve performance with individuals, groups or teams. It can help clients tackle difficult situations in meetings. It can be used as part of action planning.

What skills does the coach or mentor need?

The coach or mentor will need to model skills of empathy, assertiveness and negotiation. The ability to role-play will also be required. Alongside this, the coach or mentor needs to inspire the client with the confidence to 'have a go' at role-playing a conflict situation.

The coach or mentor can offer the model when a client experiences a conflict situation at work. It could be useful to go through all the stages of the model, rehearsing some of the skills and behaviours involved. This would require the coach or mentor to do some role-play in which they are the 'other party' in the negotiation. This would give the client invaluable practice and insight into ways in which the other party might experience them. It may be useful to reverse roles. The client is invited to get 'under the skin' of the other party by taking on their role, and the coach or mentor plays the role of the client. The debriefing of this exercise is important, in order to identify the learning points and to set goals for practising new ways of being assertive, and negotiating desired outcomes.

How is it used?

Box 9.1 demonstrates the process in full.

Box 9.1 The CAN model

 Conflict → Assertiveness → Negotiation

CONFLICT

Conflict occurs when two or more parties want different things.
1   Understand the differences: ideas, values, power, processes, outcomes.
2   Listen carefully to the other party to find out where they are coming from.
3   Show that you empathize with their point of view or their expectations.

ASSERTIVENESS

Assertiveness means clearly, positively and realistically stating what you want.
1   Prepare your own case and consider how the other party will approach things.
2   Present yourself carefully: appearance, posture, facial expression.
3   Know what you want and be prepared to state it clearly and positively.

NEGOTIATION

Negotiation involves movement between different interests.
1   Be clear about what you want and need. List in order of priority what you could give to the other party without too much cost to yourself or to your organization and what you may not be able to give under any circumstances.
2   Negotiate. Acknowledge others' wants and needs alongside your own. Separate the person from the issue. Ask questions, find out what is behind the stated position. Be flexible to offers and creative alternatives.
3   Aim for win-win, but accept that compromise can also be a successful outcome. In many negotiations the relationship as well as the outcome is important.

Note: negotiation will work only if both parties are prepared to adjust to different interests.

What are the advantages?

If the model is rehearsed within a coaching or mentoring session, it is an excellent opportunity for the coach or mentor to observe how the client might behave in a negotiation. Direct feedback can then be given and goals set for practice of assertiveness and bargaining skills.

What are the disadvantages?

Real life can never be completely replicated in a coaching or mentoring session. It is important to have a follow-up session with the client to check how the negotiation went in real life and the learning from this. Forewarned is forearmed. Some of the recommended reading deals in more depth with reasons why all the best skills won't always work!

Are there any useful references?

Fisher, R. and Ury, W. (1987) *Getting to Yes*. London: Arrow.
Kennedy, G. (1992) *The Perfect Negotiation*. London: Century.
Stone, D., Patton, B. and Heen, S. (1999) *Difficult Conversations: How to Discuss What Matters Most*. London: Michael Joseph.

Critical Path Analysis

What is it?

Critical path analysis is a technique frequently used when planning large, complex projects with interdependent activities and timescales. A simplified version can be used in coaching and mentoring to help the client to identify the action sequence necessary to achieve their goal.

When should it be used?

Critical path analysis is used in action planning when the client is considering the details of how they will implement their strategy and achieve their goal.

How does it work?

The client is asked to draw a horizontal line and mark their goal, with a date for completion at the extreme right. Working backwards from that

1 Sept	10 Sept	15 Sept	8 Oct	15 Oct	23 Oct
Book venue	Meet facilitator	Circulate draft programme	Discuss with department	Circulate final programme	Team awayday

Figure 9.8   Critical path analysis

date, they are then asked what needs to be done *before* that date in order to meet the goal deadline, and what needs to be done before that, and so on. The key actions and dates are plotted on the line, from right to left, eventually reaching the current date – i.e. the start point. The resulting line represents key actions and milestones along the path to achieving the goal. So, assuming today's date is 1 September, an example of using this technique might look like Figure 9.8 where a client is planning a team away day on 23rd October.

What skills does the coach or mentor need?

The coach or mentor may need patience and persistence in helping the client to stay focused on this task. Some may find it laborious, or over-detailed, and it may prove challenging for those, whether helping or being helped, who get bored easily or dislike detail.

What are the advantages?

A skilful coach or mentor helps the client to ensure the best possible chance of success when they act, and this technique can be a powerful aid. It identifies all the tasks which need to be completed, any that are interdependent and the timeframe associated with each. So, it enables the client to check the feasibility of goals and deadlines and helps them to clarify whether goals are achievable. The client may discover that their timescales need adjusting, or the goal refining, or that a critical step in the process needs more detailed consideration. Alternatively, this technique may confirm that the goal is achievable, and give the client a clear set of action steps. For longer-term goals, it is helpful in defining interim milestones.

What are the disadvantages?

The client may become disheartened if the goal proves unachievable in the timescale, and may need to be supported in redefining the goal or timeframe.

It is important that they do not see this as a failure, but rather as a smart piece of advance planning.

Action planning does not always mean the end of a coaching or mentoring journey. In many cases the client will return to the next coaching or mentoring session to tell the story of what happened when they implemented their action plans. It is important that they feel adequately supported to return, even if plans have not gone entirely as anticipated, without feeling that they have 'failed'.

Are there any useful references?

www.mindtools.com describes critical path analysis and other planning techniques.

Summary

In this chapter we have:

- Evaluated 12 tools and techniques which are used by coaches and mentors.
- Used a series of questions to evaluate each tool or technique.
- Explained the skills which would be needed by the coach or mentor and indicated where each tool or technique might be used within the coaching or mentoring process.
- Outlined the advantages and disadvantages of each tool or technique.

PART 4
Coaching and Mentoring Practice

10 What are some ethical issues?

Introduction

This chapter explores ethical issues and dilemmas in coaching and mentoring. It sets out to answer questions often asked by coaches and mentors. These include the following:

- What are the practical and professional issues that might arise?
- What sort of dilemmas might I face?
- What principles will help me to resolve them?

It illustrates, with case examples, the ways in which coaches and mentors might work with their clients in managing such issues.

How is ethics relevant?

Ethics can be defined as a set of moral values or principles. 'Moral' relates to the difference between right and wrong and what is considered good or bad behaviour. Questions of ethical practice may be familiar territory to the lawyer or to the medical practitioner. However, 'ethical practice' might not seem relevant to the manager asked by their organization to mentor several staff as part of a corporate management development programme, or to provide one-to-one coaching sessions.

Nevertheless, our experience is that consideration of ethical principles forms an important keystone which supports safe and effective practice, as illustrated in the example below.

> **Louise, a partner in a consultancy,** is approached by Raoul, a promising young executive in the firm, and asked for some mentoring sessions. After working together for several months, it has become clear that Raoul, while apparently successful at work, is just about coping. He is struggling with a demanding workload and the domestic pressures of a young family. At a partners' meeting it emerges that Raoul is being considered for promotion to a challenging new role, and Louise is unexpectedly asked to comment: 'You know him quite well, what do you think?' Louise wonders about the right thing to do. Here are some of her thoughts:
> - What would be best for Raoul? Surely more stress wouldn't help him at the moment?
> - What have I agreed with Raoul about confidentiality? Can I say anything at all about the pressure he's under? Maybe I should make a general remark without going into specifics?
> - Perhaps I'm taking too much responsibility here – it's Raoul who has to decide whether he wants the job. But what if he felt he had to accept a promotion and then couldn't cope?

 How do you think Louise should respond?

Below are some moral principles that Louise might refer to.

- Beneficence: what achieves the greatest good?
- Non-maleficence: what avoids or minimizes any harm?
- Autonomy: what gives the best opportunity for each person to implement their own choices?

- Fidelity: what keeps promises made?
- Justice: what is the fairest?

Each principle is worthy in its own right. The difficulty comes, however, when one principle seems to conflict with another. This can leave the coach or mentor struggling to decide the best course of action.

> **Louise** has reflected on the potential conflict between:
> - Keeping promises (what did we agree was confidential?) and avoiding harm (but if I say nothing, he may be pressured to accept a job that he can't cope with)
> - Doing good (maybe a discreet word in the right ear . . .), autonomy (isn't it really up to Raoul to decide?) and justice (what about other candidates who don't happen to have their mentor in the room?)
>
> Louise is a wise mentor who is aware that she has a tendency to take too much responsibility for others. She decides that she shouldn't assume responsibility for Raoul, or for how he might react to the job offer. Moreover, it would be inappropriate for her to break mentoring confidentiality. She thinks that it is important to be seen by her colleagues as someone who is clear about mentoring boundaries. So, she says, 'I do know Raoul quite well, but he knows himself best, so why don't you sound him out about this promotion?'

This example illustrates the special quality of relationship that develops in effective coaching and mentoring. A coaching or mentoring conversation can be very different from the usual work conversation. It is often about emotions and personal issues. However, coaching and mentoring are neither counselling nor therapy. Clarity about boundaries, and about how moral principles apply, will help the coach or mentor and client to stay on track. It will help to create learning relationships that will be productive and robust enough to cope with any difficulties that may arise, and proactive enough to anticipate tricky issues and plan ahead.

There is much discussion about professional regulation and ethical standards within coaching and mentoring. Many of the organizations involved publish their own codes of ethics and conduct, and there is a list of some websites in the Appendix. These codes are of general interest, and may be particularly helpful for the coach or mentor setting up their own practice. In addition, purchasers of coaching and mentoring services may wish to consider the ethical frameworks of prospective providers.

What are the responsibilities of the coach or mentor?

The effective coach or mentor is responsible for considering their ethical perspective, and agreeing with the client how they will work together. It is the responsibility of the coach or mentor to create a climate where ways of working can be discussed. It is their responsibility to monitor their standards of practice and reflect on how they are working with clients. It is also their responsibility to be aware of other sources of help which they or their client might call upon if needed.

Being clear about ethical principles is important for several reasons. Firstly, clarity guides the coach or mentor to work safely without doing any harm (unintentional or otherwise) to the client.

> **Marco is an experienced coach:** I have a responsibility to be clear about the commitments I make, and to honour them. For example, confidentiality is very important. If I promise confidentiality and then let slip something that a client has told me, they will feel confused and let down and possibly even betrayed. When I am clear about what issues I might not be able to keep confidential, then the client understands this from the start and can take informed responsibility for what they tell me. Clarity applies to other areas too. I cannot normally undertake telephone coaching, and I say this early on, so that a client will not ring me up 'on the off chance', and feel hurt or rejected if I cannot speak to them. I've learned to be clear about what I can realistically offer, and not to make promises which I can't keep.

Secondly, when the coach or mentor is clear about their principles and preferred ways of working, they express themselves clearly to the client, and in so doing they encourage the client to do likewise.

> **Marco:** Occasionally a coaching relationship hits a bumpy patch – it's not unusual and it can be a real learning opportunity for me and the client. I used to worry about this, but nowadays I'm upfront with clients and say that if either of us is having difficulties with the way things are going, we'll talk to each other first, before we talk to anyone else. I think it's been really helpful to say this, because it's made it okay, and given both of us permission to raise issues and learn from them.

Thirdly, clarity encourages the coach or mentor to be aware of and sensitive to issues of difference and diversity, and how these may impact on the relationship with the client, as well as the fair provision of services. An effective coach or mentor monitors their own potential blindspots.

Marco: I worked with a client whose cultural perspective was very different from mine. This was challenging, for us both, and made me think hard about some of the beliefs that I had assumed were 'givens'.

Finally, clarity about ethical principles serves as a reference point to inform the decisions a coach or mentor makes and actions they take.

Marco: There have been some situations which were difficult. I've had to weigh up the risks of taking no action versus the risks of maybe acting too quickly or inappropriately. I've found it useful to reflect on the principles, sometimes in supervision, and it's helped me to steer a path and create some clarity for myself.

Important as the principles are, they are not always the natural start point. A coaching or mentoring relationship is usually approached with a mixture of hope, anticipation, concerns and questions, not a list of moral or ethical principles. Principles may seem to be rather tricky issues, best left unspoken, and yet asking questions such as 'How will we work together?' and 'What's important to each of us?' as well as 'What if . . .?' questions is often an excellent start point for clarifying principles.

Establishing a practical, ethical working agreement

The client's issue

A natural place to start a coaching or mentoring conversation is to ask the client what they want to talk about. The coach or mentor asks this for several reasons. It encourages the client to clarify for themselves the issues and to begin to explore them. It communicates the coach or mentor's respect for the client and their agenda, and puts the client 'centre stage'. It checks that the issues are appropriate. The context of coaching and mentoring is *work*. Warning bells might ring if a client wants, for example, to unpack long-standing relationship difficulties with their partner, albeit that these are affecting their work. Coaches and mentors are not relationship counsellors and to accept this kind of assignment may risk the coach or mentor and the client getting out of their depth.

The working relationship

In addition to asking what issues are on the client's mind, the initial conversation should always include a discussion of how the coach or mentor and client are going to work together. Talking about 'how' gives the coach or mentor a chance to clarify any ethical and professional issues, to understand more about the client's concerns and perspective, and to jointly agree a way of working. The 'what' conversation is, for most people, the more natural one. The 'how' conversation may be less natural and even a little strange or uncomfortable at first. However, one way in which mentors and coaches are helpful is to make the undiscussable a little more discussable. Talking about 'how' helps to resolve uncertainties.

Getting started: coach, mentor and client questions

Hidden concerns or questions which stay hidden may create distraction and impede the coaching or mentoring process. The following example illustrates how one coach addressed an unspoken question and established one aspect of a working agreement.

> **Brian** has agreed, with some encouragement from his boss, to some coaching sessions with an external coach, but he has doubts about the process and whether working with the coach will have any real benefits. At their first meeting, Brian is surprised and relieved when the coach says, 'I imagine you may be wondering whether coaching is right for you. I suggest that we take stock after three sessions to see how we're doing, and decide at that point whether we want to continue. How does that sound to you?' Brian responds positively, and they then start to talk about what would constitute benefits of coaching, how they would assess 'how we're doing', and what 'progress' would look like from Brian's perspective.

Here the coach has taken the initiative, perhaps picking up some cues from Brian. In discussing 'how', the coach has helped to bring a hidden question to the surface and make it discussable. He has also demonstrated openness and shared accountability for the coaching process.

In the next example, the original agreement seems unclear, and has led to difficulties.

> **Adeola,** a health professional, has agreed to offer mentoring to a newly-promoted colleague, Tim, and at their initial session they establish that they will meet for an hour every fortnight. Tim frequently arrives rushed and late, with the result that sessions start late and overrun the hour. Adeola has begun to feel irritated and

resentful and is concerned that mentoring is taking too much time in her already busy schedule. She finds herself being rather short with Tim and looking meaningfully at her watch. In a review session she shares her concerns with Tim. He is finding the mentoring very useful and has been unaware of the knock-on effect of late finishes. Adeola explains that while she is happy to set aside an hour a fortnight, she cannot overrun the finish time. They agree that, in future, regardless of when Tim arrives, they will finish on time. This establishes the principle of autonomy on both sides. Tim is responsible for arriving on time or, if not, having a shorter session. Adeola is responsible for keeping the agreed time slot free. Both are relieved to clarify their arrangement.

A clear working agreement

There are, as these examples illustrate, several advantages to a clear working agreement. In particular, it:

- establishes a joint basis for ongoing review;
- demonstrates the coach's or mentor's willingness to share responsibility;
- clarifies what each party can expect from the other;
- creates the opportunity to discuss questions that might otherwise remain hidden;
- establishes a precedent and a ground rule of openness and collaboration in the relationship;
- pre-empts confusion and unnecessary ambiguity.

While it may be useful to have the working agreement written down (and professional coaches and mentors would normally include this as part of a formal contract), a written document is no substitute for a conversation. A robust working agreement will usually address the following issues:

- confidentiality;
- boundaries and role conflict;
- place, time and timescale;
- way of working;
- ongoing review;
- expectations and limitations.

We say more about the working agreement in Chapters 2 and 3.

The working agreement: confidentiality

Limitations

Both client and coach or mentor need to be clear about what confidentiality is being offered and being sought. They should be aware of obligations and constraints imposed upon them by the law and by their profession or organization. Members of professional bodies will be required to adhere to codes of ethics and standards. Many organizations have policies and procedures which impact on coaching and mentoring. Coaching and mentoring schemes have guidelines and protocols.

It is unwise and unrealistic to offer or accept an assurance of total confidentiality. Rather, the coach or mentor should consider carefully what limits of confidentiality they can offer and sustain. The client should consider what confidentiality they want and be prepared to explore this with their coach or mentor. Both parties should consider how they would work in a situation where the limits were tested. In what circumstances, and how, might confidentiality agreements need to be reviewed?

> **Mari works within the human resources (HR) function** of a large consultancy firm and offers confidential coaching for senior managers and partners, with the understanding that there is no feedback to the organization. In the course of a coaching session, it emerges that her client is struggling with an alcohol problem and her work is suffering. The client asks Mari to keep this information 'strictly confidential'. Mari believes that her first duty of care is to the client, but she is also concerned about the client's staff and colleagues, and the firm's reputation. Mari and the client together clarify the corporate policy on alcohol misuse. They explore the possibility of involving the local HR manager to help the client to get treatment. Reassured, the client contacts the HR manager.

Organization feedback

Where coaching or mentoring is sponsored by an organization, or is part of a change process or development initiative, the organization may ask for feedback. What information will be given, to whom, and in what format, needs to be agreed at the outset. Here is an example of how one coach responded to such a request.

> **Simon was asked to provide coaching for several senior executives** in a large financial institution. This was intended to

support a leadership development and culture change programme which the chief executive had initiated. Simon saw each executive for eight sessions over the course of a year. The chief executive was interested in any themes emerging which might impact on the overall development programme. She understood the need to respect individual confidentiality. Simon agreed that at the end of the year he would feed back to the chief executive his perception of any general themes emerging from coaching sessions, but in a way that protected individual confidentiality.

Public or private?

Another aspect of confidentiality concerns how public or private the coaching or mentoring relationship is within the organization. Confidentiality is often easier for external coaches or mentors to manage, since they will usually hold meetings on their own premises. It is important that the coach or mentor and client share the same understanding of who knows about the relationship. This will be different in differing contexts. For example, MBA students at a university were assigned a coach/mentor as a part of their study arrangements, and this was common knowledge. In contrast, in a healthcare setting, a mentoring scheme offered mentoring for all staff. Anyone could request a mentor, and the relationship was kept confidential unless the person wished to disclose it.

Confidentiality applies to smaller as well as more substantial issues, as this example illustrates.

> **A mentor happened to meet a client in a workplace setting** a few days after a mentoring session. In a misguided attempt to show that he had been fully attentive in the previous session, the mentor asked the client how he was getting on with issues they had discussed. The client looked embarrassed, and the mentor learned the lesson that he could not assume that it was appropriate to discuss mentoring issues anywhere other than within mentoring sessions.

Note-taking

Confidentiality also applies to any notes made during coaching or mentoring sessions. The purpose of note-taking should be clarified. If notes are to be taken, who and what are the notes for? Who will make them? Who will keep them? If the coach or mentor is keeping the notes, they should be stored securely and separately from any personal details or contact information about the client. Both parties should agree what will happen to the notes at the end of the coaching or mentoring relationship.

Supervision

In supervision, the identity of the client is not normally disclosed, and the focus is on the coach or mentor, not the client. When clients understand this, they can be reassured that their coach or mentor is paying attention to professional development and maintaining standards.

In this section we have discussed aspects of confidentiality that may be addressed in the working agreement and Box 10.1 lists some useful questions about confidentiality for coach or mentor, and client.

Box 10.1 Confidentiality checklist for coaching and mentoring

- What are the legal, professional or organizational constraints, obligations or entitlements which affect confidentiality?
- What will be confidential? What will not be?
- What will we do if something cannot be kept confidential?
- How would we do this?
- Is the relationship confidential?
- What about any notes? Who takes them? What for? Where are they kept? Disposed of?
- What feedback, if any, is there to the organization? By whom? For what purpose?
- Does the coach or mentor have supervision? How is client anonymity preserved?

The working agreement: boundaries and role conflict

There can be potential or actual conflicts between the role of coach or mentor and other relationships they have with the client. Even if confidentiality boundaries have been agreed, the coach or mentor cannot 'unknow' something that has been shared in a coaching or mentoring conversation. For example:

- A mentor is asked to give a reference for a client.
- A client attends a selection panel for a job and finds that their coach is on the panel.

- Mentor and client find themselves both attending the same work meeting. A previous mentoring conversation has focused on the client's difficulties with a colleague who is at the same meeting.
- Coach and client meet unexpectedly in a social setting.

 If you were the coach or mentor in the above situations, what would you do? If you were the client, what would you want?

While it is impossible to anticipate every contingency, it is worth considering possible conflict or boundary issues and agreeing in advance how these might be handled. Below are two case examples, the first where this was done and the second where it wasn't.

> **Jaime is mentor to Alice.** While he is not her line manager, he does have indirect management responsibility for some of her work. He is likely to be asked to comment on her work for her annual performance appraisal. They agree, together with Alice's boss, that Jaime will limit any comments he makes to Alice's work performance and results achieved.

> **Chris is a coach** and his client Mike has talked quite a bit in coaching sessions about his family, in relation to career and personal development issues. Chris and Mike live in the same city. They meet unexpectedly in a café, both with their families. Both are uncomfortable, and Chris makes polite conversation and leaves as early as he can. He reflects afterwards that he had not anticipated such an eventuality, or discussed it with Mike. In future, Chris decides, he will discuss with each new client 'What if we meet socially?'

The working agreement: time and place

Time

It is important to agree where and how often meetings will take place and the number of sessions. This might be a formal contract: 'We will meet for two hours every six weeks, initially for five meetings. At our fifth meeting we will review the work we have done, and decide whether more sessions would be useful.' It may be more informal: 'Feel free to drop in whenever you want', although experience suggests that this can be an unsatisfactory arrangement on both sides. Here is an example of a very informal arrangement which did not work well.

Sheena has offered to mentor two new teachers in her school. She has suggested that they can 'drop in for a chat any time'. One frequently pops into her office, rarely takes up more than 10 minutes of her time and finds the sessions valuable. He uses Sheena as a sounding-board, to think through decisions. Sheena is pleased to offer her support, but notices that his visits are becoming more frequent and wonders whether he may rely on her too much. The other teacher has never been to see Sheena. In fact, he is struggling in his new job and is concerned about appearing to be unable to cope. He notices that Sheena hasn't called him to ask how work is going, and assumes she is busy. Sheena meanwhile is puzzled. She had tried to be encouraging to both individuals, but one has yet to contact her. She doesn't want to put pressure on him to see her, so she is reluctant to contact him.

The moral principles described earlier in the chapter include: doing most good, avoiding harm, fairness, faithfulness to promises and autonomy. Thinking back over these principles, it is clear that there are some dilemmas in this situation for the mentor.

 Imagine you are Sheena. What dilemmas do you see?

Here are some that you might have noticed:

- Should Sheena leave each person to make their own choices about if/ how often they see her? What is equally fair to both? Should she contact the teacher who hasn't been to see her?
- Should she have a discussion with the teacher whom she sees frequently? Should she share her concerns that he may be becoming over-reliant? How can she do this in a way that is not too challenging?
- What does each person understand has been agreed by 'feel free to drop in for a chat any time'? How clear is this agreement?
- Is there any agreement about confidentiality?

 Imagine that you are each of the colleagues. What would you want Sheena to do? Anything you'd prefer her not to do?

Finally, if you were Sheena, what would you do? What actions are possible? Which are preferable?

Place

The meeting place is important. Meeting in the client's office can present difficulties: interruptions are possible and job demands can intrude. Some internal
coaches and mentors use their own offices, but this can emphasize any hier-
archy/power difference between coach or mentor and client. Here too,
everyday work pressures can interrupt. Meeting in the client's home may
present difficulties: the coach or mentor is de facto a guest. If both parties are
travelling some distance, the lobby of a hotel at a midway point may be an
option. This is neutral ground, albeit with the limitations of being a public
space. Many external coaches and mentors have their own premises where
privacy and quiet are guaranteed. For internal coaches and mentors, a quiet
meeting room can be a satisfactory alternative.

In addition to agreeing where and for how long meetings will take place,
it is useful to clarify whether there will be contact *between* meetings, either by
phone or e-mail. E-coaching and e-mentoring are becoming increasingly
popular and may form part of the relationship. In agreeing time and place, it
is important that both parties honour commitments and do not cancel meetings or phone calls except in extreme circumstances. It is useful, however, to
agree in advance how they will handle a situation where this becomes
unavoidable. Box 10.2 lists some helpful questions for both parties.

Box 10.2 Time and place checklist

- Where will we meet?
- For how long?
- How many sessions will we have?
- What happens if one of us cannot make the meeting?
- What happens if the client doesn't turn up? Or is late?
- Is contact between sessions part of the way we will work?
- If not, what if an urgent matter arises between sessions?

The working agreement: ways of working and ongoing review

Setting the scene

Clients want to know, and coaches and mentors need to be clear about, what
coaching and mentoring will involve. The skilled coach or mentor will be able
to explain simply and briefly how they work, what they expect and offer, and
any models or frameworks they might use. Box 10.3 contains an extract

from a mentor's description of mentoring during an introductory session with a client.

Box 10.3 Extract from an introduction to mentoring

Let me tell you how I usually work, and then we can decide together what would suit us. These sessions are an opportunity to explore the career issues you've outlined, and to develop goals and plans in relation to these. Rather than give advice, I will try to help you to reflect on problems or opportunities, and to clarify your goals and what you can do to achieve them. Mentoring works best if you come to each session with your ideas of what you want to discuss, and we'll start each session by agreeing how we use the time. Towards the end of the session, I'll ask about any action or plans, because doing things between meetings is important. It's helpful if you make notes of these plans, and bring them to the following meeting. It's also helpful to review the way we've worked together and anything we want to change for the next time. How does that sound to you?

Professional background

The coach or mentor should be open about their own work experience and their training as a coach or mentor. They should be prepared to offer a brief description of their background and relevant qualifications and respond to client questions about these.

> **Bryony is a doctor and mentor** in a mentoring scheme for colleagues in the region. She introduces herself to potential mentees by briefly explaining her professional background and also her training as a mentor: she has attended a four-day non-accredited training programme. She tells potential mentees that she has been a mentor for a year; she has had only a few referrals but has enjoyed the mentoring work. She has supervision three times a year provided by the scheme.

Way of working

Regular review with the client is a cornerstone of safe and effective coaching and mentoring. We cannot emphasize enough the power of joint review. Box 10.4 lists some questions which might encourage a constructive and open review, so that responsibility is shared and any difficulties can be raised in a problem-solving rather than blaming fashion. Notice how some questions invite the client to reflect on their own behaviour, emphasizing that this is a joint process involving both parties reflecting on how they are doing.

Box 10.4 Questions for review of a session

- What's been helpful about this session (e.g. use of time, structure of the session, focus, pace, venue)?
- What has been unhelpful or got in the way in this session?
- Anything in particular that I've done that's helped, or got in the way?
- Anything in particular that you've done that's helped, or got in the way?
- Anything you'd like me to do differently next time?
- Anything you'd like to do differently next time?
- Anything else it would be useful to talk about?

In the following example a coach and client review, after three sessions, how they are working together.

> *Coach:* It seems as though the sessions have helped you to get focused. I notice you are always ready to challenge yourself and open to thinking afresh, and that seems to help you clarify what's important to you. A few times I've interrupted you and wondered if that was unhelpful. I'd appreciate some feedback on that.
>
> *Client:* It has been useful having this time to focus on me, and really think about where I'm going in my career. You haven't judged me or given advice, but you have helped me to question myself and some of my ideas. I didn't always want to bother to write things down at the end of sessions, but I can see that it's been powerful in keeping me focused. Perhaps I should take time to prepare before sessions as well. I like the way that you sometimes give me space and sometimes interrupt me. At first the space was a bit scary and I realize now that it is challenging – it makes me think. Your interruptions are helpful in keeping me on track. I'd like more of them if you think I'm starting to ramble!

These comments illustrate how the review process creates dialogue, as perceptions and perspectives are shared. Notice that the coach is concerned that they might be interrupting too much and the client is asking for more!

Referral

A skilled coach or mentor considers with the client the scope and nature of the work they will do, and the possibility that at some point referral elsewhere may be appropriate. As a coach or mentor it is important to be aware of other referral resources, which might include occupational health, counselling, special careers advice, training or development programmes. In our experience, clarifying areas which are not your expertise, enhances, not diminishes, your credibility as a coach or mentor.

> **Clare is coaching an able young chemist,** Hugh, who has just been appointed to lead a large project, with high corporate visibility. Hugh comes to the coaching session asking for help with thinking through the business strategy relating to this project. Strategy is not Clare's forte, and she says so. However, she is able to help Hugh create a list of potentially useful resources. On the list are names of several people in the organization, and he selects two who are particularly experienced in strategy, and agrees to contact them before the next coaching session. The list also identifies other resources, including online educational material, which might help him.

Managing endings

Who decides?

There are many reasons why coaching and mentoring relationships come to an end. Sometimes it's a planned ending, bringing to a close a productive working relationship. At other times, it may be more abrupt. For example, an unforeseen event means that the relationship has to be cut short. Reasons may range from family emergencies to sudden job transfers. Sometimes the relationship is not working and the client needs to move on. Sometimes changes in job roles produce a conflict of interest. Sometimes a referral to another helper has been arranged. The nature of the circumstances will obviously impact on the nature of the ending.

Most endings involve a mixture of loss and gain on both sides. The skilful coach or mentor involves the client in managing the ending. This is particularly important if the coach or mentor has had the initiative in ending the relationship. Involving the client helps to minimize any feelings of rejection. Conversely, if it is the client who has decided to move on, it may be that the coach or mentor experiences some feelings of rejection. However, a well-managed ending can be a time to acknowledge the relationship, work well done and goals achieved, as in this example.

Richard has decided to stop working as a coach. He gives his clients as much notice as possible. One client is particularly surprised and rather upset. Richard works with the client to acknowledge these feelings and plan what they need to do together to achieve a 'good enough' ending. He shares with the client the loss that he too is experiencing, but also the satisfaction of the work they have done together and what the client has achieved. He helps the client to identify resources to support their development, including other potential coaches.

 Think of the ending of a coaching or mentoring relationship that you were part of. Was it planned or sudden? What thoughts and feelings did you have at the time? What helped you to manage the ending? Did anything make it more difficult for you?

Endings from the beginning

Ideally, plans for endings will have been agreed at the beginning of the coaching or mentoring relationship, and be included in the working agreement. When this happens, and ongoing review is built into the relationship, the path for a good ending is smoothed. Allowing space for ongoing review will ensure that if these plans change, it will be mutually agreed and there will be no surprises. If the coach or mentor has worked in a way that encourages the client to be proactive, then the client will have ideas about their future and can discuss these. The coach or mentor will help the client to clarify plans and to explore what help they will need in implementing these.

The final session

The final session is an opportunity to affirm what has been achieved and celebrate the working relationship. Wherever possible, there will be time put aside for this review. It will include a conversation about what is next for the client, so that they are adequately supported. It will also include clarification of 'What if we meet in the street/office/at a social event?'

Managing your practice

Working reflectively and getting supervision

Safe and effective coaches and mentors take time to reflect on their practice. There are many different ways to do this, including supervision. We say more about reflective practice and supervision in Chapters 4 and 5. Coaches and mentors should know at least one person who can provide them with support or supervision.

Managing yourself

This involves monitoring your own well-being and ensuring you have adequate emotional, physical and personal resources to work effectively. Coaches and mentors may risk doing harm, and at minimum will not do their best work, when they are stressed, suffering from fatigue, or overwhelmed by personal or work crises. Anyone who does a reasonable amount of coaching or mentoring work will at some time find themselves needing to take a break and gather and replenish their personal resources. Sometimes the break may be enough, at other times additional support or supervision may be required. Box 10.5 provides a checklist of questions for assessing your well-being as a coach or mentor.

Box 10.5 A checklist for assessing well-being

- Am I too tired to concentrate during the session?
- Am I hoping the client will cancel the session?
- Are my own concerns intruding on the sessions?
- Am I finding it difficult to give my full attention during a session?
- Am I worrying continuously before/after a session?
- Have I cancelled a session for non-urgent reasons?
- Am I avoiding supervision or support?

Making ethical decisions

In ideal circumstances, the coach or mentor has time and space to consider without undue pressure the best ethical decision to make. They have time to involve the client and to consult with a supervisor or support resources. The client has time to reflect on what they want and need, and what they expect from their coach or mentor.

Bond (1993) describes a framework used in ethical decision-making. Adapting and reworking this framework, the coach or mentor might ask the following questions:

- How do moral principles inform this decision? What does most good, least harm, is faithful to any promises made, gives maximum autonomy and is fair?

- How does the law impact on this situation? What must I do? What am I entitled to do? What am I prohibited from doing? Are there any rules of my professional body or organization which define or limit my actions?
- What resources do I have at this point which might limit or enable me? How much time and energy do I have? How much capacity, mental or physical? Am I working within my competence, or at the edge? How much support am I receiving from supervision or other sources? Am I overlooking potential resources or overestimating any?
- What is my personal view of the situation? What do I want to do? What is my 'gut feeling'?

Figure 10.1 shows that each of these aspects interlock and all may contribute to making a sound ethical decision.

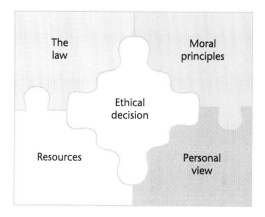

Figure 10.1 Ethical decision-making in coaching and mentoring

Sometimes the coach or mentor is faced with a decision which requires a rapid response. The following guidelines may help when making decisions under pressure.

- Don't panic. If you have just been told something difficult or troubling, that thing already exists, and the telling of it has not caused it to happen. If you have been told of something that might happen, it hasn't happened yet.
- Keep listening. It is all too easy, when anxious or concerned, to stop listening to the client and hear only our own inner voices, 'Oh heavens, what shall I do, what if . . .?' Try to keep listening.
- Take time. In almost all cases, you do not have to respond instantly. Check what you have heard.

- Listening is not necessarily agreeing or colluding. It is accepting the story of the other person and trying to understand it.
- Keep the focus on the client and give them space to arrive at their own answer.
- You have valuable perspectives to share but not to impose.
- Sometimes no action is better than the wrong action. If you decide to act, review your decision, even if only for a few minutes. If unsure, it may be best to reflect rather than act hastily.
- Create 'time out' if necessary. Having a break can give both you and the client the time to gather thoughts and consider resources.
- Get help. If you can, take the issue to supervision or support.

 Which of these actions might be easy for you? Which might you find harder to do? Are there any examples from your own experience where you have used these approaches? What was the result?

Will and his coach have been working together for several months, helping Will make the transition into a senior management role at work, which seems to be going well. The coach is surprised when Will starts a regular session by blurting out that family problems have been getting him down and this morning he felt like 'giving up'. Will is clearly upset, and says that everything seems hopeless. The coach is concerned, and in addition he knows that Will is facing a long drive that day followed by an important meeting.

 Imagine you are the coach. How are you feeling? What are you thinking? Which moral principles and ethical considerations are relevant here? What courses of action do you consider?

Imagine you are Will. What are you thinking? What are you feeling? What do you want from your coach? Anything you don't want them to do? What might help you?

The coach allows Will to talk about his feelings and about the family upset. Will has space to 'let off steam' and becomes visibly calmer as the session progresses. The coach wonders whether Will is temporarily upset or if there is something more than that, and so asks Will if he thinks he needs help from anyone else, for example a doctor. The coach does not get drawn too deeply into the family matters but helps Will to work through some strategies for coping with them. The coach checks with Will how he will manage in the meeting he is attending later that day. They discuss whether Will feels safe to drive, and also how Will could make contact with the coach before the next session if necessary.

Ethics and diversity

The effective coach or mentor is sensitive to issues of difference and diversity. These issues are important and may impact not only on an individual coaching or mentoring relationship but also on fair provision of coaching or mentoring services, and on the use of coaching and mentoring as tools for promoting equal opportunity (Clutterbuck and Ragins 2002).

If the coach or mentor is acting fairly and justly, they will want all clients to be able to access the benefits of coaching and mentoring. They will consider whether the approaches and frameworks used are equally applicable to all clients, whatever their background, ability, ethnicity or cultural expectations. Such awareness can lead to expanding and diversifying the ways in which coaching and mentoring are offered – for example, using e-coaching to reach more clients.

Clutterbuck and Megginson (2005: 42) identify coaching and mentoring as positive opportunities for developing diverse talent: 'Developmental dyads between people of different race and gender, or between able and disabled people, help to identify hidden causes of discrimination. They also provide a safe environment where people can discuss and develop tactics for dealing with cultural barriers to advancement'.

There is a huge volume of literature relating to cross-cultural differences. The work of Hofstede (2001) and Trompenaars and Hampden-Turner (1998) has been particularly influential. They identified cultural differences in perceptions of what are appropriate power and hierarchy gaps, what is gender equality and the importance of individual (rather than collective) achievement. They also found that cultures differ in their tolerance of ambiguity. Cultural differences may affect the client's expectations of the coach or mentor.

In the following example, ask yourself whether cultural differences are impacting on the situation.

A mentoring scheme offers support for overseas health professionals now resident and working in the UK. A mentoring relationship is in difficulty. The mentor sees his relationship with the client as a partnership of equals, a collaborative endeavour focused on the client's needs, to help the client take charge of their own development. He finds the client frustratingly passive and acquiescent, willing to 'go along with' him but often asking for his advice, and looking rather blank when he tries to explain that advice-giving is not his role. He describes the client as 'rather formal'. The client sees things differently. She had anticipated that the mentor, a respected figure, would steer and guide her in career choices. She cannot understand why the mentor, an older, wiser, senior member of her profession, won't provide more guidance. She is also confused by the mentor asking her about her own goals and aspirations.

Of course, it may be that the problems described above are nothing to do with cultural difference. When looking at a situation through the 'culture' lens, we have to guard against the risk of cultural stereotyping. So, effective coaches and mentors use what they know about themselves and about others from *both* individual *and* cultural perspectives. They constantly seek to increase their awareness with regard to their practice.

Hay (2007: 149) gives some prompts to coaches and mentors to raise awareness of their 'fantasies and fears' in relation to a whole range of 'difference' factors which include some of the following: sexual orientation, age, cultural background, ethnic origin, race, colour, religious background, physical disability, learning disability, social class, accent, educational experiences, employment history. In the following examples, differences are impacting on the mentoring relationship. If you were a peer supervisor how would you work with the mentors?

> **Keith is a long-serving senior manager who mentors junior staff** on a one-year leadership development programme. He has difficulty working with Pete, who expresses views such as, 'I'm only here for the short term' and 'I don't owe the organization anything'. Keith is upset. He believes that the organization has invested considerably in Pete's development. He describes him as 'typical Generation Y'.

> **Kelly is a senior academic who mentors final-year students at her university.** As a single parent, Kelly has battled hard to overcome obstacles to reach her senior position. She is mentoring Jeanette who describes herself as 'here for the social life mainly'. Jeanette has few thoughts about her career, and is intending to follow her boyfriend 'wherever he gets a job'. Kelly is infuriated at Jeanette's lack of ambition.

A final word

One of us, a bit of a worrier, has a cartoon pinned on the kitchen notice-board depicting an anxious person anticipating the possible disasters which might occur during the day, and deciding therefore to stay huddled in bed. The final caption shows the worrisome thought entering their head: 'But . . . even so . . . there is always . . . death by mattress!' The topic of ethics can seem a bit like death by mattress. The array of ethical, moral and professional considerations to bear in mind, the potential moral and legal dilemmas which might arise, could lead us to conclude that we might be better off staying in bed and not taking any risks! We are only too aware of this reaction, especially among trainee coaches and mentors, who may feel quite overwhelmed by 'what if. . .?'

In reality, many of the ethical decisions we face are not overwhelming: they are commonplace and, for a trained and reflective coach or mentor, they are manageable. Only occasionally are we faced with very difficult and complex decisions. Nevertheless, ethical practice pervades all aspects of coaching and mentoring. The more thoughtfully we consider in advance our own boundaries, the more we help the client to consider and manage theirs. When we work in this way, we are more likely to prevent ethical dilemmas occurring, or handle them wisely if they do.

Summary

In this chapter we have:

- Listed some ways in which consideration of their own ethical perspective can help the coach or mentor to work effectively.
- Described the importance of a clear working agreement.
- Offered checklists to help develop a working agreement, and discussed both ongoing review and managing endings in coaching and mentoring.
- Noted the importance of self-management and reflective practice.
- Referred to a framework for ethical decision-making and suggested some pointers for decision-making under pressure.
- Highlighted some diversity issues.

11 What are frequently asked questions?

- What if someone is sent for coaching or mentoring?
- What if the client tells me something I can't keep confidential?
- What if coaching or mentoring doesn't seem to be working?
- Can I give advice?
- What if I am asked to coach or mentor by e-mail, phone or video?
- How do I balance the needs of client and sponsoring organization?
- What if the client asks for more than I can offer?
- Can I be the client's manager, assessor, appraiser?
- Can I coach or mentor a client that I meet socially?
- How important is supervision and accreditation?

In this chapter we have listed 10 frequently asked questions about coaching and mentoring, each of which also links to one or more of the chapters so far. The useful resources and contacts in the Appendix will enable you to explore these questions and many others in more depth in your own time.

What if someone is sent for coaching or mentoring?

It is not unusual for someone to be sent for coaching or mentoring – often with a view to 'fixing' a performance or personality problem. People who are sent may be: reluctant, seeing the encounter as punishment; unrealistic, imagining that everything will be magically fixed by you; seeing themselves as a victim and blaming everyone and everything for their difficulties; or perhaps a mixture of all of these. Sometimes, an unpromising start can be turned into a productive helping relationship. Begin with the premise that people can change if they choose. Avoid bending over backwards to help: you may be colluding with your client. Avoid the other extreme, a stance of 'I can't help you unless you want to be helped': this may become a fixed position. Try to establish a 'working alliance' so that your client sees themselves as a partner in a joint venture, with a payoff for them, rather than someone who is being 'done unto'.

The value of basic active listening skills and of communicating respect, empathy and genuineness, cannot be overemphasized: some clients who are 'sent' have never had the chance to tell their story and to hear themselves without interruption, evaluation or advice. You can communicate empathy, not sympathy. You can empathically challenge the client to identify *their problem*, as distinct from *the problem*. If the client is able to own their problem and see a chink of light, something that they can work on, then perhaps progress can be made. It will help if you are clear and transparent from the outset about what information, if any, you will share with the organization which sent the client. Finally, stay realistic. These approaches don't work in every situation, and it is difficult to help someone who has decided not to be helped.

What if the client tells me something I can't keep confidential?

We want and need to offer our clients an assurance of confidentiality. However, no one can guarantee absolute confidentiality. We all work within organizational and/or professional guidelines, and so it is important to discuss boundaries and limits at the outset. Clarity about confidentiality is an essential part of negotiating a working agreement with the client. This is the opportunity to be explicit about what you can and cannot keep confidential. It is the opportunity to check the client's understanding of this, and so will benefit from time and space for discussion. If you have been clear about limits, and the client nevertheless tells you something that cannot be kept confidential, you can ask them why they have told you, and what they expect to happen now. What do they want or need from you? If they were in your shoes, what would they do? If action needs to be taken, it is best if you can agree this with the client. In rare circumstances you may judge that the risk of harm outweighs considerations of client autonomy and you may decide to act unilaterally. In this case you would normally tell the client.

When faced with an issue of something that cannot be kept confidential, it is best to seek support from supervision. Sometimes no action is better than hasty action.

What if coaching or mentoring doesn't seem to be working?

Sometimes we question whether we are helping a client. Do they really want to change? Are we the right helper? Do they need a different kind of help? We may feel that we are working harder than the client which is often a sign that something isn't quite right. Sometimes it is the client who feels that all is not well. Perhaps they see us as too challenging, or not challenging enough, or too structured, or lacking focus, or maybe just not on their wavelength. Establishing regular reviews to talk about how things are going is a powerful source of learning. Getting into the habit of reviewing is likely to make it easier to talk about any problems.

If the relationship doesn't seem to be working from your perspective, you may want to raise your concerns *in a non-judgemental way* with the client. Sometimes this can lead to a breakthrough that helps the client to move forward. Supervision can help you to look at your own part in any difficulties and to rehearse any conversation you might want to have with the client. When sharing concerns with clients, especially if you think that the client would benefit from referral elsewhere, it is important not to make the decision *for* the client. Decisions, as far as possible, should be arrived at *jointly*.

If it doesn't seem to be working from the client's perspective, remember that many clients find it difficult to 'criticize', and so regular reviews can encourage their feedback. To help this, you can ask questions that make the undiscussable more discussable. Good questions include 'What am I doing that is helping you?', 'What I am I doing that's getting in the way?' and 'If there was something that you could change in the way we work together, what would that be?' In addition, working agreements often include a 'no blame' clause that makes it clear that the client can end the relationship or request a change of coach or mentor at any time.

Can I give advice?

When we train people as coaches and mentors, we ask them to tell us, based on their own experience of being helped, what they consider to be the skills and qualities of effective helpers. Having trained many hundreds of people, we cannot recall a single instance where a group has agreed that 'giving advice' was an important skill of an effective helper. And yet, paradoxically, as soon as these same participants start to practise skills, they find themselves giving advice, often within minutes of a coaching or mentoring conversation! So although they know that advice isn't helpful, the habit is hard to break. Giving advice is tempting, especially when many of us have a professional identity based upon our expert role. The teacher, doctor, dentist, nurse, lawyer, HR professional – each is expected to give sound advice. Clients often ask for advice. Sometimes they may demand it. Our guideline is *beware of giving advice*. It rarely works, because you are not the client so you cannot know what is best for them. It can create dependence. Over time, it may diminish client resourcefulness and autonomy. And, as we all know, people often do not take advice, so you are likely to be wasting your time and theirs. And yet it is difficult to stop giving advice, when that's what you do in your day job. So, if you are tempted to give advice, ask yourself:

- Am I concerned about this client or their proposed course of action? If so, can I share my concerns with them in a clear but non-judgmental manner? Or can I create the opportunity for them to check any blindspots?
- Would the client benefit from facts or information (as distinct from advice or opinion) that I have and they don't? Is there any downside to sharing that information? Or to telling the client where to find it?
- Does the client need advice or guidance? Perhaps they need something in addition to coaching or mentoring? Would they benefit from, for example, training, supervision, staff induction or some expert help?
- Would it be useful to share my experience with the client, perhaps of a similar situation to the one they are facing? Might I say, 'This is what I did and this is how it worked out for me, but it may not be the same for you'. We would caution against sharing your experience too often because this can easily become advice-giving in disguise.

What if I am asked to coach or mentor by e-mail, phone or video?

There is a growing interest in telephone, video or e-mail coaching and mentoring. Often, this is used to supplement face-to-face sessions, perhaps when a crisis at work has necessitated an unscheduled session, or when distance or weather have prevented a face-to-face meeting. Coaches have reported the value of telephone coaching with clients who have just been to an important interview or appraisal at work and who needed some immediate debriefing. With video, there is the advantage that non-verbal communication is still partly accessible, but with phone there is only voice, and with e-mail just the written word. However, whichever of these is used, provided the coach or mentor gives the same focused attention to the client, the process can work well. It probably works best when coach and client have already worked with one another. Before embarking on distance coaching or mentoring you need to think carefully through any concerns that either you or the client may have about confidentiality. This will include sessions being on record – for example, your e-mail replies. Will you be happy that they could be accessible to other persons or organizations you do not know? Another important issue for consideration is how you will deal with distress when you do not have the normal safeguards of a face-to-face encounter in place.

How do I balance the needs of client and sponsoring organization?

Your client is the person you are coaching or mentoring. Other interested parties may be involved, and have expectations which need to be negotiated, but they are not your client. As soon as you are approached to provide coaching or mentoring, you need to ascertain who are the interested parties and what are their expectations. Do they align with each other, or do they conflict in any way? We have mentioned the importance of clear working agreements. Where there may be conflicts of interest, it is even more important to explicitly agree terms of reference at the outset, preferably in writing. For example, a manager may have arranged coaching with an external provider, for a member of staff who is underperforming. The manager arranges payment out of a departmental budget and wants a successful outcome. They ask the coach for ongoing reports, submitted at the time of invoicing. In this case, the client should be made aware of this from the outset. A meeting could be arranged with all parties, before the coaching starts, to agree who will be involved in writing the reports, and what they will and will not contain. In some coaching and mentoring schemes within organizations, there is an expectation that both the coach or mentor and client will complete 'exit evaluation' forms to help in the further development of the service. The client needs to be assured that they are not being assessed for the way they perform in the sessions and that the content remains confidential. Always be transparent with your client, respect their autonomy, and involve them in any agreements pertaining to your work with them, preferably before you start. You may decide in some instances that you cannot agree to requests for information, from organizations or employers, because your view is that this will impede the relationship. If in doubt about compromising your work with a client, you may decide that it is better to turn down an assignment, rather than take on conflicting expectations.

What if my client asks for more than I can offer?

Perhaps this has happened because you were not clear about what you could and could not offer. It is always advisable to be clear about boundaries and limitations from the outset. Then, if difficulties arise, you have a point of reference for some ongoing review and negotiation. However, some clients may be more needy than others, some may find it difficult to operate within prescribed boundaries, some are more impulsive than others, or tend to leave things to the last minute and then hope that everyone else will adjust to that. In these situations, what is happening in the coaching or mentoring relationship may be telling you something valuable about a limiting pattern in the client's life generally. For example, a client tries to cancel a booked session at the last minute. You may respond on more than one level. It could be, 'You want to cancel our session tomorrow? Yes, I can do that but I had booked out that time for you and it's too late to fill that slot now so I will have to charge for it, as we arranged in our working agreement.' This level is straightforward and business-like and maintains clear boundaries. Then it may be followed up, when the client arrives for the next session, with 'I realized that this wasn't the first time you have asked to cancel sessions very close to the date when we were to meet.' This observation offers the opportunity to work on a pattern of procrastination and over-commitment.

Some clients want to contact you outside the agreed session times, or they ask for extra sessions, or they have a habit of going over the time allocated for the session. Such issues may be sorted out by clear working agreements or they may be indicative, as in the example above, of underlying patterns. Another example of a client asking for more than you can offer is when the client expects you to do all the work and come up with all the answers. This is where you will benefit from careful reflective practice and regular supervision. It will help you to work on your own reactions to clients expecting too much from you, as well as working on ways in which you can offer supportive challenge and immediacy to your client, in order to help both of you to move forward.

Can I be the client's manager, assessor, appraiser?

This is the problem of managing possible conflicts of interest. There is no right or wrong answer here. But ethical principles can inform your decision. What would do most good and least harm to your client? What would be most just and fair? What would empower the client most? What will enable you to keep to any promises you make to your client, or what may get in the way? Generally, we would not advise having a 'power' relationship with your client, such as managing them or assessing them. However, some clients positively choose their managers or assessors because they respect and admire their integrity. In other situations at work, coaching is being offered as part of a managerial or leadership role and mentoring is being offered by someone perhaps more senior or experienced in the same department or specialty. If this is the case, then it is the responsibility of the coach or mentor to raise possible conflicts of interest at an early stage in the relationship and to ensure that the client is able to give informed consent to the implications of sharing confidences, with someone who is in a position of influence and power.

Can I coach or mentor a client that I meet socially?

This question is about boundaries. The boundary of the coaching or mentoring session usually includes a timeframe and a clock, a specific location which is appropriate for the work that needs to be done, an ambience that is conducive to the development of a sound and confidential working relationship. These boundaries provide safe containment for both client and coach or mentor. Once you step outside of these carefully constructed boundaries there is the possibility of uncertainty and apprehension in the way that you relate to one another. In the social situation you are not in the roles of client with coach or mentor, you are in the roles of friends, colleagues or acquaintances. Some people are easily able to adjust between roles and contexts. Others not so. Never assume that your client will be able to adjust because you can. If you are both aware that you may meet socially during the course of working together, do address the matter explicitly. Give space to discuss how each of you would wish to manage such a situation if it were to arise. There is a sense in which you can never be totally off-guard if you meet a client socially. You take with you the ethical responsibility to do no harm, particularly in regard to confidences that have been shared, and this responsibility lasts a lifetime, long after formal coaching and mentoring has concluded.

How important is supervision and accreditation?

If coaching or mentoring is your main work, then both supervision and accreditation are advised. They will help you and your clients to be assured of an ethical and professional service, where each of you is safeguarded because you will have regular opportunities for reflection on your work and you will have been assessed against specific competencies. We would also recommend membership of a national or international professional coaching or mentoring association to provide opportunities for updating, networking and renewal. If you are coaching and mentoring as part of another job you do at work, you will still benefit from getting into the habit of reflective practice. Depending on the extent of the coaching and mentoring you do, we would advise regular supervision either with a peer, a peer group, a qualified supervisor, or a supervision group facilitated by a qualified supervisor. If coaching and mentoring is a small part of your work you may not wish to gain accreditation but may find it useful to keep up to date with the websites of major coaching and mentoring organizations such as the ICF and the EMCC, in order to check your practice against their current codes of ethics, and their current requirements for accreditation.

12 How is a coaching and mentoring culture developed?

- Introduction
- Developing the culture: why bother?
- What is a coaching or mentoring culture?
- How do you develop a mentoring culture?
- How do you develop a coaching culture?
- What helps or hinders?
- What difference does it make?
- How do you assess your organization?
- Summary

Introduction

In this final chapter we share with you the voices of people involved in coaching and mentoring initiatives in organizations. We hear from them the possibilities and problems; the costs and benefits; the highs and lows; the resistances and the rewards. Their experience encompasses both coaching and mentoring, delivered both internally and externally. They are:

Wendy Briner	Leadership coach and researcher, Ashridge Management College
David Harrison	Headteacher and consultant headteacher
Malcolm Hurrell	Director, New Mindsets Ltd, leadership performance coach
Shaun Lincoln	Associate director, Leadership & Management LSN
Nancy Redfern	Consultant anaesthetist, Newcastle upon Tyne Foundation Trust and dean director (1994–2010), Northern Postgraduate Medical and Dental Deanery

Wendy Briner describes the results of research into how different organizational cultures respond to leaders who have coaching as part of their leadership
development. David Harrison shares how he has developed a coaching and
mentoring culture in his own school and how, as a consultant headteacher, he
shares best practice with other schools. Malcolm Hurrell tells how AstraZeneca
developed both coaching and mentoring as complementary learning and
development methodologies within an organization which constantly seeks to
achieve both individual and organizational learning. Shaun Lincoln shares his
experience from the learning and skills sector, providing evidence that a
programme called 'Leaders as Coaches' is influencing culture change. Dr Nancy
Redfern shares a journey of culture change in a large city hospital where
consultants trained as mentors. They supported one another and gradually
influenced key stakeholders to recognize the need for mentoring and to give
resources for a hospital-wide mentoring scheme for doctors.

Developing the culture: why bother?

Coaching and mentoring are increasingly being recognized as powerful
learning and development tools. Carole Gaskell describes the experience of
using a positive coaching approach alongside internal performance review:

> Coaching can have a dramatic impact on an organisation's culture,
> people and bottom-line. When woven into the fabric of a business, the
> benefits of coaching are there for all to see. It can accelerate the develop-
> ment of talent, improve staff retention and create a high-performance
> culture that offers a company a real competitive advantage.
>
> (Eglín 2006: 6)

The 2006 annual CIPD learning and development survey noted that 80
per cent of respondents using coaching claim that their organization aspires
to develop a coaching culture, and 75 per cent report investing time, resources
and effort into achieving this aim. 93 per cent of those using coaching 'believe
that a coaching culture is either "very important" or "important" to the
success of their organisation', with individual and business performance cited
as the main objective for developing such a culture (CIPD 2006: 10). By the
time the 2010 survey was published, it was evident that coaching took place
in 82 per cent of organizations, although only a third had a system for
evaluating it. A key finding was that 46 per cent of organizations surveyed
identified that the major organizational change affecting learning and talent
management in the next five years would be 'a greater integration between
coaching, organizational development and performance management to
drive organizational change' (CIPD 2010).

The consulting firm Blessingwhite (2009) produced the results of a global survey entitled *The Coaching Conundrum*. It found that:

> Few have succeeded in creating cultures where coaching of employees is a regular, fully supported, and rewarded managerial practice . . . The majority of leaders seem to be caught up in a tug of war of competing priorities, well-meaning goals around coaching, and an ambivalent organizational culture.

But what about developing a mentoring culture? Our research (Connor *et al.* 2000) highlighted two problems in implementing mentoring in the NHS: a culture where mentoring is viewed as a sign of weakness, and a lack of resources, particularly time. However, the climate is changing. For example, there has been an exciting initiative designed to create a coaching and mentoring culture, not just within an organization, but across NHS health organizations in London. In their report *The First Five Hundred* (Viney and Paice 2010) the London Deanery Coaching and Mentoring Service describe theirs as probably the largest NHS scheme, for doctors and dentists, in the UK. Between 2008 and 2010 they saw 500 clients. They have a comprehensive programme of training, supervision and accreditation using external resources to develop clinicians and managers as coaches, mentors and facilitators. They aim to eventually resource training and supervision internally. They have learned lessons from others' experiences: 'What is needed is not just a handful of allocated or even fully-trained mentors but an overall paradigm shift to a culture of coaching, with role models, positive constructive feedback, and good staff management principles' (Hutton-Taylor 1999: 318).

In *The First Five Hundred* report there is a section on sustaining and embedding the service:

> The challenge for the service is to encourage and embed a culture of coaching and mentoring across London's NHS. Initiatives that the service will be pursuing to promote this aim include:
>
> • Training in mentoring and coaching for teams of senior staff from the same NHS organizations.
> • Training for multi-professional groups including Human Resources, Medical Education and Nurse Practitioners.
> • Forming partnerships with other organizations encouraging coaching and mentoring such as Royal Colleges and Medical Schools.
> • Training of some mentors in team-building and team-coaching.
>
> (Viney and Paice 2010)

Two factors which seem to support the development of coaching and mentoring in organizations are:

1   A culture of openness, learning and development within the organization.
2   A culture which acknowledges that resources are needed for coaching and mentoring, not just externally, but also internally. These include time, training, development and rewards.

Some organizations encourage coaching and mentoring as part of learning and development for all; some embed it in the everyday processes and activities of the organization; some view it as only for those with problems; others see it as a perk for high-flyers. Increasingly, organizations are moving towards developing internal coaches and mentors with selective use of external resources.

David Harrison is a headteacher, who is developing a coaching and mentoring culture in his own school and who is also appointed to give external support to headteachers and senior staff in other schools. The National College for School Leadership (Creasy and Paterson 2005: 43) produced criteria for reviewing coaching culture in a school. These include:

✓   There are strong models for good coaching practice.
✓   Senior leaders and staff welcome and actively seek feedback.
✓   People are able to engage in constructive and positive confrontation.
✓   Coaching is seen primarily as an opportunity rather than as a remedial intervention.
✓   Time for reflection is valued.
✓   The links between personal growth, team development and school improvement are clearly understood.

David views coaching and mentoring as an integral part of his philosophy of distributive leadership, where staff are encouraged to feel ownership and part of the success of the school:

●   Every member of staff is a coach and mentor to others, even though one senior person has a designated mentoring role to support newly-qualified teachers and staff new to the school.
●   Staff are both leaders and learners. Leadership is shared according to expertise, rather than seniority. All teachers are subject leaders. They learn from one another as they collaborate in lesson observations, scrutiny of lesson plans and moderation of assessments. Their aim is to identify good practice and areas for development.

This requires the skills and qualities to give and receive honest feedback that is both supportive and challenging, to coach and be coached.

- Professional working relationships are thus built on honesty, trust, and respect. This ethos takes time to establish.
- All staff are encouraged to both share with, and learn from, other schools.

Difficulties which David identifies as hindering the development of a coaching and mentoring culture include: time constraints; differing levels of experience; matching coach/mentor and client styles of learning and personality; keeping the balance between teaching roles and leadership roles; having a culture where mistakes are accepted as part of learning.

The National College for School Leadership notes that one hallmark of an embedded coaching culture is the links made between a school and the external community. In his role as external consultant headteacher, David shares good practice with other schools and helps them to identify areas for development. He finds that what works well is to 'listen and share' rather than to 'advise and go'. He finds that each school has to adapt good practice ideas in order to fit into their structure and ethos. One model does not fit all. His coaching style is to maintain a supportive presence, to be called upon for help when necessary. This may, for example, be to assist with a school development plan or to prepare for an Ofsted (Office for Standards in Education) inspection. He reports the positive outcomes that can result from structural and cultural changes in leadership and management:

✓ A culture of self-analysis, evaluation and accountability develops.
✓ Senior leaders take ownership. They develop the confidence that they can now do what were previously seen as insurmountable tasks.
✓ Senior management teams become proficient in recording and analysing school data and communicating the facts to staff.
✓ Middle leaders are developed and take responsibility for subject areas and teams.

What is a coaching or mentoring culture?

Clutterbuck and Megginson (2005: 19) define a coaching culture as one where 'coaching is the predominant style of managing and working together, and where a commitment to grow the organisation is embedded in a parallel commitment to grow the people in the organisation'. We would include mentoring in that definition. They view coaching and mentoring as complementary learning and development opportunities. They refer to Alison Hardingham's characteristics of a coaching culture in which there is an emphasis on teams, not just on individuals (Hardingham *et al.* 2004: 187–8). Alison highlights: cross-company teams; rotating leadership of teams according to specific purpose; and an atmosphere of openness, trust and respect. She also highlights frequent goal-setting in all aspects of the life of the organization. Clutterbuck and Megginson list six areas which they identify with a coaching culture, and Megginson *et al.* (2006) do the same for a mentoring culture. Both are shown in Table 12.1.

Coaching culture (Clutterbuck and Megginson 2005: 28)	Mentoring culture (Megginson *et al.* 2006: 7)
1 Coaching linked to business drivers	1 Clear link to a business issue, where outcome is measured
2 Being a client is supported and encouraged	2 Part of a culture change process
3 Provide coach training	3 Senior management involved as clients and mentors
4 Reward and recognize coaching	4 Link to long-term talent management established
5 Systemic perspective	5 Clients in the driving seat
6 The move to coaching is managed	6 Light-touch development of individuals and scheme
	7 Clear framework, publicized, with stories
	8 Scheme design-focused on business issues and change agenda

Table 12.1 Characteristics of coaching and mentoring cultures

Malcolm Hurrell talks about the coaching and mentoring culture at AstraZeneca and there are links with some of the cultural factors shown in Table 12.1.

Optimizing the performance of people in every position in the company is a strategic priority, owned and sponsored by the senior executive team. There is a long history of supporting both coaching and mentoring in the organization, each seen as being distinctly different in approach and accountability of those involved, but being highly complementary.

Coaching
A process carried out by the line or project manager in order to enhance the performance and development of an employee in their existing role. Seeks to build capability through increased awareness and responsibility, sometimes applied in a skills transfer model in technical areas whilst also applied in managerial settings through questioning from a position of support.

Mentoring
A relationship where one person with more experience of the issue and able to provide organization-wide thinking and context works with a colleague, with the focus more on broader and longer-term development. We recommend it is carried out by someone outside the line or functional relationship and it is often linked to future capability or to people beginning new and challenging positions, possibly in a new environment (e.g. international assignee). In simple terms the organization seeks to use the coaching process to build capability in role whereas the mentoring process facilitates reflective learning to enhance awareness, understanding and wisdom that can be applied to a broader perspective. Both processes are essential if the company is to achieve the aim of being a learning organization able to constantly reinvent itself.

AstraZeneca sees coaching as a core process, expected to be used by all, whereas mentoring is taken up on a voluntary basis, both by mentee and mentor. As a learning organization, acquiring the skills of mentoring is viewed as a critical capability of high-performing experienced professionals across the organization. The process provides the opportunity for people to learn from each other, mutual benefit being afforded to both parties and to organizational and team performance.

How do you develop a mentoring culture?

The previous example illustrates how coaching and mentoring develop as a result of corporate strategy aimed at optimizing the performance of the organization by continually developing the talents and strengths of its people. However, cultural change can develop from the bottom up as well as the top down. It can evolve through the initiative of employees. The next example highlights how volunteer mentors are changing a medical culture in a large inner-city acute hospital trust.

Dr Nancy Redfern describes an employee-driven mentoring initiative which illustrates that developing a mentoring culture takes time.

Newcastle upon Tyne Foundation Trust is a large NHS acute hospital providing care to the population of Newcastle, with tertiary referrals from the North East and beyond. It employs 700 consultants, many of whom are academics at Newcastle Medical and Dental Schools.

Being a consultant in the NHS has always been a responsible job. But doing the job well and meeting the expectations of an increasingly well-informed public while achieving the targets and throughput expected by the NHS was taking its toll. This pressure was even more challenging for our junior staff, who did not yet have the security of a permanent consultant post. We were aware that many trainees looked to their consultants as role models, and thought we should be better prepared than we were for the role. Thus, when an opportunity to attend a mentor development programme presented itself several of us were keen to take this up.

The course was a great success. We spent six days (a day a month) learning the skills of mentoring and we used The Skilled Helper framework to guide discussions. Spending time working together, using as our material the challenges and opportunities we faced at work, made us realize the power of mentoring for ourselves. So, having come on the course with the aim of providing mentoring for our trainees, many of us left thinking that we might do better to use our skills among our colleagues.

The next move was to set up a mentoring scheme within the Trust. Offering mentoring to all of the consultants seemed overwhelming, and rather beyond our still nascent skill set. We retreated from this, choosing to use our skills between ourselves while we built up our numbers.

We realized that mentoring is of most use at a time of change, and decided our first focus should be a scheme for newly-appointed consultants. The aims were to provide an opportunity for consultants to have confidential conversations with someone from outside their area of work, to help them settle into the role of consultant, to manage their work most effectively and achieve their full potential.

In the longer term, we hoped that building up the numbers of trained mentors and mentees would create a learning culture in which people would make time to question their own practice, where it would be normal to ask when you don't know something, and where giving and receiving support from colleagues is seen as a sign of strength.

What was achieved?

Each newly-appointed consultant is offered the opportunity of having a mentor, and nearly all meet one of the mentors who introduce them to the scheme and describe how others use mentorship.

Mentoring is described on the consultant induction programme, and some of the experienced mentors explain how we use the scheme among ourselves. Examples of common topics discussed with mentors are outlined and include influencing, managing difficult situations or working with colleagues, team-building, change management, and organizing and prioritizing work or work–life balance.

As the scheme has become more established, the Trust offers a mentor to doctors facing difficult professional situations, or those who are struggling. Thus we are developing some expertise in supporting colleagues in difficulty. Mentoring appears to help people become engaged in making changes in their practice and to develop skills to prevent further difficulties, rather than feeling isolated and 'looking over their shoulder'.

The number of consultant mentors has grown gradually, and now 10 per cent of consultants in the Trust are trained mentors. Mentors now also include nurses, midwives, pharmacists, university academics and managers.

Some reflections

By nature, doctors and senior NHS managers prioritize patient care over their own professional and personal development. They have professional values and training based on taking individual responsibility, and a tradition of 'coping' rather than asking for help. For those who do not have a burning issue to discuss, there can be a reluctance to prioritize mentoring for themselves over a busy clinical workload.

So, it takes time for a scheme to become established. Informal feedback from people who have used the mentoring scheme or trained as mentors, about what they gained personally, seems to be the most effective publicity.

In earlier years, a few senior consultants expressed the view that 'mentoring was for the needy, weaker characters, and not something they would entertain'. Either this view has died out as personnel have changed, or the culture is now one in which such opinions are rarely heard. However, for some, there may always be a perception that asking for help is regarded as weakness.

How do you develop a coaching culture?

In the mentoring example above, the culture change happened through training a critical mass of volunteer mentors over a period of several years. In the example which follows, the driver for change was that a new type of leadership development was needed to improve performance and deliver results. This culture change had strong commitment from leaders in the organization.

> **Shaun Lincoln** delivered the Leaders as Coaches (LAC) programme and worked with Sean Mileusnic, head of leadership and development at Greater Manchester Police (GMP). They explain how they work together and how a coaching culture is developing (adapted from Hilpern 2006: 42–5).
>
> There is an ever-increasing need for leadership within the organization to meet rising performance targets, and to enable people to develop and reach their potential. GMP therefore took the decision to develop a positive culture change around leadership that would have an impact on everyone – not just those in supervisory positions. A new leadership charter was developed to manage expectations, while coaching, mentoring and 'buddy' schemes were introduced alongside leadership programmes aimed at staff with high potential.
>
> Each person on the Leaders as Coaches programme goes on to coach three people at any one time. The idea is to bring about a fundamental culture change whereby coaching eventually becomes part of the ethos of the organization, and all police officers – and indeed all police staff – feel confident in their leadership skills as a result.
>
> Some employees already report feeling more competent, confident and in control of their own development. 'In a perfect world, we'd like to have coaches professionally trained right across the organization, but that's impossible in terms of resources,' admits Sean. 'In fact, that was one of our earliest lessons: not to be unrealistic about

what we can do. Not every individual will be a coach or coachee, but we hope that indirectly they will benefit from the coaching culture,' Sean says.

Shaun Lincoln believes the programme is working well largely because leadership coaches within GMP aren't necessarily line managers. 'Sometimes it's actually better that coaches aren't line managers because individuals can usually be open with their coach in a way that perhaps they couldn't be with a line manager,' he says. Coaching at GMP even cuts across ranks. 'Like many organizations, GMP is quite hierarchical, yet you have people coaching people higher up the ranks than them,' Sean says. 'The great thing about this is that to create a real coaching culture, you need to have coaching working in four ways: the ability to coach each other and yourself, and to coach upwards and downwards.'

What helps or hinders?

A CIPD survey found several reasons why, despite positive attitudes to coaching and mentoring, a successful culture may not develop:

> competing business pressure (66%) forms the main barrier to developing a coaching culture. This is followed by some of the more usual suspects – lack of expertise (52%), lack of investment (48%) and poor senior management commitment (48%).
>
> (CIPD 2006: 12)

Where there is senior management commitment to leadership development across the organization there is a strong possibility that a coaching and mentoring culture will develop.

Wendy Briner has carried out research into what happens to participants of the Ashridge Leadership Process who have ongoing coaching as part of the programme. She finds that coaching is a vital component in leadership development but that the sustainability of behaviour change in leaders back at work varies according to their leadership culture.

Ashridge Leadership Process was so christened because development takes place over six months. Coaching is integrated into this process, starting with a telephone conversation prior to the workshop, with two meetings during the workshop and two meetings in the subsequent six months. We set up a developmental network of coaches whose aim was to enable participants to make sense of the self-awareness, ideas and aspirations that the workshop provided, so that they could become self-sustaining in developing their leadership in practice.

The coaching approach we use is primarily solutions-focused, complemented by appreciative enquiry. Coaches value and have confidence in their client capacities. They encourage clients to identify and elaborate what is constructive in them and their situations. They ask clients to consider who they are, what they have and what they want. They aim to help them to focus on what they can do and want to do in their context.

What leaders value most in their development process

They tell us there are four interactive and integrative learning processes that make most difference to their development in practice. These are shown in Figure 12.1.

Development is a social and practical process so the opportunities to discuss, reflect and try out alternatives, while focusing on a future that is seen as in some way better, generates tangible benefits. Leadership coaching is one of those processes and leaders value its unique contribution.

Leaders say they value coaching because:

● It is one-to-one, confidential and a period of time that is separate from the frantic activity of everyday work. They can stop the

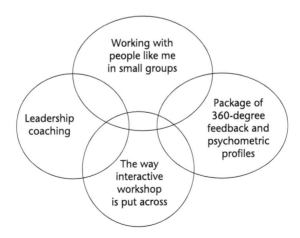

Figure 12.1 Four interactive and integrative learning processes

clock and step outside to reflect on what they're doing and the impact they're having.

- Your coach is a professional in listening, asking the right provoking questions, summarizing and running developmental discussions. The coach is interested in you but impartial and not implicated in other aspects of your life.
- It provides a focus and brings clarity around your own agenda and you find your own solutions that do make a difference.
- It is affirming and enables you to use your capabilities to make more effective contributions.

Culture can help or hinder coaching

We compared four organizations and the impact of coaching, and, where the organization culture is seen to value 'relational leadership', coaching is seen to be useful and compatible. By relational leadership we mean doing things with people in a participatory way to deliver results – i.e. meetings which are participatory, bouncing ideas off one another, using awaydays. In these organizations, change is in tune with the culture and is more acknowledged, valued and sustained.

Among leadership cultures where delivery is based on structure and consistent processes, coaching is seen to be relevant, but less durable. Likewise, in cultures where professional autonomy, rather than teamwork, is emphasized, coaching is personally useful but has little impact on the culture. In these cultures, there were changes in individuals' leadership style as a result of coaching, but there was less appreciation by, for example, colleagues, of its relevance. A colleague might wonder, 'Shouldn't she or he be tougher?' or, 'This more participatory approach may be OK for today's problem but will it work in the future?'

Reflections for leadership development

- Coaching enables leaders to construct a bridge from having good intentions to putting them into practice in their complex context. Having some time to do this in a personalized and bespoke way recognizes how necessary this apparently simple step is in bringing about significant positive development and impact.
- Many developers underestimate the impact that coaching has with the individual and the organization. They see workshops, content and exercises as most important in fostering development. Feedback from leaders suggests that workshop and group sessions have a part to play in orienting, stimulating and supporting leaders in their development, but leadership coaching is much more valued. It is a vital component in a leadership development process.

Shaun Lincoln develops coaching with further education colleges as well as with police organizations. He recognizes some helpful and unhelpful factors in organizational cultures.

What helps?

1   Agreement on the need for culture change and for senior management to actively support this.
2   For senior management to understand what coaching is and the benefits it can bring.
3   Senior management team commitment to achieving this and being trained as coaches themselves so they are part of the change they want to see.
4   Time and space for the coaching to happen.
5   A clear need for culture change to happen as the result of feedback such as the outcome of an external inspection, or external drivers to improve performance.
6   A request for coaching from potential coachees themselves – typically via staff surveys.
7   After an initial coaching cohort, coaching is reported to make a clear difference, and even better if it is seen to deliver to the bottom line (and thus represent a return on investment).
8   Our work at creating coaching cultures has worked best where the initial training has been high impact and created a 'wow' factor, and where this was immediately followed up by participants formally coaching people they do not line manage for four to six months, even if their long-term goal was to coach their own teams.
9   Not taking a deficit approach to coaching – for this reason we use a solutions-focused coaching model. This builds on what managers already have, rather than working with deficits.

What hinders?

1   A lack of all the above.
2   The cost of using external coaches.
3   Coaching being seen as imposed, with little buy-in or consensus.
4   Lack of understanding of what coaching is by senior management team.
5   Lack of buy-in from coachees if there has been no prior consultation with them, and fear that coaching is remedial: 'If you are being coached you have a problem'.
6   After the training, just relying on managers to then use these new skills informally with their own teams, without then developing confidence and expertise via formally coaching two or three people they do not line manage.
7   Lack of resources.

What difference does it make?

In this section there are examples of some of the observable differences in organizations when coaching and mentoring cultures develop.

Shaun Lincoln quotes leaders in the further education sector to illustrate some outcomes of the Leaders as Coaches (LAC) programme.

The examples below focus specifically on how we have worked with organizations to develop a coaching leadership style and in some cases a coaching culture. The programme can be used in two ways:

1   Manager-coach version – helping managers in the organization develop an informal coaching leadership style with the staff they manage.
2   Internal coach version – developing individuals to act as a formal pool of coaches available to colleagues on a no-line manager basis.

One key aspect of creating a coaching culture via the LAC programme is the team-building between the coaches themselves, as well as between coach and coachee: 'We undertook the LAC programme so that the senior management team could offer coaching support to middle managers. This proved to be extremely powerful in terms of both self-awareness and team awareness, and it generated a terrific "wow" factor and a buzz. Even experienced managers learned from this experience and carried it into their teams. We've seen positive development right across the piece, an impact right across the board. Coaching can certainly be a catalyst to trigger step change. The team awareness aspect has been particularly interesting. Managers are learning about themselves and appreciating that they have their own roles to play in the team, and that they may in fact be part of the problem, which previously they would have sought to externalize' (David Pomfret, principal, Boston College).

Another outcome is that several of the senior management teams now use coaching techniques in their meetings. Some structure their meetings around such techniques. The solutions-focused approach has led to culture change, to greater sharing of problems, focusing on what works and finding solutions

'The main impact I would describe is that firstly it has had an impact on management behaviour in terms of how they have approached managing their staff. Secondly it has changed the language of dialogue about issues in the organization. People are recognizing that as culture is beginning to change, people are expected not only to present problems but also to present solutions as well. This does not mean that the solutions identified are "soft", they are often addressing very difficult issues that require the effective use of performance management tools, for example capability and discipline. Middle managers are more challenging in a positive solutions-oriented approach. This has been challenging, in a positive way, to the senior management team' (Paul Head, principal and chief executive, College of North East London).

Another difference is that coaching has often been most successful where a pool of internal coaches has been developed. This enables staff to discuss with coaches aspects or concerns about their work that they would be less likely to discuss with their line manager. In this way they can obtain many of the benefits of external coaching in a way that the organization can afford. It also increases the likelihood that this organizational learning is retained and acted on. Key to this has been using a non-directive coaching approach, as in the example earlier in the chapter from GMP.

Malcolm Hurrell shares some learning from initiatives taken at AstraZeneca where the GROW model is used for internal coaching by all core staff.

Goal
The coach engages the employee in identifying the overriding goal – what is the longer-term change in performance/development we are seeking to achieve?

Reality
The coach helps the employee by getting them to tell the story of what is currently happening, helping to deepen awareness and from increased awareness identify potential new options. The coach can help the employee to understand the issues; challenge beliefs and misconceptions; help break down the tasks; and focus on what will have greatest impact on performance.

Options
The coach helps the employee to see what good performance would look like and to explore different ways to achieve this. It is an opportunity to share personal experience and insight and to establish clear outcomes to be achieved. Finally the coach guides the employee to a clear choice of what to work on.

Will

The coach helps the employee move towards and commit to action by planning ways to deliver the desired performance. Once decided, this forms a detailed plan of action alongside agreed ways to monitor and evaluate progress.

A senior director in finance talks about some of the outcomes of a coaching programme: 'I am more curious, more questioning, more demanding and stretching in my questions. I have seen a real difference in my team and in their approach to learning. We are embedding coaching in performance management targets. The performance of my direct reports is increasing. We are using a common language around capability and learning. I have now taken up an executive coach as ongoing complementary learning.'

A coaching intervention was implemented in AZ Information Systems. It used three key statements, that the organization should focus on:

- What it is passionate about.
- What it is best at.
- Delivering recognizable value.

The programme introduced coaching, based on applying these key statements at a personal level:

- Providing coaching to individuals using the 'Now Discover Your Strengths' approach devised by Gallop, which provides insights on your 'natural talents' which you will therefore be passionate about and can turn into strengths.
- Providing coaching to individuals using 360-degree feedback which helps individuals understand what they are 'best at' in other people's eyes.
- Requiring individuals to present back to groups on the 'value they had delivered'.

External coaches led groups of leaders over three days, followed by one-to-one external coaching sessions, wrapped up by re-forming the leaders' groups for a two-day session, nine months later. What was the impact on individuals and on the business?

From a business perspective, 77 per cent of line managers stated that they had seen an improvement in leadership contribution. From an individual perspective, both the principles and the results from 'Now

Discover Your Strengths' brought about some significant changes. These were either to the approach that leaders took to their roles or to their decisions in changing roles – sometimes quite radically. Some leaders left the organization while others applied for, and got, more senior posts.

Two important lessons were learned. Firstly, there is power in the simple message that we should be 'developing our talents into strengths' rather than trying to become 'fully rounded people by always focusing on our weaknesses'. This message breathes new life into individual development and the approach it can take. Secondly, that the organization needs to be ready for the amount of internal people movement and sometimes turnover that occurs as a result of deep-searching individual coaching.

How do you assess your organization?

If the benefits of coaching and mentoring at work are to be fully effective, then the culture of the organization will encourage, sustain, support and reward those who lead and manage these forms of learning and development. Clutterbuck and Megginson (2005: 96) identify four progressive stages on this journey: *nascent*, where there is little commitment in evidence; *tactical*, where the organization recognizes a need but does not show understanding about what will be necessary; *strategic*, where managers are involved in coaching as part of everyday work and where this is rewarded; and *embedded*, where coaching and mentoring are an integral part of learning and development and where all levels are involved in both the delivery and the receipt of coaching and mentoring.

The questions below have been developed from the experiences described in this chapter. They reflect some of the factors which have been highlighted as significant when developing a coaching or mentoring culture. They may help you to reflect upon the development of a coaching and mentoring culture in your organization. The topics which they address include: the relationship between coaching and mentoring; developing a culture of learning, valuing and achievement; the link between individual development and organisational performance; the impact of coaching and mentoring on leadership and talent-management in the organisation; team-working; resourcing and embedding coaching and mentoring. These topics throw light on the way in which values, structures, systems and processes contribute to organisational culture.

Box 12.1 Assessing the coaching and mentoring culture of your organization

---

1   Are both performance and development a strategic priority?
2   Does your organization link individual development to business performance?
3   Does senior management actively sponsor individual development? How?
4   What systems, procedures or processes support individual development? How well do these operate?
5   Are coaching and mentoring viewed as learning and development? If not, how are they viewed?
6   Are coaching and mentoring encouraged throughout the organization? If so, in what ways?
7   Do senior managers talk about using coaches and mentors themselves?
8   Do leaders and managers coach and mentor staff?
9   How would you describe the style of leadership in your organization? How does it fit with coaching and mentoring values?
10 In what ways are teamwork and participation encouraged and rewarded?
11 Is there a 'blame' culture anywhere in the organization?
12 Is there a culture where 'everything is a learning opportunity' operating anywhere in the organization?
13 Are there any forms of learning – for example, action learning and e-learning – that support coaching and mentoring?
14 Is coaching and mentoring non-hierarchical: downwards, upwards, peers?
15 Do managers embed coaching and mentoring in the way they work? How?
16 What resources are available for training and support of coaches and mentors?
17 Can you access both internal and external coaching and mentoring?
18 In what ways are coaching and mentoring used as part of talent management and developing potential?
19 How are the outcomes of coaching and mentoring reported?
20 What would be your main recommendations for your organization now that you have completed this questionnaire?

Summary

In this chapter we have:

- Argued that in order for coaching and mentoring to be effective they must be integrated into the whole learning and development culture of the organization.
- Reported the experience of five contributors who have been involved in coaching or mentoring in public and private sector organizations.
- Identified key features of coaching and mentoring cultures and highlighted factors which help and hinder the development of coaching and mentoring at work.
- Concluded with a self-assessment questionnaire, based upon the experience of the contributors, to help you identify the coaching and mentoring culture in your organization.

Appendix: useful contacts and websites

AC: The Association for Coaching
www.associationforcoaching.com

APECS: Association for Professional Executive Coaching and Supervision
www.apecs.org

BACP Coaching: British Association for Counselling and Psychotherapy
www.bacpcoaching.co.uk

BPS: British Psychological Society (see Special Group in Coaching Psychology)
www.sgcp.org.uk

CIPD: Chartered Institute of Personnel and Development
www.cipd.co.uk

Coaching and Mentoring Network
www.coachingnetwork.org.uk

EMCC: European Mentoring and Coaching Council
www.emccouncil.org

ICF: International Coaching Federation
www.coachfederation.org

Mindtools
www.mindtools.com

National College for School Leadership
www.ncsl.org.uk/coaching

Bibliography

AC (Association for Coaching) (2007) *Coaching Supervision: Analysis of Survey Findings*, www.associationforcoaching.com.

Adair, J. (1986) *Effective Teambuilding*. London: Pan.

Bandura, A. (1969) *Principles of Behaviour Modification*. New York: Holt, Rinehart & Winston.

Barden, S. (2006) The team: the heart of executive coaching, *Coach and Mentor: The Journal of the Oxford School of Coaching and Mentoring*, 6: 6–7.

Bayne, R. (2004) *Psychological Types at Work: An MBTI Perspective*. London: Thomson.

Belbin, M. (2000) *Beyond the Team*. London: Butterworth-Heinemann.

Belbin, M. (2003) *Team Roles at Work*, 2nd edn. London: Butterworth-Heinemann.

Berg, I and Szabo, P. (2005) *Brief Coaching for Lasting Solutions*. London: Norton & Co.

Berglas, S. (2002) The very real dangers of executive coaching, *Harvard Business Review*, 80(6): 86–92.

Berne, E. (1972) *What Do You Say After You Say Hello?* London: Corgi.

Berne, E. (1976) *Beyond Games and Scripts*. New York: Ballantine.

Bion, W.R. (1961) *Experiences in Groups*. London: Tavistock.

Blanchard, K. (1994) *Leadership and the One-Minute Manager*. London: Harper Collins Business.

Blatner, A. (1996) *Acting-In: Practical Applications of Psychodramatic Methods*, 3rd edn. New York: Springer.

Blessingwhite (2009) *The Coaching Conundrum: Building a Coaching Culture that Drives Organisational Success*, www.blessingwhite.com.

Bluckert, P. (2006) *Psychological Dimensions to Coaching*. Maidenhead: Open University Press.

Bluckert, P. (2010) The Gestalt approach to coaching, in E. Cox, T. Bachkirova and D. Clutterbuck (eds) *The Complete Handbook of Coaching*. London: Sage.

Bolles, R.N. (2002) *What Color is Your Parachute? A Practical Guide for Job Hunters and Career Changers*. Berkeley, CA: Ten Speed Press.

Bond, T. (1993) *Standards and Ethics for Counselling in Action*. London: Sage.

Boyatzis, R., Smith, M. and Blaize, N. (2006) Sustaining leadership effectiveness through coaching and compassion: It's not what you think, *Academy of Management Learning and Education*, 5(1): 8–24.

Burgoyne, J. (1990) Doubts about competence, in M. Devine (ed.) *The Photofit Manager*. London: Unwin Hyman.

CIPD (Chartered Institute of Personnel and Development) (2006) *Learning and Development: Annual Survey Report*. London: CIPD.

CIPD (Chartered Institute of Personnel and Development) (2008a) *Mentoring Factsheet*. London: CIPD.

CIPD (Chartered Institute of Personnel and Development) (2008b) *Coaching and Buying Coaching Services*. London: CIPD.

CIPD (Chartered Institute of Personnel and Development) (2009) *Taking the Temperature of Coaching and Mentoring. Annual Survey of Learning and Development*. London: CIPD.

CIPD (Chartered Institute of Personnel and Development) (2010) *Coaching and Mentoring Factsheet*. London: CIPD.

Clutterbuck, D. (2001) *Everyone Needs a Mentor*. London: CIPD.

Clutterbuck, D. and Megginson, D. (2005) *Making Coaching Work*. London: CIPD.

Clutterbuck, D. and Megginson, D. (2010) Coach maturity: an emerging concept, *International Journal of Coaching and Mentoring*, 8(1): 4–12.

Clutterbuck, D. and Ragins, B.R. (2002) *Mentoring for Diversity*. London: Butterworth-Heinemann.

Connor, M. (1994) *Training the Counsellor*. London: Routledge.

Connor, M. (1997) *Mentoring for Medics*. York: University College of Ripon and York St John.

Connor, M. and Pokora, J. (2007) *Coaching and Mentoring at Work*. Maidenhead: Open University Press.

Connor, M., Bynoe A.G., Redfern N., Pokora, J. and Clarke, J. (2000) Developing senior doctors as mentors: a form of continuing professional development. Report of an initiative to develop a network of senior doctors as mentors, 1994–99, *Medical Education*, 34: 747–53.

Cooperrider, D.L. and Whitney, D. (1999) Appreciative enquiry: a positive revolution in change, in P. Holman and T. Davane (eds) *The Change Handbook: Group Methods for Shaping the Future*. San Fransisco, CA: Berrett-Koehler.

Cooperrider, D., Whitney, D., Stavros, J. and Fry, R. (2003) *Appreciative Enquiry Handbook*. San Fransisco, CA: Berrett-Koehler.

Covey, S.R. (1989) *The Seven Habits of Highly Effective People*. London: Simon & Schuster.

Creasy, J. and Paterson, F. (2005) *Leading Coaching in Schools*, Leading Practice Seminar Series, National College for School Leadership, www.ncsl.org.uk.

Critchley, B. (2009) Relational coaching: taking courage and making a difference, *International Journal of Mentoring and Coaching*, 7(2): 25–35.

De Bono, E. (1992) *Serious Creativity*. New York: Harper Business.

Downey, M. (2003) *Effective Coaching: Lessons from the Coaches' Coach*, 2nd edn. London: Texere.

Easterby-Smith, M., Burgoyne, J. and Araujo, L. (eds) (1999) *Organisational Learning and the Learning Organisation*. London: Sage.

Eaton, J. and Johnson, R. (2001) *Coaching Successfully*. London: Dorling Kindersley.

Egan, G. (2002) *The Skilled Helper*, 7th edn. Belmont, CA: Thomson Brooks/Cole.

Egan, G. (2006) *Essentials of Skilled Helping*. Belmont, CA: Thomson Wadsworth.

Egan, G. (2010) *The Skilled Helper*, 9th edn. Belmont, CA: Brooks/Cole Cengage Learning.

Eglin, R. (2006) Building a more efficient society, *The Sunday Times*, 14 May, p. 6.

EMCC (European Mentoring and Coaching Council) (2004) *Guidelines on Supervision: An Interim Statement*, www.emccouncil.org.

EMCC (European Mentoring and Coaching Council) (2005) Press release EMCC19, December, www.emccouncil.org.

EMCC (European Mentoring and Coaching Council) (2009) *EQA Information Guide*, www.emccouncil.org.

Fisher, R. and Ury, W. (1987) *Getting to Yes*. London: Arrow.

Flood, R.L. (1999) *Rethinking the Fifth Discipline*. London: Routledge.

Francis, D. (1994) *Managing Your Own Career*. London: HarperCollins.

Fraser, S. and Greenhalgh, T. (2001) Complexity science: coping with complexity, educating for capability, *British Medical Journal*, 323: 799–803.

Fritchie, R. and Leary, M. (1998) *Resolving Conflicts in Organisations*. London: Lemos & Crane.

Fritts, P.J. (1998) *The New Managerial Mentor*. Palo Alto, CA: Davies Black.

Gallwey, T. (2000) *The Inner Game of Work*. London: Orion.

Garret-Harris, R. and Garvey, B. (2005) *Towards a Framework for Mentoring in the NHS*, evaluation report on behalf of the NHS. Sheffield: Sheffield Hallam University.

Garvey, B. and Garret-Harris, R. (2005) *The Benefits of Mentoring: A Literature Review*, report for East Mentors Forum. Sheffield: Mentoring and Coaching Research Unit, Sheffield Hallam University.

Gergen, K.J. (2003) *An Invitation to Social Construction*. London: Sage.

Goldsmith, M., Lyons, L. and Freas, A. (eds) (2000) *Coaching for Leadership: How the World's Greatest Coaches Help Leaders Learn*. San Francisco, CA: Pfeiffer.

Goleman, D. (1998) *Working with Emotional Intelligence*. London: Bloomsbury.

Greene, J. (2003) *Solution Focused Coaching*. Ashland, OR: Momentum.

Grimley, B. (2010) The NLP approach to coaching, in E. Cox *et al.* (eds) *The Complete Handbook of Coaching*. London: Sage.

Hardingham, A., Brearley, M., Moorhouse, A. and Ventner, B. (2004) *The Coach's Coach: Personal Development for Personal Developers*. London: Chartered Institute of Personnel Development.

Harris, A. and Harris, T. (1985) *Staying OK*. London: Pan.

Hawkins, P. and Shohet, R. (2000) *Supervision in the Helping Professions*. Buckingham: Open University Press.

Hawkins, P. and Smith, N. (2006) *Coaching, Mentoring and Organizational Consultancy*. Maidenhead: Open University Press.

Hawkins, P. and Smith, N. (2010) Coaching supervision, in E. Cox *et al.* (eds) *The Complete Handbook of Coaching*. London: Sage.

Hay, J. (2007) *Reflective Practice and Supervision for Coaches*. Maidenhead: Open University Press.

Hilpern, K. (2006) Bringing law to order, *Coaching at Work*, 1(2): 42–5.

Hofstede, G. (1994) *Cultures and Organisations*. London: Harper Collins Business.

Hofstede, G. (2001) *Culture's Consequences: Comparing Values, Behaviours, Institutions and Organizations Across Nations*, 2nd edn. Thousand Oaks, CA: Sage.

Honey, P. and Mumford, A. (1992) *A Manual of Learning Styles*. Maidenhead: P. Honey Publications.

Honey, P. and Mumford, A. (2006) *The Learning Styles Questionnaire: 80 Item*. Maidenhead: P. Honey Publications.

Hutton-Taylor, S. (1999) Cultivating a coaching culture, *British Medical Journal*, 318.

Inskipp, F. and Proctor, P. (1989) *Skills for Supervising and being Supervised*. St Leonards-on-Sea: Alexia Publications.

Jackson, P.Z. (2002) *The Solutions Focus*. London: Nicholas Brealey.

Jacobs, M. (1989) *Psychodynamic Counselling in Action*. London: Sage.

James, M. and Jongeward, D. (1971) *Born to Win*. Reading, MA: Addison-Wesley.

Jarvis, J. (2004) *Coaching and Buying Coaching Services – a CIPD Guide*. London: CIPD.

Johnson, S. (1985) *Characterological Transformation*. New York: Norton

Karpmann, S. (1968) Fairy tales and script drama analysis, *Transactional Analysis Bulletin*, 7(26): 39–43.

Katzenbach, J.R. and Smith, D.K. (1993) *The Wisdom of Teams: Creating the High-performance Organization*. Boston, MA: Harvard University Press.

Kauffman, C., Boniwell, I. and Silberman, J. (2010) The positive psychology approach to coaching, in E. Cox *et al.* (eds) *The Complete Handbook of Coaching*. London: Sage.

Kelly, G. (1963) *A Theory of Personality*. New York: W.W. Norton.

Kennedy, G. (1992) *The Perfect Negotiation*. London: Century.

Kirkpatrick, D.L. (1994) *Evaluating Training Programs: The Four Levels*. San Francisco, CA: Berrett-Koehler.

Kolb, D. (1984) *Experiential Learning*. Englewood Cliffs, NJ: Prentice Hall.

Kolb, D. and Fry, R. (1975) Towards an applied theory of experiential learning, in C.L. Cooper (ed.) *Theories of Group Processes*. London: Wiley.

Korzybski, A. (1994) *Science and Sanity: An Introduction to Non-Aristotelian Systems and General Semantics*, 5th edn. Brooklyn, NY: Institute of General Semantics.

Kotter, J.P. (1998) *What Leaders Really Do*. Boston, MA: Harvard Business School Press.

Lambert, M. (1992) Implications for outcome research for psychotherapy integration, in J. Norcross and M. Goldstein (eds) *Handbook of Psychotherapy Integration*. New York: Basic Books.

Launer, J. (2002) *Narrative-based Primary Care*. Oxford: Radcliffe.

Lewin, K. (1951) *Field Theory in Social Science: Selected Theoretical Papers*, ed. D. Cartwright. New York: Harper & Row.

Luft, J. (1969) *Of Human Interaction*. Palo Alto, CA: National Press.

Luft, J. (1970) *Group Processes: An Introduction to Group Dynamics*. Palo Alto, CA: National Press Books.

Maslow, A.H. (1970) *Motivation and Personality*, 2nd edn. New York: Harper & Row.

Matthews, G. (undated) *Summary of Recent Goals Research*. Dominican University of California, www.dominican.edu/dominicannews/study-backs-up-strategies-for-achieving-goals.html.

McKay, M., Davis, M. and Fanning, P. (1981) *Thoughts and Feelings*. Richmond, CA: New Harbinger Publications.

Mead, G.H. (1967) *Mind, Self and Society: From the Standpoint of a Social Behaviorist*, ed. C.W. Morris. Chicago, IL: University of Chicago Press.

Megginson, D., Clutterbuck, D., Garvey, B., Stokes, P. and Garret-Harris, R. (2006) *Mentoring in Action: A Practical Guide for Managers*. London: Kogan Page.

Myers, I. with Myers, P. (1980) *Gifts Differing*. Palo Alto, CA: Consulting Psychologists Press.

Neenan, M. and Dryden, W. (2002) *Life Coaching: A Cognitive Behavioural Approach*. London: Routledge.

Neenan, M. and Palmer, S. (2001) Cognitive behavioural coaching, *Stress News*, 13(3): 15–18.

NHS Finance Staff Development (2004) *Mentoring Guidance Pack for Mentoring in the NHS Finance Function*, unpublished.

Parsloe, E. (1992) *Coaching, Mentoring and Assessing: A Practical Guide to Developing Competence*. London: Kogan Page.

Parsloe, E. (1999) *The Manager as Coach and Mentor*. London: Institute of Personnel and Development.

Parsloe, E. and Wray, M. (2000) *Coaching and Mentoring: Practical Methods to Improve Learning*. London: Kogan Page.

Pask, R. and Joy, B. (2007) *Mentoring-Coaching: A Guide for Education Professionals*. Maidenhead: Open University Press.

Pedler, M. and Aspinwall, K. (1996) *Perfect PLC?* Maidenhead: McGraw-Hill.

Pedler, M., Burgoyne, J. and Boydell, T. (1991) *The Learning Company: A Strategy for Sustainable Development*. Maidenhead: McGraw-Hill.

Pedler, M., Burgoyne, J. and Boydell, T. (1994) *A Manager's Guide to Self Development*. Maidenhead: McGraw-Hill.

Perls, F. (1951) *Gestalt Therapy: Excitement and Growth in the Human Personality*. New York: Julian.

Phillips, A. and Pokora, J. (2004) Diagnostic versus active listening, unpublished presentation to GP Leadership Programme, Northern Deanery.

Pokora, J. and Briner, W. (1999) Teams and the learning organisation, in R. Stewart (ed.) *Gower Handbook of Teamworking*. Aldershot: Gower.

Rawlinson, J.G. (1986) *Creative Thinking and Brainstorming*. Aldershot: Gower.

Revans, R. (1983) *ABC of Action Learning*. Bromley: Chartwell-Bratt.

Rich, J.R. (2003) *Brainstorm: Tap Into Your Creativity to Generate Awesome Ideas and Tremendous Results*. Franklin Lakes, NJ: Career Press.

Rickards, T. (1997) *Creativity and Problem Solving at Work*. Aldershot: Gower.

Robbins, A. (1992) *Awaken the Giant Within*. Riverside, NJ: Simon & Schuster.

Rodenburg, P. (2007) *Presence*. London: Michael Joseph.

Rogers, C.R. (1961) *On Becoming a Person*. London: Constable.

Rogers, C.R. (1983) *Freedom to Learn in the 80s*. Columbus, OH: Charles Merrill.

Rogers, J. (2008) *Coaching Skills*, 2nd edn. Maidenhead: Open University Press.

Schein, E. (1990) *Career Anchors: Discovering Your Real Values*. San Francisco, CA: Jossey-Bass/Pfeiffer.

Schön, D.A. (1983) *The Reflective Practitioner: How Professionals Think in Action*. London: Temple Smith.

Seligman, M. (2002) *Authentic Happiness*. New York: Free Press.

Senge, P.M. (1992) *The Fifth Discipline*. London: Century Business.

Starr, J. (2003) *The Coaching Manual*. London: Pearson Education.

Steiner, C. (1974) *Scripts People Live*. New York: Bantam.

Steven, A., Oxley, J. and Fleming, W.G. (2008) Mentoring for NHS doctors: perceived benefits across the personal–professional interface, *Journal of the Royal Society of Medicine*, 101: 552–7.

Stone, F.M. (1999) *Coaching, Counselling and Mentoring*. New York: American Management Association.

Stone, D., Patton, B. and Heen, S. (1999) *Difficult Conversations: How to Discuss What Matters Most*. London: Michael Joseph.

Sulaiman, T. (2006) How to mentor: it's a shared experience, *The Times*, 11 May.

Trompenaars, F. and Hampden-Turner, C. (1998) *Riding the Waves of Culture: Understanding Cultural Diversity in Global Business*, 2nd edn. New York: McGraw-Hill.

Tuckman, R.W. (1965) Developmental sequences in small groups, *Psychological Bulletin*, 63: 384–99.

Vickers, A. and Bavister, S. (2005) *Teach Yourself Coaching*. London: Hodder Arnold.

Viney, R. and Paice, E. (2010) *The First Five Hundred. A Report on London Deanery's Coaching and Mentoring Service 2008–2010*, www.londondeanery.ac.uk.

Whitmore, J. (2002) *Coaching for Performance: GROWing People, Performance and Purpose*, 3rd edn. London: Nicholas Brealey.

Whitworth, L., Kimsey-House, H. and Sandahl, P. (1998) *Co-Active Coaching: New Skills for Coaching People Toward Success in Work and Life*. Mountain View, CA: Davies Black.

Zdenek, M. (1983) *The Right Brain Experience*. London: Corgi Books.

Zeus, P. and Skiffington, S. (2000) *The Complete Guide to Coaching at Work*. North Ryde, NSW: McGraw-Hill.

Index

COACHING POSITIVELY
Lessons for Coaches from
Positive Psychology

Matt Driver

9780335241156 (Paperback)
July 2011

eBook also available

Coaching is a positive practice which focuses on building people's resourcefulness and positive beliefs about themselves. Recent research into positive psychology supports and builds upon current coaching practice and also refines it. Like many other coaches, managers and consultants, Matt Driver has found this relatively new field to be inspiring and to offer practical insights into his work. It is proving to be of enormous value to people who are interested in what works rather than what does not and who aim to fulfil themselves by developing their natural strengths.

Key features:

- Brings together substantial psychological research
- Includes examples from coaching clients that shows what has worked best for them
- Stresses the importance of relationships, autonomy and achievement in the coaching process

www.openup.co.uk

OPEN UNIVERSITY PRESS
McGraw - Hill Education

LEADING AND COACHING TEAMS TO SUCCESS
The Secret Life of Teams

Phil Hayes

9780335238521 (Paperback)
July 2011

eBook also available

"Coaching remains an underused leadership style. This book offers a usable, practice-led guide to developing the skills to broaden your leadership repertoire. Phil draws on his years of experience as both a leader and a coach to provide insight into coaching successfully, not just with individuals but also with teams. A welcome addition to the expanding coaching canon."
Andy Firth, Senior Consultant, Roffey Park Institute, UK

Key features:

- Provides case studies with questions and learning points for the reader
- Contains practical, easy-to-assimilate tips and strategies
- Links story format to each chapter with practical lessons from each story

www.openup.co.uk

 OPEN UNIVERSITY PRESS
McGraw - Hill Education

COACHING SKILLS
A Handbook
Third Edition

Jenny Rogers

9780335245598 (Paperback)
March 2012

eBook also available

The first and second editions of this book have been described by many training organisations as 'The Coach's Bible'. This new, thoroughly revised and updated edition offers friendly, accessible and practical advice, which any coach can adapt to his or her own work. The book is brought to life using case studies and examples, helping readers to acquire the skills that are essential for becoming an outstanding coach.

Key features:

- New case studies added throughout
- New sections on: Ending the coaching relationship, Coaching as a line manager, Technique of 'Clean Language' and Kogan Leahey approach
- Contains an interactive E-book with selected videos from a new coaching video resource

www.openup.co.uk

 OPEN UNIVERSITY PRESS
McGraw - Hill Education

EXECUTIVE COACHING
A Psychodynamic Approach

Catherine Sandler

9780335237937 (Paperback)
October 2011

eBook also available

This beautifully-written book, by one of the UK's most experienced and highly-regarded executive coaches, provides a clear and concise introduction to psychodynamic concepts and their practical application to executive coaching. The book illustrates the value of this perspective for coaches and allied professionals and shows how they can incorporate it into their work.

Key features:

- Clarifies the difference between coaching and psychotherapy
- Gives coaches the psychological knowledge they need to become advanced practitioners
- Underlines the central importance of the coach's own self-reflection, self-awareness and self-management

www.openup.co.uk

OPEN UNIVERSITY PRESS
McGraw - Hill Education

The **McGraw·Hill** *Companies*

What's new from Open University Press?

Education... Media, Film & Cultural Studies

Health, Nursing & Social Welfare... Higher Education

Psychology, Counselling & Psychotherapy... Study Skills

Keep up with what's buzzing
at Open University Press
by signing up to receive
regular title information at
www.openup.co.uk/elert

Sociology

 OPEN UNIVERSITY PRESS

McGraw - Hill Education

31690574R00167

Made in the USA
Lexington, KY
22 April 2014